$8.95

ECONOMIC REGULATION OF DOMESTIC AIR TRANSPORT THEORY AND POLICY

GEORGE W. DOUGLAS and JAMES C. MILLER III

Airlines have become the dominant means by which Americans travel between the nation's cities. Having grown rapidly since 1938, when the Civil Aeronautics Board began to regulate them in the public interest, airlines are now big business, partly because they have been promoted—by subsidies and other techniques—as an infant industry. Thus it has become appropriate to ask whether the promotional and organizational goals that were paramount in shaping past regulatory policies are still appropriate.

To investigate that question, George W. Douglas and James C. Miller III, working from a model that describes how the airline industry works under regulation, compare the present behavior of the airlines and the regulating authority with the way both would behave if economic efficiency were the major objective of policy. By that criterion, they find that present fares are far too high and that various inefficiencies are built into the fare structure. They also find that the public interest would not be served if the airlines, by agreement among themselves, or the CAB, by exercising its regulatory powers, were to control the capacity of the industry. They review recent CAB policy actions and conclude with specific suggestions that, in their view, would improve the performance of both the industry and the regulating authority.

This book is the tenth of the Brookings Studies in the Regulation of Economic Activity series. George Douglas and James Miller, members of the economics faculties at the University of North Carolina and Texas A&M University, respectively, wrote it as members of the Brookings associated staff.

Studies in the Regulation of Economic Activity
TITLES PUBLISHED

Studies in the Regulation of Economic Activity

387.71
D734

Economic Regulation of Domestic Air Transport: Theory and Policy

GEORGE W. DOUGLAS

JAMES C. MILLER III

The Brookings Institution / Washington, D.C.

Library of Congress Cataloging in Publication Data:
Douglas, George W   1938–
 Economic regulation of domestic air transport.

 (Studies in the regulation of economic activity)
 Includes bibliographical references.
 1. Aeronautics and state—United States.
2. Aeronautics, Commercial—United States.
3. United States. Civil Aeronautics Board.
I. Miller, James Clifford, joint author.
II. Title.   III. Series.
HE9803.A4D68   387.7'1'0973   74-17435
ISBN 0-8157-5724-7

9 8 7 6 5 4 3 2 1

THE BROOKINGS INSTITUTION is an independent organization devoted to nonpartisan research, education, and publication in economics, government, foreign policy, and the social sciences generally. Its principal purposes are to aid in the development of sound public policies and to promote public understanding of issues of national importance.

The Institution was founded on December 8, 1927, to merge the activities of the Institute for Government Research, founded in 1916, the Institute of Economics, founded in 1922, and the Robert Brookings Graduate School of Economics and Government, founded in 1924.

The Board of Trustees is responsible for the general administration of the Institution, while the immediate direction of the policies, program, and staff is vested in the President, assisted by an advisory committee of the officers and staff. The by-laws of the Institution state, "It is the function of the Trustees to make possible the conduct of scientific research, and publication, under the most favorable conditions, and to safeguard the independence of the research staff in the pursuit of their studies and in the publication of the results of such studies. It is not a part of their function to determine, control, or influence the conduct of particular investigations or the conclusions reached."

The President bears final responsibility for the decision to publish a manuscript as a Brookings book or staff paper. In reaching his judgment on the competence, accuracy, and objectivity of each study, the President is advised by the director of the appropriate research program and weighs the views of a panel of expert outside readers who report to him in confidence on the quality of the work. Publication of a work signifies that it is deemed to be a competent treatment worthy of public consideration; such publication does not imply endorsement of conclusions or recommendations contained in the study.

The Institution maintains its position of neutrality on issues of public policy in order to safeguard the intellectual freedom of the staff. Hence interpretations or conclusions in Brookings publications should be understood to be solely those of the author or authors and should not be attributed to the Institution, to its trustees, officers, or other staff members, or to the organizations that support its research.

Foreword

AIRLINES in the United States have been regulated by the Civil Aeronautics Board and its predecessor since the passage of the Civil Aeronautics Act of 1938. Unlike many other industries regulated in the public interest, the airlines have also been promoted as an infant industry. The CAB has served as the agent of Congress in expanding scheduled air service with subsidies and by other techniques. Today, as a result of technological change and rapid growth, the industry dominates intercity commercial passenger transport. Hence the promotional and organizational goals that were paramount in shaping past regulatory policies may no longer be appropriate.

This book examines a broad range of regulatory issues affecting the airline industry: the efficient levels of capacity, the efficient structure of prices, the role of charters, and policies toward merger, entry, exit, and collusion. It also reviews the CAB's recent Domestic Passenger Fare Investigation and summarizes its major findings. Finally, it considers at length the role of competition in spurring market efficiency.

In the authors' view, the CAB's regulation of the domestic trunk air carriers does not fit the usual pattern of public utility regulation. The Board presides over markets often distinguished by a high degree of competition rather than monopoly, which implies that regulatory policies ought to be judged by how well they promote or retard competition. Thus, while in monopoly regulation control over prices constitutes fairly direct control over profits, regulation in a competitive market more often leads to changes in the quality of service and costs. The authors find analytically and empirically that price regulation in the airline industry has led to a far from efficient pattern of prices, quality, and costs. For that reason, and because the airline regulator now faces problems fundamentally different from those of the industry's developmental period, the authors conclude that the CAB's primary attention should be devoted to policies that would improve the economic efficiency of air service.

George W. Douglas, of the economics faculty at the University of North Carolina (currently on leave at the University of Texas), and James C. Miller III, of Texas A&M University (currently a senior staff member of the Council of Economic Advisers), prepared this study as members of the Brookings associated staff. They express their indebtedness to Samuel L. Brown, George C. Eads, John Evans, William A. Jordan, William A. Kutzke, Paul W. MacAvoy, Roger G. Noll, Joseph A. Pechman, Roy Pulsifer, Roger Sherman, V. Kerry Smith, Robert D. Tollison, and Joseph V. Yance for helpful suggestions, encouragement, and advice during the research. Of course, the authors accept responsibility for any errors that may remain. The manuscript was checked for accuracy by Evelyn P. Fisher and edited by Herbert C. Morton; the index was prepared by Florence Robinson.

This book is the tenth in the Brookings series of Studies in the Regulation of Economic Activity. The series presents the findings of a program of research focused on public policies toward business. The program is supported by a grant from the Ford Foundation and is directed by Joseph A. Pechman, director of the Brookings Economic Studies program, and Roger G. Noll, formerly a Brookings senior fellow and now professor of economics at the California Institute of Technology.

The views expressed in this book are solely those of the authors and should not be ascribed to the trustees, officers, or other staff members of the Brookings Institution or to the Ford Foundation.

KERMIT GORDON
President

August 1974
Washington, D.C.

Contents

Text Tables

Appendix Tables

Figures

CHAPTER ONE

Introduction

IN RECENT YEARS economists have been assessing the performance of regulated industries and reexamining the rationale for government regulation. Such an endeavor is particularly appropriate in the transportation industries, since technological developments have altered significantly the character of transport markets and services while the goals and practices of the regulatory agencies have remained substantially the same.[1] In air transport, economic regulation arose in response to alleged conditions of competitive instability when the industry was in its infancy forty years ago. The industry is now mature, and the underlying structural weaknesses of the 1930s no longer obtain. Moreover, the legislative "Declaration of Policy" in the Federal Aviation Act of 1958[2] admonishes the regulator to "promote" the industry as well as to regulate it in the public interest. This mandate of promotion, while perhaps justified when the industry was very young, bears reexamination today.

Another reason for reassessing airline regulation is that economists and other social scientists have been developing new theories for explaining and predicting regulated-industry behavior. This book represents another such effort, and we believe that the approach developed here can be generalized to provide useful analyses of other quasi-competitive industries under government regulation.

Although it deals exclusively with the airlines, ours is not a conventional industry study. While at times we will consider matters of industry structure and conduct, our principal concern is with economic performance, more specifically *economic efficiency*.[3] By concentrating on a description of the

1. The Interstate Commerce Act, pertaining to the regulation of surface transportation, was enacted in 1887. The airlines were brought under federal regulation by the Civil Aeronautics Act of 1938.
2. Federal Aviation Act of 1958, sec. 102 (72 Stat. 740).
3. For an analysis of the U.S. domestic airlines which discusses industry structure and conduct in some depth, see Richard E. Caves, *Air Transport and Its Regulators: An Industry Study* (Harvard University Press, 1962).

1

characteristics of an efficient airline market and developing a descriptive model of industry behavior, we are in a better position to frame proposals for changes in regulatory policy and structure.

Our emphasis on economic efficiency derives from its appeal as a policy objective. A first aspect of economic efficiency is "technical efficiency." A production process is technically efficient if, through appropriate selection and combination of inputs, the given rate of output of a given quality is produced at the lowest total cost. A second aspect of economic efficiency is "allocative efficiency." Allocative efficiency measures whether the combination of goods and services flowing from the production process appropriately reflects the desires of consumers. Allocative efficiency exists if no other combination of outputs, output qualities, and output distribution could improve the welfare of some market participant without diminishing the welfare of some other participant.[4]

Of course, economic efficiency need not be the only rational public policy objective. In fact for over thirty years other goals have been considered in commercial aviation, including: (a) "the promotion, encouragement, and development of civil aeronautics," (b) "the promotion of safety in air commerce," and (c) meeting "the present and future needs of the foreign and domestic commerce of the United States, of the Postal Service, and of the national defense."[5] As noted by Richard E. Caves, these objectives are ambiguous and mutually contradictory.[6] For example, an air transportation system adapted specifically to domestic commerce would not necessarily maximize its contribution to national defense.

Another important public policy goal is "equity." For example, the practice of charging children less than adults for the same airline service is so widely accepted that no serious efforts have been made to change it. Yet such discounts usually violate narrowly defined efficiency conditions. Another example, which, incidentally, shows changing public attitudes toward equity, is airline discounts for youth and the elderly. Because of the backlash against student agitation in the late 1960s, the public has become less in favor of youth-fare discounts and more sympathetic to discounts for the elderly.

The important thing to note is that whereas these and other possible policy goals are often consistent with achieving economic efficiency, they do on occasion conflict. One important role of an economist is to indicate

4. For a further discussion of economic efficiency, see Chapter 5.
5. From the Board's "Declaration of Policy" (72 Stat. 740).
6. Caves, *Air Transport,* pp. 126–27.

the economic costs of pursuing such "noneconomic" goals. Thus, in our view, economic efficiency is a highly appropriate starting point for industry evaluation.[7]

Scope of the Analysis

The main features of the analysis may be summed up as follows. First, we develop an economic model of airline competition which stresses the predominant role of nonprice rivalry. Second, given this model, we show how the regulator can and does affect industry equilibrium through changes in its policies toward rates. Third, we present a method for estimating the combination of price and service quality which, within given restraints, would maximize economic efficiency; we then compare the efficient price and service combination with that under regulation. Finally, we describe an important regulatory case in which the analysis developed here was proffered to the regulator, and we discuss how the regulator responded.

We are concerned almost exclusively with the domestic "trunk" airlines and their regulation by the U.S. Civil Aeronautics Board (CAB or Board). The trunk airlines currently account for over 90 percent of U.S. intercity air passenger traffic.[8] These carriers are not regulated monopolists, but rather they are regulated competitors, with routes between major cities, or "city-pair markets," such as Boston–New York or Chicago–Los Angeles, being served by two or more airlines. They have been subject to economic regulation by the CAB or its predecessor since 1938 and to specific safety and operational regulation by the Federal Aviation Agency and its successor, the Federal Aviation Administration (FAA), since 1958.[9] Moreover, they have been assisted by federal and local governments which provide and operate airports and airway facilities. The major restraints on the organization and provision of service are, however, those initiated and maintained by the Board. Thus, our focus on this regulatory body.

7. Accordingly, it should be kept in mind that in this study the analysis and conclusions are consistent with a regulatory policy of maximizing economic efficiency.

8. Measured in revenue passenger-miles. See U.S. Civil Aeronautics Board, *Handbook of Airline Statistics, 1971 Edition* (1972), p. 23. The other major domestic airline group, the local service carriers, was the subject of analysis in George C. Eads, *The Local Service Airline Experiment* (Brookings Institution, 1972).

9. Before 1958, safety regulation was vested with the CAB. Responsibility for investigating accidents remained with the Board until transferred to the National Transportation Safety Board under the 1966 Department of Transportation Act.

The economics of scheduled air transportation is complex, and the usual economic criteria for market efficiency cannot be applied in a straightforward manner. The principal complicating factor is that scheduled service cannot be stored; current consumption must come entirely from current production. Because capacity can be produced in only discrete units, because the demand for scheduled service at any time is uncertain, and because the present pricing structure encourages schedule augmentation as a means of nonprice competition, the scheduled air transportation system tends to be characterized by some unused or "excess" capacity. However, such excess capacity is useful to users of the system, being a crucial determinant of overall quality as measured by frequency of service and the probability of obtaining a seat on the desired flight. Of course, excess capacity can be obtained only at a cost, which usually means higher fares. It is the nature of this trade-off between service quality and price—and the way in which the Board can, does, and should influence the ultimate combination if it wishes to maximize economic efficiency—that forms the central theme of this study.

For example, even casual observation reveals that in recent years the capacity of the airline industry has grown significantly relative to the amount demanded, causing per-passenger costs to rise and placing great upward pressure on fares. Is this excess capacity desirable? Or would it be preferable to operate the system with less excess capacity and achieve normal profits with significantly lower fares, as in the intrastate markets in California?[10] Our analysis suggests an answer to this important question by attempting to quantify the interrelationships among price, quality, and quantity and by attempting to identify an efficient market outcome.

Outline of the Study

The book is divided into nine chapters and an appendix. The appendix summarizes the industry's history, its industrial organization, and the powers and responsibilities of its regulators. A reader not familiar with the airlines may find it helpful to peruse this appendix before reading further. Following the introduction, there are two brief chapters on the costs of producing and on the demand for scheduled air services. In both chapters

10. For an analysis of this market and what it suggests about the efficiency of CAB regulation, see William A. Jordan, *Airline Regulation in America: Effects and Imperfections* (Johns Hopkins Press, 1970).

the emphasis is on the characteristics most relevant to defining an efficient market equilibrium; neither chapter is meant to be an exhaustive survey of research in the field.

Chapter 4 presents our descriptive model of how the industry reaches market equilibrium under CAB regulation and how this equilibrium responds to changes in regulatory policy. The next three chapters identify the characteristics of an efficient airline market and compare this configuration with industry experience. The *qualitative* aspects of airline market efficiency are discussed in Chapter 5. In Chapter 6, we estimate *quantitatively* the optimal price-quality combination, using a special model designed for this purpose, and contrast this estimate with the existing market combination. This chapter also discusses other efficiency aspects of airline pricing. Chapter 7 surveys Board policy in nonprice areas, including entry, exit, mergers, and collusion. Basically, its function is to describe the nature of nonprice restraints on competition and how these affect the relative efficiency of the regulated-market equilibrium.

Chapter 8 is a case study in economics advocacy. During 1970 and 1971, we prepared testimony and exhibits on behalf of the U.S. Department of Transportation in the CAB's Domestic Passenger Fare Investigation.[11] Those presentations consisted largely of preliminary versions of the economic analysis contained in Chapters 4–6. How the Board responded to these arguments is fully described.

Finally, there is a concluding chapter in which we summarize the major efficiency costs of regulation and suggest how these might be reduced or eliminated through feasible changes in Board policy and legislation.

11. CAB Docket 21866. (The authors do not necessarily endorse all of the department's presentation in that case, nor does the department necessarily endorse all of the analysis contained in this study.)

CHAPTER TWO

Costs of Producing Scheduled Air Service

A DETERMINATION of industry costs lies at the heart of the regulatory process. Whenever the Civil Aeronautics Board makes a decision of economic consequence, the question of costs—past, present, and future—is of primary concern. Costs affect Board policy toward profits, prices, entry, and mergers, as discussed below.

In a broad sense, the regulator seeks to ensure that firms in the industry do not earn profits which exceed a "reasonable" rate of return on their investment. On the other hand, the Board is charged by the Federal Aviation Act with promoting air transportation, which in many cases is interpreted as requiring the maintenance of a "healthy" industry. To chart a course between the extremes of inadequate returns (an unhealthy industry) and excessive profits, the regulator must know actual costs and, presumably, what costs will be under various circumstances in the future.

A determination of efficient or optimal fares for the industry ultimately depends on a description of the costs of production. These include the relation of cost to distance, aircraft size and speed, congestion, measures of utilization, and tangible aspects of service quality such as space per seat, meals, and other amenities.

A rational policy of entry into the industry and into specific city-pair markets rests ultimately on an assessment of the cost function. To restrict entry on grounds that the market's size will support only a limited number of firms is an implicit statement of belief that there exist significant economies with respect to consolidation of service in that particular market.

To offset the presumed loss of competition occasioned by a merger, the regulator must assess among other things the benefits to be gained from any hypothetical savings in cost due to consolidation of markets. In addition, most mergers are to varying degrees "end-to-end," expanding the total number of markets served by the carrier, and this raises the traditional question of scale economies or diseconomies.

The issues raised above suggest two major reasons for studying airline costs. First, to determine an appropriate *structure* of airline prices we must have some understanding of the structure of costs, that is, how the cost of a passenger trip depends on the market and service characteristics. Second, to appraise the remaining issues we must understand the characteristics which affect the firm's aggregate cost *level*. The remainder of this chapter explores the major cost characteristics which are crucial in the determination of regulatory policy.[1]

Categories of Airline Costs

As an initial overview of the composition of airline costs, Table 2-1 presents the aggregated costs of the domestic trunk carriers for the year ending June 30, 1971.[2] The individual cost categories in the table are those adopted by the Board, but, in addition, to glean more economic relevance we have grouped them into four components: operating costs, ownership costs of the capital (principally aircraft), passenger and freight traffic costs, and overhead expenses.

From this aggregative data an important relationship can be discerned: the largest share of the costs of operating a scheduled air transport system are those involved in generating capacity on the scheduled routes. The sum of the first two groups, which might be considered to represent the long-run costs of generating scheduled capacity, account for almost three-quarters of the total costs during the period. On the other hand, the costs attributed directly to the volume of traffic carried amount to only one-fifth the total, and the overhead costs to considerably less.

Categorizing airline costs in this fashion emphasizes the conceptual distinction between costs primarily related to capacity and those primarily

1. In this chapter we limit our discussion of airline costs by assuming that the prices firms pay for inputs such as labor, fuel, and equipment are given. While the nature of factor markets is important in determining an industry's costs, we will postpone our discussion of these issues until Chapter 7.

2. In Table 2-1, and throughout this study, we adopt the cost levels achieved by the regulated carriers as our basic cost standard. This is appropriate, given our emphasis on allocative efficiency and given that our analysis has particular relevance to efficiency within the existing regulatory institution. For a discussion of how economic regulation may affect cost levels and particularly the rates paid for certain inputs such as labor, see Chapter 7.

Table 2-1. Operating Costs of All U.S. Domestic Trunk Carriers, Year Ending June 30, 1971[a]

Cost category	Total cost (millions of dollars)	Percent of total	Cost per available seat-mile (cents)	Cost per passenger-mile (cents)
Aircraft operating costs				
Flying operations	1,900	27.2		
Direct maintenance	526	7.5		
Indirect maintenance	448	6.4		
Aircraft and traffic servicing	1,152	16.5		
Subtotal	4,026	57.6	2.02	4.21
Aircraft ownership costs				
Depreciation of flight equipment	562	8.0		
Capital costs[b]	567	8.1		
Subtotal	1,129	16.1	0.57	1.18
Traffic costs				
Passenger service	673	9.6		
Promotion and sales	730	10.4		
Subtotal	1,403	20.0	0.71	1.47
Overhead costs				
General and administrative	293	4.2		
Amortization of developmental and preoperating expenses, etc.	49	0.7		
Depreciation of nonflight equipment	92	1.3		
Subtotal	434	6.2	0.22	0.45
Total	6,992	100.0	3.51	7.30

Sources: Civil Aeronautics Board, *Air Carrier Financial Statistics* (June 1971), pp. 2, 28; and *Air Carrier Traffic Statistics* (June 1971), p. 2. Calculations were made from data before rounding.

a. Data include operations of Pan American World Airways, which is certificated for international operations only but which carries some domestic traffic in connection with its international operations.

b. Estimated as 10.5 percent of average adjusted investment in all domestic trunk carriers, year ending June 30, 1971. As of that date, 10.5 was the Board-determined reasonable rate of return; we do not contend that this constituted a normal rate of return.

related to servicing passengers and freight. It is, moreover, a principal contention of this study that the per-passenger cost of air transportation can vary markedly with changes in the relative balance between scheduled capacity and actual traffic. The ensuing discussion will follow this principal division between the capacity costs and traffic costs.

Capacity Costs

Airline capacity is usually measured in "available seat-miles" or "available ton-miles." To illustrate, a 100-mile flight of an aircraft having 100 seats and a payload capacity of 10 tons would generate 10,000 available seat-miles and 1,000 available ton-miles.[3]

The cost per seat-mile or ton-mile of capacity produced varies with aircraft type, size, and with the characteristics of the markets served. (The technique of airline cost analysis utilized in later chapters is described in the appendix to this chapter.)

Aircraft Technology

Production technology has undergone considerable change in the past twenty years with the advent of turbojet and turbofan engines and the associated modifications in airframe design. Perhaps the most remarkable aspect of this technological revolution is that the jet era aircraft dominated their predecessor types in all relevant dimensions: speed, comfort, and economy.[4] Hence, by the 1970s, virtually the entire fleet of the trunk airlines had been converted to jet aircraft. Moreover, while jet-powered transports can be designed to operate at various cruising speeds, a rather small range (from about 500 to 580 miles per hour at optimum altitudes) appears to dominate any other design.[5]

3. Measuring output in such an aggregative way has its hazards, as it implicitly assumes that all seats are of a standard size and that other aspects of quality are equal. Moreover, it is not simply available seats or available tons that the firm seeks to sell; it is rather capacity from point A to point B at some specified time. Hence, we should be aware that the firm does not, in general, seek to minimize the costs of producing X units of output. The carrier, instead, acquires a fleet of aircraft and adopts scheduling and routing patterns over its authorized markets consonant with the pattern of demands it faces. The process of fleet selection, scheduling, and routing has been treated extensively in the operations research literature, and will not be addressed in that manner here. (See, for example, James C. Miller III, "A Time-of-Day Model for Aircraft Scheduling," *Transportation Science,* Vol. 6 [August 1972], pp. 221–46; and William A. Jessiman and Donald E. Ward, *Intercity Transportation Effectiveness Model,* Final Report [Boston: Peat, Marwick, Mitchell and Co., December 1970].) Instead, we will describe in a more general way the characteristics of production costs as related to the fleets and schedules adopted.

4. Technological changes in aircraft design are not always of this character, as witness the operating and proposed supersonic transports. These aircraft are characterized by much higher speeds, but are associated with higher unit costs.

5. That is, while aircraft of a given size could be designed to operate with less power, but with wings designed for greater lift, the reduction of operating costs per hour would be overwhelmed by the reduced speed, causing an increase in the cost of capacity per ton-mile. Similarly, increases in speed are obtained at a very high cost, due to the rapid increase in air resistance and structural requirements as the speed approaches that of sound.

Aircraft Size

Economies with respect to aircraft size arise from at least two sources: crew costs and costs related to aircraft equipment and structure.[6] While the crew requirements on large aircraft are somewhat greater than on the smaller types, the relationship is less than proportional. In the latter case, there are many equipment costs that are independent of aircraft size, such as avionics, and others which are not strictly proportional to size, such as galleys. Moreover, the simple relationship between volume and area, that is, cubed dimensions versus squared dimensions, might be expected to impart some economies with respect to increasing aircraft size.

One can gain some impression of size economies from the operating cost data for representative aircraft types shown in Table 2-2. Since the average costs reported in Table 2-2 reflect a number of factors other than size, not all of the difference in average cost can be attributed to aircraft size alone.[7]

Flight Distance

Flight distance figures into the cost of producing capacity in two ways. First, for each aircraft type there is a "design range"—the maximum distance it can fly (with appropriate fuel reserves) with its design payload of passengers, baggage, and freight. While the aircraft may be able to carry additional fuel and fly a greater distance, it would do so at the expense of payload. In general, unit costs of capacity flown increase with the aircraft's design range. This occurs because to carry a given payload over a given distance an aircraft with a design range of 4,000 miles must have a greater gross weight and more powerful engines than one with a design range of, say, only 1,500 miles.[8]

For flights of a given aircraft type, however, there exists a much more significant inverse relationship between distance and unit costs. Economies with respect to distance arise principally from the "fixed cost" aspect of

6. By "economies," we mean decreasing costs per available ton-mile or available seat-mile.

7. A lucid description of aircraft operating costs and design factors which affect unit costs is contained in two papers by Robert W. Simpson: "An Analysis of Airline Costs," and "Technology for Design of Transport Aircraft," both reprinted in "Proceedings of the NASA/MIT Workshop on Airline Systems Analysis" (Massachusetts Institute of Technology, Flight Transportation Laboratory, November 1972; processed). See particularly his description of the effects aircraft size have on average cost in "Technology for Design," especially p. 29.

8. An illustration of this effect is given by Simpson in ibid., p. 30.

Table 2-2. Average Operating Costs and Performance of Turbofan Aircraft, 1971

Costs in dollars except where noted

Cost or performance item	Four-engine wide body	Four-engine regular body	Three-engine regular body	Two-engine regular body
Costs				
Direct operating costs per block hour[a]				
Crew	272.83	197.53	177.72	149.46
Fuel and oil	378.24	209.30	154.43	107.50
Other	65.06	9.87	9.46	7.86
Total flying operating costs	716.12	416.71	341.61	264.82
Maintenance costs per block hour[a]				
Airframe	127.15	58.03	50.76	43.16
Engine	166.04	39.01	39.22	31.05
Burden	130.90	93.78	75.82	57.85
Total maintenance costs	424.08	190.82	165.80	132.07
Depreciation and rentals per block hour	546.08	180.67	141.14	112.31
Total direct operating expenses per block hour	1,686.29	788.20	648.55	509.20
Total direct operating expenses per seat-mile (cents)	1.135	1.408	1.674	1.988
Performance				
Daily utilization (hours)	8.92	8.38	7.21	6.53
Capacity (average seats)	328.6	133.9	106.9	84.5
Capacity (average tons)	52.7	19.0	14.1	10.8
Average stage length (miles)	1,986	1,070	545	312
Average airborne speed (miles per hour)	507	474	432	378
Average block speed (miles per hour)	463	428	368	309

Source: Civil Aeronautics Board, *Aircraft Operating Costs and Performance Report* (August 1972), p. 1. Figures may not add to totals because of rounding.

a. A block hour begins when the aircraft leaves the origin gate and ends when the aircraft stops at the destination gate.

each flight. The direct costs of operating the aircraft on any flight are roughly proportional to the time elapsed between the departure from the origin gate to the arrival at the destination gate—that is, the "block time."[9] Since for a flight of any length some time is required for taxiing before

9. For further discussion, see the appendix to this chapter.

takeoff, climbing to cruising altitude, and taxiing after landing, there is a fixed cost component for each trip. Hence, average block time per mile flown and average direct costs per mile both fall with increases in flight distance, at least up to the design range of the aircraft.[10]

Other Factors

A number of other factors may affect the cost of producing capacity in any market. For example, the total number of hours an airline is able to fly its aircraft in revenue service affects its average cost of capacity, since aircraft ownership costs have a fixed annual component. This fact must be borne in mind when evaluating the costs of a firm that specializes in extensive charter or freight services which are less sensitive to a daily demand cycle, thus allowing the carrier to realize significantly higher levels of utilization. Similarly, airlines which operate on routes that are subject to frequent weather delays may be expected to experience higher unit costs.

Traffic Costs

While most of the costs incurred in producing scheduled air services are directly related to the generation of capacity, some are related to the quantity of passengers and freight actually carried. Many of the firm's costs are related to reservations, sales, and service to passengers and shippers. Some of these expenses are independent of the trip length, or at least have a fixed component, thus reinforcing the fixed costs which generate economies with respect to distance. Expenses of this type would include baggage handling, reservation expenses, and costs of processing passengers at the terminal. Other expenses, such as food and stewardess services, are related to the flight time or distance. Table 2-3 shows average costs of these traffic-related services.[11]

10. Since, as noted above, average costs also increase with design range, costs are minimized when the design range equals the flight distance. Since airlines fly many routes of varying distances, this is seldom the case, but rather a typical fleet may contain a mixture of short-, medium-, and long-range aircraft consonant with the airline's route structure.

11. The use of averages in this context implies that the cost function is characterized by constant returns to scale. We make this assumption here only for purposes of illustration, explicitly considering its accuracy in a subsequent discussion.

Table 2-3. Average Traffic-Related Costs, Air Coach Passengers, 1970
Dollars

	Cost per passenger trip	
Traffic-related cost item	Fixed	Variable (per mile)
Stewardesses	0.24	0.00097
Food	0.38	0.00151
Other passenger in-flight services	...	0.00135
Traffic servicing	1.93	...
Baggage service	1.05	...
Reservations and sales	0.68	0.00425
Advertising and publicity	...	0.00160
General and administrative	...	0.00318
Total	4.28	0.01286

Source: Derived by authors from data contained in direct exhibits of CAB, Bureau of Economics, CAB Docket 21866-9 (Nov. 20, 1970).

Cost Characteristics of the Passenger Trip

The cost per passenger of a representative trip from origin to destination depends greatly on the number of passengers carried per flight, since the capacity costs of the flight are approximately the same whether the aircraft flies empty or fully loaded. The ratio of passengers carried to available seats, the "average load factor," is thus the single most important determinant of the average cost per passenger. The relationship between average load factor and per-passenger cost for a representative air trip is reported in Figure 2-1 as curve *AC*. In this example—based on a hypothetical market with 800 daily passengers and a distance of 600 miles—average cost per passenger is 27 percent higher at an average load factor of 50 percent, typical of the industry in 1970, than at an average load factor of 75 percent.

While this relationship between average cost and realized average load factor is widely recognized by the Board and by the carriers, until recently it had not been regarded by either as subject to control.[12] As the following chapters show, however, the actual load factor is predictably related to the Board's pricing policies and can be a source of important cost savings to the carriers as well as the public.

Scale Effects of Firm Size

Issues of merger and restraint on entry raise questions of scale economies. In a number of areas one might anticipate lower unit costs as the

12. On this recent change in attitude, see Chapter 8.

Figure 2-1. Costs per Passenger Trip as a Function of Average
Load Factor, Hypothetical Market, 1970

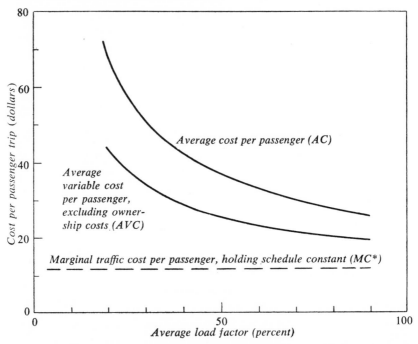

Source: Based on a hypothetical market with 800 daily passengers and distance of 600 miles.

firm's level of output rises. For example, maintenance operations require large inventories of parts and specialized labor. Moreover, scheduling maintenance is a task in which the "lumpiness," or discrete aspect of the problem, diminishes with increases in fleet size. (The existence of scale economies in such an activity as maintenance does not necessarily imply similar economies to the air carrier if, as is often the case, these activities can be contracted out to other specialist firms.) Other activities with potential scale economies include reservations, advertising, and scheduling. On the other hand, the airline is not immune to the increasing costs of information and control often found in large enterprises. Hence, whether scale economies exist must be determined empirically.

A number of previous studies of airline costs indicate that returns to scale are approximately constant.[13] The analysis of aggregate costs presented here and the conclusions generally confirm the earlier studies.

13. These include George Eads, Marc Nerlove, and William Raduchel, "A Long-Run Cost Function for the Local Service Airline Industry: An Experiment in Non-

Table 2-4. Average Ton-Miles, Operating Expense per Ton-Mile, Stage Length, and Aircraft Capacity, by Carrier Group, 1971

Item	Big four trunks	Other trunks[a]	Local service carriers
Average available ton-miles (millions)	4,980	1,363	244
Total operating expense per available ton-mile (dollars)	0.2144	0.2068	0.3639
Average stage length (miles)	673	483	160
Average aircraft capacity (tons)	17.4	17.4	8.8

Sources: CAB, *Air Carrier Financial Statistics* (December 1971), and *Air Carrier Traffic Statistics* (December 1971).
a. Includes domestic operations of Pan American World Airways. See Table 2-1, note a.

As noted above, the air service production function and its associated cost functions are not amenable to direct estimation, given the complexity of the outputs which affect costs. However, we can make a start by analyzing broad statistical cost aggregates. First, we compare the gross average costs of producing available ton-miles of capacity for the "big four" trunk carriers—American, Eastern, Trans World (TWA), and United—the smaller trunks, and the local service carriers. These comparisons, shown in Table 2-4, indicate that the average costs of capacity for the large and small trunk carriers are approximately equal, while the costs of the local service carriers are a great deal higher. This finding reflects the effects of much shorter average flight distances and the smaller aircraft used by the local service carriers.

Second, we analyze these aggregated costs using cross-section multiple regression techniques. Such an analysis, however, is severely limited and its results must be treated with caution. The first restriction is a conceptual one: the production function, and hence the cost function, is not appropriately specified with one output, or even a small number of outputs. The analysis of aggregated or average costs with aggregated or average ex-

Linear Estimation," *Review of Economics and Statistics,* Vol. 51 (August 1969), pp. 258–70; Robert J. Gordon, "Airline Costs and Managerial Efficiency," *Transportation Economics,* A Conference of the Universities–National Bureau Committee for Economic Research (Columbia University Press for the National Bureau of Economic Research, 1965), pp. 61–94; and Mahlon R. Straszheim, *The International Airline Industry* (Brookings Institution, 1969), Chap. 5, and App. B.

planatory variables introduces a number of errors if the underlying component functions are nonlinear. However, this limitation does not restrict the analysis from drawing at least qualitative inferences about the overall production process.

Another limitation encountered in the analysis is the paucity of observations with respect to the number of explanatory variables that should be employed. That is, in recent times there have been only eleven trunk carriers, which constitute a reasonably homogeneous data set, so that for a given time period there are only eleven observations. In order to increase this number, one is forced to pool time-series with cross-section data, which opens new statistical hazards. Principally, the problem is that over the time period changes occur in input costs, the relative utilization of inputs, and possibly in the production function itself. A first-order correction for most such changes is obtained by the use of time period dummy variables, and we choose for analysis a period in which we believe that the production process has remained virtually unchanged. Multicollinearity between important independent variables, such as available ton-miles and revenue ton-miles, also hampers the estimation.

The results of a cross-section time-series analysis for 1964–70 are:[14]

(1) $TOE/ATM = 1.29 + Ann \cdot Dummy + 0.016\,ATM - 0.002\,ATM^2$
$$(2.67) \qquad\qquad (2.00)$$

$$- 0.069 \log LEN + 0.015\,HUB - 0.155 \log ACAP$$
$$(3.83) \qquad\qquad (5.00) \qquad\qquad (4.84)$$

$$R^2 = 0.722; \text{ degrees of freedom} = 65.$$

(2) $DOE/ATM = 0.524 + Ann \cdot Dummy + 0.005\,ATM - 0.000\,ATM^2$
$$(1.67)$$

$$- 0.043 \log LEN + 0.006\,HUB - 0.040 \log ACAP,$$
$$(5.38) \qquad\qquad (6.00) \qquad\qquad (2.67)$$

$$R^2 = 0.734; \text{ degrees of freedom} = 65.$$

where

TOE/ATM = total operating expense per available ton-mile

DOE/ATM = direct operating expense (flying operations + direct maintenance + depreciation on flight equipment) per available ton-mile

ATM = available ton-miles flown (billions)

LEN = average flight stage length

---

14. Derived from data in CAB, *Handbook of Airline Statistics, 1971 Edition* (1972).

HUB = percent of flight departures from major hubs
$ACAP$ = average aircraft capacity (tons)

and the numbers in parentheses are the t-statistics.

Average stage length is strongly significant in the manner hypothesized—that is, average cost decreases as average stage length increases. Since operations in high density airports require greater time and expenditures than in others, we have employed as a proxy measure the proportion of aircraft departures for each carrier from airports characterized by the FAA as "large traffic hubs" (42 large urban centers, each of which generates more than 1 percent of total national enplanements). The effect of this variable on unit costs is also significant and of the appropriate sign. We have accounted for economies in aircraft size by the inclusion of this measure as an independent variable, again with strong significance and the appropriate sign. Finally, the coefficients for output, available ton-miles flown, and output-squared are close to zero, and indicate slightly increasing, then decreasing, unit costs with output.[15] The absolute size of this effect, however, is quite slight; at the average values taken by the independent variables, an increase in output by 10 percent would increase average unit costs by approximately 1.5 percent. This result is broadly consistent with most prior investigations of airline costs—that no important scale economies exist in the production of aggregate output over the range of sizes represented by the existing trunk carriers.

A final, though highly imperfect, test of scale economies is a comparison of achieved profit rates, as reported in Table 2-5. As can be seen, the larger carriers seem to have fared relatively less well than the smaller trunks. This evidence is further bolstered by the viability of a small, unregulated carrier that successfully and profitably competes with large trunks in the intrastate California markets, exhibiting production efficiencies not generally realized by the larger carriers.[16]

These results, together with those outlined in the appendix to this chapter, support our assuming in this study that the airlines are characterized by constant returns to scale for relevant ranges of output. Moreover, they strongly suggest that horizontal mergers are not likely to achieve any significant economies of operating costs; that when profit incentives exist for such a merger, the effects are primarily on the demand side.

15. Note too that the t-statistics are fairly small, raising questions about the possibility of no size effect whatsoever.

16. See William A. Jordan, *Airline Regulation in America: Effects and Imperfections* (Johns Hopkins Press, 1970), pp. 178–225.

Table 2-5. Rate of Return on Investment, Domestic Operations of Trunk Air Carriers, in Order of Increasing Carrier Size, 1965–70

Carrier or group	Carrier size measured by available ton-miles, 1970 (millions)	Rate of return (percent)[a]					
		1965	1966	1967	1968	1969	1970[b]
Northeast Airlines	604	[c]	3.7	−15.5	1.1	−66.8	−57.1
National Airlines	906	19.6	15.9	17.1	12.8	9.1	−1.8
Braniff Airways	1,027	14.1	15.9	2.2	5.0	5.9	3.4
Western Air Lines	1,180	14.7	15.9	10.6	6.2	−0.4	4.0
Northwest Airlines	1,217	20.4	16.0	14.2	10.4	7.7	3.8
Continental Air Lines	1,472	19.1	20.9	13.6	5.1	4.4	5.1
Delta Air Lines	2,636	23.6	28.7	18.7	14.6	12.8	11.8
Eastern Air Lines	3,139	11.5	6.0	6.5	0.8	3.0	3.6
Trans World Airlines	4,261	9.9	7.2	3.9	1.0	1.1	−4.8
American Airlines	5,307	9.4	9.8	6.6	6.1	6.4	−0.4
United Air Lines	7,337	8.9	6.7	6.9	5.0	5.8	0.7
Big four trunks	...	9.7	7.6	6.1	3.7	4.4	−0.1
Other trunks[d]	...	19.3	18.9	12.0	9.1	5.3	4.6
All trunks[d]	...	12.2	10.9	7.7	5.3	4.7	1.6

Source: Civil Aeronautics Board, *Handbook of Airline Statistics, 1971 Edition* (1972), pp. 120–31, 391.

a. Defined as net profit after taxes but before interest payment on debt as a percent of equity-plus-long-term-debt; excludes investment tax credits.

b. Includes operations in Alaska and Hawaii as well as the other forty-eight states.

c. Not computed due to smallness of base.

d. Includes domestic operations of Pan American World Airways. See Table 2-1, note a.

Summary

The per-passenger cost of air service depends on several factors. First, total cost for a given aircraft increases with greater distance, but at a decreasing rate of increase; thus, cost per passenger-mile is lower the longer the flight. Second, per-passenger cost is generally lower the larger the aircraft. Since the larger aircraft tend to be used on the longest routes, this reinforces the effect of lower per-mile costs of greater travel distance. Third, and most important for this study, average cost is affected significantly by aircraft utilization. When load factors are high, per-passenger cost is low, and vice versa. Finally, for the trunk carriers, size of the firm per se does not have a significant impact on the level of average cost. In short, the airline industry is characterized by reasonably constant returns to scale.

Appendix: A Scheduled Air Service Cost Function

The Civil Aeronautics Board, in common with most regulatory agencies, obtains a large volume of cost data from the industry it regulates. Air carriers file quarterly reports with the Board in a standard accounting format (CAB Form 41), and the Board, in turn, makes these publicly available and regularly publishes individual carrier costs by accounting category. While the data are rich in many aspects, their specification and design are more in accordance with the needs of audit than with the needs of econometric studies of air service cost functions. Generally, the data are aggregated excessively, typically over the firm's entire operation. Moreover, the measurement of certain costs may reflect the application of arbitrary cost allocation rules, generally proportional to some output measure, and if used uncritically to test cost relationships may only confirm these arbitrary accounting conventions. Nevertheless, with the foregoing caveats, we shall discuss below a typical analytic technique for describing air transport costs.

Capacity Costs

The direct costs for a trip over a given route for aircraft type i typically are represented as a function of the operating time. Two measures of operating time are commonly used: block time and airborne time. Block time begins when the engines are started at one terminal and ends when the engines are shut down at the next; airborne time is self-explanatory. Conceptually, it would appear that an accurate representation of costs should embody both airborne time T_a and ground time T_g (that is, block time minus airborne time), since at the very least fuel consumption is lower while taxiing than while airborne. If the form is linear, we would expect then that direct trip costs would be of the form:

$$(3) \qquad C_{t_i} = \alpha_{0_i} + \alpha_{1_i}T_a + \alpha_{2_i}T_g.$$

Most analyses of airline costs, however, express direct trip costs as a function of block time T, where $T = T_a + T_g$, and suppress the constant:[17]

$$(4) \qquad C_{t_i} = \alpha_{3_i}T.$$

This simple expression of cost as a constant proportion of block time may serve as a good approximation of equation (3) if in the system's operations ground time T_g is approximately constant at some level $\bar{T}_g$. If so, then equation (3) may be written:

17. This is the approach taken by Simpson in "An Analysis of Airline Costs," and "Technology for Design"; by Theodore E. Keeler, "Airline Regulation and Market Performance," *Bell Journal of Economics and Management Science,* Vol. 3 (Autumn 1972), pp. 399–424; and by the Board's Bureau of Economics (CAB Docket 21866-9, Nov. 20, 1970). Direct trip costs represented here do not include the landing fees and services provided at the gate. These are estimated separately.

(5) $$C_{t_i} = \alpha_{0_i} + (\alpha_{2_i} - \alpha_{1_i})\bar{T}_g + \alpha_{1_i}(T_a + \bar{T}_g).$$

The first two terms on the right-hand side of equation (5) then become the constant, which might well be approximated by zero since we assume that $\alpha_{1_i} > \alpha_{2_i}$.

While the above assumptions are in principle testable, the source of data is not suitable for a test of great discrimination. The Board does publish operating costs by aircraft type and by carrier, but since it is aggregated over all the carrier's flights involving the aircraft, we have at the outside only one observation per carrier.

For the Boeing 727-200, an aircraft that is widely represented in the trunk carriers' fleets, we fit the following regressions:[18]

(6) $$T_{c_i} = -73.30 + 1584T_g + 410T_a,$$
$$(2.2) \qquad (3.7)$$
$$R^2 = 0.81;\ \text{degrees of freedom} = 9.$$

and

(7) $$T_{c_i} = 19.94 + 519T,$$
$$(5.7)$$
$$R^2 = 0.76;\ \text{degrees of freedom} = 10.$$

where time is measured in hours. The explanatory power of the single-variable equation (7) is about the same as the two-variable equation (6), and the small constant is not significantly different from zero, lending support to the use of a proportional trip cost model (that is, total capacity cost as a function of time in transit).[19]

A proportional trip cost model then works quite simply. Average costs per block hour are estimated for each aircraft type. The direct operating cost for a trip of distance d_j is then simply the cost per block hour of aircraft type i times the expected trip time T_j for distance d_j. Trip time (block time) can be estimated quite accurately as a linear function of distance:

(8) $$T_j = T_0 + \beta d_j.$$

From the reported averages by aircraft type and carrier, we can estimate the required coefficients. First, from the reported average block speed and average trip distance for each carrier, we compute the average trip time. Each carrier having aircraft of the type analyzed generates then a single

18. The data are from U.S. Civil Aeronautics Board, *Aircraft Operating Cost and Performance Report for Calendar Years 1970 and 1971* (August 1972).

19. Where ground times diverge significantly from the average, such as at congested airports, one would do better to estimate the costs attributable to ground and airborne times separately.

observation (T_j, d_j). To illustrate, data for the Boeing 727-200 for the year 1971 were used to estimate the coefficients of equation (8):

$$(9) \qquad T_j = 22.1 + 0.12d,$$
$$R^2 = 0.93.$$

where T_j is measured in minutes.

Alternatively, one can regress scheduled trip times published by the carriers against distance. For the 727-200, Simpson reports that scheduled trip time may be represented as:[20]

$$(10) \qquad T = 26 + 0.11d.$$

The Board's Bureau of Economics costing model uses a similar expression for the 727-200:[21]

$$(11) \qquad T = 29 + 0.106d.$$

The proportional time cost model then generates distance economies as a result of the "fixed cost" in time per trip. It should be noted that this time intercept not only includes an estimate of ground time, but also includes the effect of the lower speeds associated with climbing and descending.

The direct flight cost function implied is then linear with respect to distance:

$$(12) \qquad C_{T_j} = c_0 + c_1 d_j.$$

The coefficient estimates for the 727-200 in 1971 are:

$$(13) \qquad C_{T_j} = \$240.71 + 0.985d_j.$$
$$(4.2)$$
$$R^2 = 0.64; \text{ degrees of freedom} = 10.$$

More frequently, the data are insufficient to estimate equation (12), and the coefficients are generated by estimating the coefficients T_0 and β of equation (8), computing the average cost per block hour, α_3, for the observations available on aircraft i, and setting $c_0 = \alpha_3 T_0$, and $c_1 = \alpha_3 \beta$. Other ground expenses, such as servicing the aircraft at the gate and landing fees, are related to the unit of operation, rather than flight time. Adding estimates of these constants to the constant term in the direct flight cost function gives a direct trip cost function:

$$(14) \qquad C_{ij} = \lambda_i + \rho_i d_j.$$

20. Simpson, "Technology for Design," p. 32.
21. CAB Docket 21866-9, direct exhibits of the Bureau of Economics.

Estimates of the direct operating cost parameters for various current air-craft types are reported in Table 2-6.[22]

Traffic Costs

The costs of providing services to travelers and shippers is generally assumed to be proportional to some direct measure of activity, such as revenue passengers enplaned or revenue passenger-miles. This assumption of proportionality, of course, is analogous to the assumption of constant long-run average costs. Such an assumption, we believe, is reasonably justifiable as a good approximation for two reasons. First, the relationship may be determined explicitly by contract or by practice. For example, the sales commission "expense" is established as a fixed percentage of the fare; since the latter can be approximated as a linear function of distance, commission expenses are by definition a function of revenue passenger-miles. Similarly, stewardesses, baggage handlers, and other personnel directly engaged with the public are required by contract or by practice to perform their duties with regard to passenger block hours (number of passenger-hours in the aircraft) or passengers enplaned. Second, in defining "output" of these services one should bear in mind its relationship with "quality." In lieu of an appropriate, detailed study of the production of services standardized for quality (which is related to, if not defined by, dollars expended), the heuristic relationship of average cost by unit activity (Table 2-6) is the best available approximation of these costs.

Cost Characteristics of the Passenger Trip

In converting capacity costs per flight to capacity costs per passenger trip, it must be recognized that each flight produces typically three kinds of output: first class traffic, coach class traffic, and air freight. Since capacity costs are common to all services, an issue in the determination of average costs per unit of output is the allocation of these common costs to each

22. One principal adjustment is made in the reported costs to reflect more accurately the long-run costs of capacity. The CAB accounts for depreciation expense and aircraft lease expense are replaced by a more general ownership expense which includes both depreciation and an imputed reasonable return on capital. This we have estimated by the annual payments required to amortize the capital cost over a useful life of fourteen years at a discount rate of 18 percent in order to yield a 12 percent return on investment. (This is current Board practice; we do not necessarily endorse these figures.)

Table 2-6. Direct Flight Operating Cost Parameters, by Type of Aircraft, 1971

Costs in dollars

Cost parameter	Boeing 747	Douglas DC-10	Douglas DC-8-63	Boeing 727-200	Boeing 737-200	Douglas DC-9-30
Aircraft costs						
Purchase price (millions)	28.7	23.0	13.0	8.4	6.0	5.4
Ownership, annual[a] (millions)	5.65	4.53	2.56	1.65	1.18	1.06
Total direct operating costs, per hour, α_3	3,025	2,843	1,576	1,046	838	733
Ownership[a]	1,885	1,510	854	552	394	355
Flight	1,140	1,333	722	494	444	378
Ground expense, per departure, g_1	620.54	358.34	244.82	143.99	86.24	86.24
Landing fees, per departure, g_2	146.64	90.43	53.74	36.54	23.81	23.81
Coefficients						
Trip time (hours)						
Fixed time component, T_0	0.6833	0.6833	0.6833	0.3693	0.3693	0.3693
Distance, β	0.00181	0.00181	0.00181	0.0020	0.0020	0.0020
Trip cost						
Fixed	2,834	2,391	1,375	567	420	381
Variable	5.475	5.146	2.853	2.092	1.676	1.466

Sources: Purchase prices are the averages of aircraft sales prices as reported by Robert W. Simpson, "Technology for Design of Transport Aircraft," in "Proceedings of the NASA/MIT Workshop on Airline Systems Analysis" (Massachusetts Institute of Technology, Flight Transportation Laboratory, November 1972; processed), pp. 48, 49. Direct flight costs are average costs for domestic trunks for flying operations and maintenance, as reported in CAB, *Aircraft Operating Cost and Performance Report* (August 1972), pp. 13–17, except for DC-10, which is from CAB, direct exhibits of Bureau of Economics, Docket 21866-9, cited in Table 2-3. Ground expense and landing fees are from Docket 21866-9. The trip time coefficients are derived from text equation (6). The fixed cost coefficients = $\alpha_3 T_0 + g_1 + g_2$; the variable coefficients = $\alpha_3 \beta$.

a. Ownership costs are depreciation and return on capital, amortized over a life of fourteen years at a discount rate of 18 percent, to yield a 12 percent return on investment. Hourly costs assume 3,000 hours annual utilization per aircraft.

activity. As we discuss in Chapter 5, in the long run the production process is flexible as to output composition, and thus the various outputs should be treated as common products, rather than joint products or by-products. One way to simplify the issue is to estimate costs based on a single output, such as coach service, and then indicate the trade-off between coach capacity and other services, first class and freight. Since coach class traffic and revenues overwhelmingly dominate the others, we will base the following synthesis of costs on coach service alone. Further, while recognizing that the size of the coach seat and the space used are variable, we will take as a standard the typical dimensions prevailing at this time: a width of 18 inches and a pitch fore and aft of 34 inches.

In general form, we may express the cost per passenger trip as:

$$(15) \qquad P_{ij} = [(\lambda_i + \rho_i d_j)/N_i] + \gamma + \delta d_j,$$

where

P_{ij} = per passenger cost of trip, aircraft i, market j

λ_i = fixed capacity cost per trip, aircraft i

ρ_i = variable capacity cost per mile, aircraft i

d_j = distance (in miles), market j

N_i = number of passengers, aircraft i

γ = fixed (passenger) traffic cost per trip

δ = variable (passenger) traffic cost per mile.

Table 2-7 shows estimates of capacity costs per seat by aircraft type, along with traffic costs per passenger. Figure 2-1 illustrates the aforementioned economies with respect to distance for typical aircraft, assuming, for illustrative purposes, a 60 percent average load factor. (First class service costs may be estimated by multiplying coach capacity costs per seat by the ratio of the difference in floor space, approximately 1.6, and further by adjusting food service costs by a factor of approximately 2.4 and stewardess service cost by a factor of approximately 3.0.)

The factor of greatest importance for average trip cost per passenger,

Table 2-7. Estimated Cost Parameters per Passenger Trip, Domestic Trunk Air Coach, 1971

Costs in dollars

Type of aircraft	Total seats[a]	Capacity costs per seat		Traffic costs per passenger	
		Fixed	Variable (per mile)	Fixed	Variable (per mile)
Boeing 747	397	7.14	0.0138	4.28	0.01286
Douglas DC-10	280	8.54	0.0184	4.28	0.01286
Douglas DC-8-63	213	6.45	0.0134	4.28	0.01286
Boeing 727-200	148	3.83	0.0141	4.28	0.01286
Boeing 737-200	102	4.12	0.0164	4.28	0.01286
Douglas DC-9-30	97	3.93	0.0151	4.28	0.01286

Source: Calculations as described in text, using as data source CAB, *Aircraft Operating Cost and Performance Report* (August 1972).

a. 100 percent coach equivalent.

however, is the average load factor achieved. Equation (15) can be expressed equivalently as:

(16) $$P_{ij} = \{[\lambda_i/S_i + (\rho_i/S_i)d_j]/ALF\} + \gamma + \delta d_j,$$

where S_i is the number of seats in aircraft i, and where ALF = average load factor = N_i/S_i. Thus, for a given route, the relation between average cost per passenger and average load factor is hyperbolic, as shown in Figure 2-1.

We can also approximate the marginal costs of changing output composition, both in the short run and in the long run. If schedules are held constant, the very short-run (or market-period) marginal cost to the firm of carrying an additional passenger in an unfilled aircraft approaches zero. That is, since an unanticipated increase in the number of passengers carried would not cause a staffing change of the carrier's personnel who provide passenger services, the out-of-pocket change in cost in the market period would be only the food and beverages consumed in flight, plus some small additional wear and tear on the upholstery. Stating the conditions this way points out that the additional costs are not borne solely by the firm, but also by the other passengers in the diminished service quality they receive. The additional (unanticipated) passenger's demand for service would increase delays at the gate, cause more congestion and crowding on the aircraft, increase baggage handling delays, and decrease the individual services received from the stewardesses.

An "intermediate-run" marginal cost may be defined relative to an anticipated change in passengers, holding scheduled capacity constant. In this case, the marginal cost to the firm would comprise those traffic costs discussed above, at their average values if we assume constant returns. These "marginal costs," estimated for a representative 600-mile trip, are shown as MC^* in Figure 2-1. Note again, however, that here we have measured only the marginal cost to the firm, and not the total or social marginal cost of the service. The additional passengers carried, holding capacity fixed, diminishes the quality of service received by the other passengers in a different dimension. Although as described more extensively later, as the load factor of the scheduled service increases, the probability of being able to travel at one's most desired time is reduced. Hence, the intermediate marginal cost, MC^*, does not in fact measure the marginal cost of the same quality of service.

One can more closely estimate the marginal cost of carrying an additional passenger on a scheduled transport system while holding service quality constant by holding the average load factor constant.[23] In this case, we are defining the long-run marginal cost of changing both capacity and traffic proportionately. If the cost function is characterized by constant costs, then long-run marginal cost is equal to long-run average cost for the load factor (quality level) chosen.

At least one other cost concept is of considerable interest—intermediate-run average variable cost. That is, suppose we consider the fleet to be fixed, yet the schedules are not. Thus, in considering fluctuations in output over the year, for example, it is useful to know the average variable costs, omitting the "sunk" ownership costs of the fleet and other capital. These can be estimated by subtracting "ownership costs per hour" from "direct operating costs per hour" in Table 2-6 to obtain the average variable cost of capacity with fleet size held constant. An example of the average variable cost per passenger trip is shown in Figure 2-1 with the curve labeled AVC.

23. Assume for now that average load factor is the only dimension of service quality.

The Demand for Scheduled Air Service

IN WELL-FUNCTIONING competitive markets the desirable rate and quality of production are determined directly by the interplay of supply (costs) and demand (benefits), but in the domestic airline market a regulator is interposed between producers and consumers. As we will describe in Chapter 4, the decisions made by the regulator profoundly affect the character of the system. Thus, to judge the regulator's performance in representing the public, a rather detailed description of demand is required.

With the aim, then, of characterizing the demand for air transportation as an indicator of benefits to travelers, we will describe in this chapter how it may be analyzed and will draw inferences which are essential to enlightened regulation.

Nature of the Demand for Scheduled Air Travel

Underlying many analyses of the demand for air travel is an important assumption—that air travel is generally an "intermediate good." It is simply a means of moving from one point to another for some other purpose. Thus, while the Sunday afternoon drive and the cruise to nowhere represent examples of the consumption aspect of travel, the trip by commercial airline is not usually thought of in and of itself as consumption. By characterizing air travel as an intermediate good it is possible to hypothesize a decision process followed by travelers from which many important characteristics of air travel demand can be inferred.[1]

The travel decision can be separated conveniently into three components: (a) whether to travel at all, or how often, (b) by what mode: air,

1. That is, air travel can be analyzed as a derived demand.

auto, bus, or other, and (c) at what time. Once the decision to travel has been made, the individual's choice of mode and timing are assumed to be based on the desire to minimize the cost and inconvenience of travel. Put another way, the traveler minimizes his "full cost" of travel, such full cost including price or monetary cost, trip time, and schedule convenience.[2]

For example, consider an individual in city A who needs to be in city B for a 1:00 P.M. meeting. If his options are to drive a personal car or take a scheduled flight, the decision process may be portrayed in the following way. Suppose the time en route by car is five hours and the variable expenses of operating the car are $15. The time en route by air is one hour and the fare is $25. However, the total time of the trip by air also includes the time required to reach the airport at city A, the required check-in time, the time to deplane and possibly claim baggage, and also the travel time from the airport at city B to the final destination. Similarly, one must add to the air fare the costs of the trip to and from each airport to determine the total monetary cost of the air trip. In short, the decision to take a trip by public transport must include an assessment of the access and egress times and costs.

After accounting for access and egress, the air trip price may be $30 and the time two hours door to door. When compared with the auto alternative, the total cost would be less by air if the traveler valued his time above $5 per hour.[3] That is, at a time value of $5 per hour, the full cost of travel by each mode is $40 (that is, auto: $15 + $25; and air: $30 + $10). For trips of this nature a traveler valuing his time at, say, $6 per hour would probably choose to travel by air *provided there were space on a conveniently timed departure* and if he were indifferent to the relative comforts of air and auto travel.

From such a priori reasoning a number of useful inferences can be drawn about the demand for travel. First, since the air mode has typically had a time advantage over surface transport but a slight fare disadvantage, the value of time is an important determinant of the choices of travelers between air and other modes. Similarly, air travel demand appears highly income elastic, that is, it responds disproportionately to given percentage changes in income level. This derives not only from the positive income elasticity of travel generally, but also from the growth of the relative share

2. It is this hypothetical full cost of travel which then is weighed against the benefits to be gained from traveling in determining whether or how often one travels.
3. A further allowance may be made for the value of food and drink, and for relative comfort and safety.

of air travel caused by the increase in per capita income and thus higher time value. That is, studies uniformly show a positive relationship between the individual's income level and the value he places on his time.

Second, the relative advantage of the air mode increases with trip distance. The reason is that the time saving of air travel over surface alternatives grows faster than the money saving of surface over air. A general "break point," or discontinuity, occurs at a distance which can be driven comfortably in a day, since beyond this distance the cost of the auto trip must include lodging. Hence, over long distances the air mode has a greater advantage. Those who travel long distances by auto do so for some direct purpose of consumption, such as viewing the scenery or visiting en route, taking additional passengers without incurring additional cost, or because their time is of low value.

Third, reductions in the air fare cause a reduction in the critical time value (above which the total trip cost by air is less than by one of the alternatives). This causes a greater number of people to travel by air. Further, a reduction in the total trip cost for all air travelers enhances demand. Fourth, time en route by air decreases as aircraft speeds increase, or as the number of stops en route is reduced, or both. Such a change, of course, enhances the relative advantage of the air trip, and could be expected to increase air travel at the expense of other modes, as well as air travel in general. In response to all these described effects, air travel grew over the twenty-year period 1950–70 at a compound annual rate of 13.4 percent.[4]

While the role of price and trip time is commonly recognized in the discussion of air travel demand, another and often overlooked factor of considerable importance is the convenience of the scheduled service. What follows emphasizes the role service plays in travelers' decisions and its significance in the determination of an efficient airline market.

In transportation, the timing of the service usually affects its desirability to the traveler. That is, each traveler typically has some preferred time of departure or arrival for any specific trip. For the traveler, a convenient schedule is one where a departure with an available seat coincides with his most preferred time of departure. Conversely, an inconvenient schedule is one which causes him to depart at a less preferred time. By this definition, all forms of private transport offer the greatest possible schedule convenience: one simply schedules the departure for the most preferred time. Sup-

4. Revenue passenger-miles for the domestic trunk carriers grew from 7.8 billion in 1950 to 95.9 billion in 1972. U.S. Civil Aeronautics Board, *Handbook of Airline Statistics, 1971 Edition* (1972).

pose the traveler wishes to depart at 11:00 A.M. While he may have preferred flying to driving if there were a flight at or close to 11:00, the flight alternative becomes less attractive if he must take a flight at 9:00 A.M. or must postpone his trip until noon. It is quite conceivable that the inconvenience of an earlier or later departure would cause him to revise his plans and travel by auto or perhaps not take the trip at all.

More important, the concept of convenience thus defined becomes measurable. For a given day in a particular city-pair market the most preferred departure times of potential travelers vary from early morning to late at night. While many travelers' preferences are similar, thus generating peaks in the time pattern of demand, there is generally sufficient variation to ensure that with a given number of flights many or most travelers will be unable to depart precisely at their most preferred time. Such travelers are obliged to adjust their departure time to the closest scheduled flight with an available seat.

For any given schedule travelers must make adjustments if they use the scheduled system. Since for the individual traveler the convenience of the service is indicated by the difference between his preferred departure time and his actual departure time, the overall convenience of service in this market is the average of this time difference over all passengers, that is, the adjustment per passenger. We have defined this difference as "schedule delay." The expected schedule delay per passenger is then a measurable surrogate for schedule convenience in the market.

In air transport the level of schedule delay can and does vary considerably. For example, at one end of the scale some high-salaried executives may avoid schedule delay entirely by using a personal or business jet aircraft. At the other end of the scale passengers traveling in a group charter a plane, accepting substantial schedule delay in order to cut their fare.[5] Scheduled transport, of course, lies between these two poles, but the level of service convenience can vary widely across markets. Generally, heavily traveled markets are likely to have lower expected schedule delays than more lightly traveled markets, since the former have more frequently scheduled departures. However, as we shall develop in greater detail in Chapter 6, schedule delays depend on other factors besides daily flight frequencies, such as the availability of seats.

5. Where the members' travel plans coincide anyway, such as an alumni group traveling to a football game or a business group traveling to a convention, the aggregate schedule delay may in fact be very small.

Use of Demand Analysis

Through empirical analysis it is possible to estimate the effect on air travel demand of some specific change in one or more of its independent determinants. Thus far, the Civil Aeronautics Board has focused its demand analysis on two areas: the forecasting of air travel in future years as an aid to planning, and the study of the sensitivity of air travel demand to changes in price. While price elasticity is one of the principal determinants of the quantity of a good or service demanded (and thus is essential for good forecasting), most of the Board's preoccupation with price elasticity is inappropriate. That is, as we shall discuss more thoroughly in Chapter 5, fares should be determined primarily by the costs of production, and only in unusual cases should they be influenced by demand elasticity.

A knowledge of the sensitivity of quantity demanded to changes in price is, however, quite important in another way. When used in conjunction with the sensitivity of demand to some other characteristic, one can infer the implicit value of that characteristic measured in dollars. For example, the size of the aircraft's seats and the amount of leg room, or "pitch," affect the comfort of the traveler. By increasing the seat dimensions and enhancing comfort, air travel would become more attractive, and presumably more people would fly, ceteris paribus. Suppose it were found that an increase of, say, two inches in both seat width and pitch would increase by 1 percent the quantity of air travel demanded. Suppose that from a knowledge of the price sensitivity, one could calculate that a $2 fare reduction, taken alone, could also increase by 1 percent air trips demanded in the same market. One could then infer that travelers are willing to trade off the increment of comfort of the larger seat for $2. (Whether the seat dimensions should be changed, of course, depends on the additional costs attendant on changing the configuration and reducing the number of seats in the aircraft.) Similar trade-offs could be defined for other characteristics which determine the demand for air travel, such as speedier baggage claim, broader aisles, and more expensive meals.

Economists have evidenced a continual interest in the implicit valuation of time en route, as one example, since it plays such a key role in determining the relative share of travelers choosing each mode. Moreover, the analysis would be simplified if the implicit value of time could be estimated by the hourly wage rate of the travelers. (Hence, the sensitivity of demand to price and time in future years could be projected if the income level and distribution of the population were known or could be forecast.) A study by Reuben Gronau in 1970 found that travelers' choices can be explained fairly accurately by assigning a time value equal to the passenger's wage rate.[6] A notable application of this methodology for demand forecasting is the 1966 study of the proposed supersonic transport by the Institute for Defense Analyses.[7]

As we shall develop in subsequent chapters, a principal ramification of the CAB's pricing regulation has been the effect on the service convenience of the scheduled air system. Since the regulator can control the level of convenience and cost, the efficient policy toward price and service quality can be shown to depend crucially on the perceived benefits of extra convenience.

Ideally, one could infer from an appropriate demand analysis the traveler's implicit value of convenience or avoidance of schedule delay. Consider again the example of the traveler who wishes to depart at 11:00 A.M. Suppose, moreover, that he is the marginal air traveler who values his time en route at just barely over $5 an hour and who would choose to fly only if he could depart at 11:00 A.M. Suppose, however, that there were no 11:00 A.M. departure, the closest being at 10:00 A.M. He faces a one-hour schedule "delay," which presumably would cause him to choose driving over flying. But if he were offered a reduced air fare that compensated him for the cost he places on the inconvenience of one hour's schedule delay, he might again decide to travel by air. A demand analysis does not portray a single individual's decision, however, but the aggregate decision of many travelers. The trade-off between convenience and money would thus be defined as the fare reduction which would be necessary to compensate for the effect on daily demand of a one-hour increase in expected average schedule delay per passenger.[8]

We should emphasize again at this point the distinction between the

6. Reuben Gronau, *The Value of Time in Passenger Transportation: The Demand for Air Travel* (Columbia University Press for the National Bureau of Economic Research, 1970).

7. Norman J. Asher and others, "Demand Analysis for Air Travel by Supersonic Transport," Vols. 1, 2 (Arlington, Va.: Institute for Defense Analyses, 1966; processed). Noting that the projected sale of SSTs was highly sensitive to the hypothesized time value, the FAA "encouraged" the authors of the study to value travelers' time at 1.5 times their wage rates! See ibid., pp. 4–23, 58.

8. Specifically, this trade-off rate is defined as $(\partial N/T_s)/(\partial N/P)$, where N is the quantity of air trips demanded per time period, T_s is expected schedule delay, and P is price.

traveler's value of *time en route* and his value of *timing* as represented by schedule delay. The former almost certainly exceeds the latter, since the time represented by schedule delay has alternative uses; it need not be spent in waiting,[9] whereas the alternative uses of time en route are quite limited. Thus, one would expect to assign a higher value to time en route than to schedule delay.

Time Pattern of Air Travel Demand

Travel demands fluctuate over time in response to preferences of the travelers. There are seasonal demand patterns that reflect primarily the time patterns of other economic and personal activities—daily cycles, weekly cycles, and an annual pattern. Table 3-1 indicates the daily cycle of service demanded for the domestic trunk air carriers and average load factors, that is, the proportion of seats filled. While this pattern varies somewhat over markets—depending on whether they are primarily North-South, or East-West and thus crossing time zones—it does represent the average peaking behavior of traffic over the course of the day.[10] Two peaks are discernible: one around 9:00 A.M. and another at the close of the business day, from 5:00 P.M. to 7:00 P.M.

The weekly pattern is illustrated in Table 3-2, and the annual cycle of demand in Table 3-3. The variation in demand over the week is considerably less than over the year, the trough day averaging approximately 84 percent of the demand of the peak day in the weekly cycle, while the trough month's average daily demand is approximately 66 percent of that of the peak month. Thus, carriers tend to maintain a rather steady schedule over the days of the week, while altering schedules in response to seasonal variation over the year.

As will be shown in some detail in Chapters 5 and 6, the peaking of demand does introduce a pricing issue which has yet to be satisfactorily addressed by the Board in regulating the structure of fares.

In addition to the predictable level and timing of demand, there is a random, or stochastic, component. As will be described in Chapter 6, a

9. Exceptions might include emergency travel, where the arrival at or before a specific time is of great value.

10. Since the data reflect passengers carried, the time profile is of necessity constrained by the actual timing and quantities of capacity offered (for example, observe that load factors tend to peak along with traffic in Table 3-1).

Table 3-1. Daily Cycle in Air Traffic and Average Load Factors, Domestic Trunk Carriers, Sample Periods, 1969

Hour of departure	Traffic as percent of peak hour	Average load factor (percent)
1:00 A.M.	15.2	45
2:00	5.7	31
3:00	4.1	36
4:00	2.8	43
5:00	2.3	44
6:00	2.5	a
7:00	29.0	42
8:00	71.2	48
9:00	92.5	55
10:00	77.2	57
11:00	65.7	51
12:00 noon	74.4	66
1:00 P.M.	70.6	58
2:00	63.8	55
3:00	74.4	63
4:00	78.3	66
5:00 (peak)	100.0	64
6:00	99.1	64
7:00	95.8	61
8:00	57.6	53
9:00	55.8	44
10:00	37.1	44
11:00	21.7	38
12:00 midnight	14.9	46

Sources: Traffic—U.S. Department of Transportation, CAB Docket 21866-9, Exhibit DOT-D-34 (sample period covered all of 1969); average load factors—Department of Transportation, CAB Docket 21866-6, Exhibit DOT-D-1, p. 1 (sample period covered February and November 1969).
a. No flights scheduled at this hour during load factor sample period.

knowledge of this random aspect of air travel demand is essential to a determination of optimal market characteristics.

Demand Studies and Their Estimates

For long-range planning, the airlines, the CAB, and the Department of Transportation require forecasts of future levels and trends in air travel and its spatial patterns. For these purposes demand analysis usually employs aggregative data on the annual revenue passenger-miles flown, the average real fare, total population, gross national product, and so on. These time series analyses are useful in forecasting the major trends but are not satis-

Table 3-2. Weekly Cycle in Air Traffic and Average Load Factors, Domestic Trunk Carriers, Sample Periods, 1969

Day of week	Traffic as percent of peak day	Average load factor (percent)
Monday	90.0	63
Tuesday	88.4	51
Wednesday	92.8	53
Thursday	97.7	57
Friday (peak)	100.0	56
Saturday	84.2	58
Sunday	98.0	53

Sources: Traffic—U.S. Department of Transportation, CAB Docket 21866-9, Exhibit DOT-D-56 (sample period covered all of 1969); average load factors—Department of Transportation, CAB Docket 21866-6, Exhibit DOT-D-4, p. 1 (sample period covered February and November 1969).

Table 3-3. Monthly Cycle in Air Traffic and Average Load Factors, Domestic Trunk Carriers, Sample Periods, 1969

Month	Traffic as percent of peak month	Average load factor (percent)
January	86.2	...
February	66.0	58
March	85.6	...
April	94.6	...
May	92.9	59
June	98.6	...
July	95.2	...
August (peak)	100.0	71
September	83.3	...
October	86.7	...
November	79.2	55
December	93.7	...

Sources: Traffic—U.S. Department of Transportation, CAB Docket 21866-9, Exhibit DOT-D-78 (sample period covered all of 1969); average load factors—Department of Transportation, CAB Docket 21866-6, Exhibit DOT-D-7, p. 1 (sample period covered February, May, August, and November 1969).

factory in measuring the characteristics of demand that are required for efficient price and quality regulation. That is, such aggregative analysis merely reveals the effects on demand one would expect from observed variations in the character of individual city-pair markets.[11]

11. Other forecasting techniques in use include input-output analysis. However, these analyses shed little light on the issues of relevance to efficient pricing. Another rather ambitious method, which indicates considerable promise in principle, attempts to explain travel demands for all modes in a given region with the relative prices and

For an analysis of regulatory issues, forecasting needs are secondary, and a much more modest partial analysis of demand is suitable. Two recent cross-section, or market-by-market, analyses of air travel provide both a general confirmation of the demand decision process described earlier and some of the estimates needed in guiding optimal regulation. The objective of the cross-section analysis is to explain statistically the different levels of air travel among the city-pair markets served by the airlines. These differences can be attributed to those characteristics which would be expected a priori to have a determining influence on the demand for air travel: the population of the cities, their distance apart, their per capita incomes, the fare level, and the air travel time.[12]

One study of the demand for air travel by Arthur S. De Vany employed 1968 data collected by a CAB origin-destination survey, with observations on 572 markets.[13] Another CAB staff study by Samuel L. Brown and Wayne S. Watkins employed similar data on 438 markets for 1969.[14] Both models used a multiplicative, or log linear specification, that has proved fruitful in analyzing many spatial phenomena. (Sometimes these are called "gravity models.")[15] The economic implication of this specification is that the elasticity of any variable may be read directly as that variable's coefficient.[16]

---

quality characteristics of each, along with the demographic, or travel-generating, characteristics of the region studied. These techniques are of particular relevance in predicting the effects of a substantial change in the transport system, such as the introduction of a high-speed rail service.

12. A major shortcoming of the two studies described in this section is that neither analyzes the effect on demand of expected schedule delay. However, such an analysis would introduce serious problems of simultaneity and collinearity which it might be impossible to overcome with the current data base.

13. De Vany, "The Revealed Value of Time in Air Travel," *Review of Economics and Statistics,* Vol. 56 (February 1974), pp. 77–82.

14. Brown and Watkins, "Measuring Elasticities of Air Travel from New Cross-Sectional Data" (paper delivered at the annual meeting of the American Statistical Association, 1971; processed).

15. So named because of their similarity to the Newtonian specification of the force of gravity as being related to the product of the masses divided by the square of the distance between them.

16. For example, one model specification used by Brown-Watkins is as follows:

$$Q_{ij} = A \cdot F_{ij}{}^{B1} \cdot P_{ij}{}^{B2} \cdot T_{ij}{}^{B3} \cdot D_{ij}{}^{B4} \cdot C_{ij}{}^{B5} \cdot (Y_i Y_j)^{B6} \cdot e,$$

where $Q_{ij} = i\text{--}j$ traffic, A = constant, F_{ij} = first class fare per mile, P_{ij} = coach fare per mile, T_{ij} = en route time per mile, D_{ij} = distance of route $i\text{--}j$, C_{ij} = daily telephone calls (community of interest), $(Y_i Y_j)$ = income products, and e = error term. (We have changed the Brown-Watkins notation for comparative purposes.)

De Vany's specification was similar, but did not constrain the elasticities (ex-

Table 3-4. A Comparison of Cross-Section Estimates of the Elasticity of Demand for Air Travel

Independent variable and statistic	De Vany (1968), coach trips	Brown-Watkins (1969), all trips
First class fare	...	0.10
Coach fare	−1.07[a]	−1.30
Trip time	−0.45[a]	−0.63
Time value per hour (dollars)		
First class	...	11.97[a]
Coach	7.28[a]	8.09[a]
Correlation coefficient[b] (R^2)	0.50	0.70

Sources: From or derived from Arthur De Vany, "The Revealed Value of Time in Air Travel," *Review of Economics and Statistics*, Vol. 56 (February 1974), p. 80; Samuel L. Brown and Wayne S. Watkins, "Measuring Elasticities of Air Travel from New Cross-Sectional Data" (paper delivered at the annual meeting of the American Statistical Association, 1971; processed), p. 9.

a. Evaluated at mean trip distance and fare.

b. Proportion of variations in observations from the mean explained by the model.

The results of the De Vany and Brown-Watkins regression analyses are shown in Table 3-4. Note that both studies find the demand for air travel to be price-elastic: a percentage change in price elicited a greater percentage change in quantity demanded. Both studies conclude that demand has an inelastic response to changes in travel time: a percentage reduction in travel time increased travel, but by a lesser percentage. Finally, De Vany estimated the average value travelers place on their time at $7.28 per hour at the mean trip distance and fare, whereas the Brown-Watkins results imply time values of $11.97 for first class passengers, and $8.09 for coach passengers.[17]

As noted before, because of statistical problems (simultaneity and collinearity) and inadequate data (insufficient variations in the observations), many other variables of importance and interest have not been analyzed. Some of these may be of only negligible interest to the regulator, such as the

---

ponents) to be constant in all markets. (Brown and Watkins did test the variability of elasticities by market distance by separately estimating the fare elasticities with the data stratified by mileage blocks; however, this test failed to discern any significant differences among these elasticities.) De Vany's model is as follows:

$$Q_{ij} = A \cdot P_{ij}{}^{a+bM_{ij}} \cdot T_{ij}{}^{c+dM_{ij}} \cdot M_{ij}{}^F \cdot (N_i N_j)^g \cdot (Y_i Y_j)^h \cdot e,$$

where N_i = population of city i, M = distance from city i to city j, and the other notation is as defined above.

17. Since for reasons given earlier we would expect schedule delay to be valued at a lower rate than time in transit, these estimates should be interpreted as upper bounds on the valuation of schedule delay. This is of particular relevance to our estimation of optimal price-quality level and structure in Chapter 6.

effect of seat size postulated earlier, since firms have strong incentives to seek out their optimal values without direction. However, as noted earlier, convenience of the service and the implicit value placed on it by travelers should be of the greatest interest to the regulator. In later parts of this study we will devote considerable attention to this particular issue.

Summary

An understanding of air travel demand is essential for an identification of efficiency of scheduled service and for the design of optimal regulatory policies. The patterns of demand during the day, week, and year and the random aspect of demand create two basic pricing problems which regulation has by and large ignored. On the one hand, the peaking of demand over daily, weekly, and yearly cycles suggests a need for peak load pricing. Moreover, as is emphasized throughout this study, the convenience of the scheduled service is affected by regulatory policy. Service convenience can be measured, and if the regulator is to elicit an optimal level of service convenience and associated fare, the marginal value of service, as perceived by the traveler, must be weighed against its marginal cost.

CHAPTER FOUR

A Model of Industry Behavior under Economic Regulation

A DESCRIPTION of airline competitive dynamics and industry equilibrium can take one of two approaches. One is a descriptive or positive analysis of the response of the market to the exogenously determined policies of the regulator. This is the appropriate starting point for developing a theory of regulatory control and for describing optimal regulatory policies, given the legal and institutional framework. Alternatively, a more general description of the industry and its equilibrium can be attempted, hypothesizing an endogenous relationship between the regulator and the industry.[1]

We will focus here primarily on the former approach, that of describing how the industry reaches, or moves toward, a market equilibrium within the given constraints and policies set down by the regulator.[2] In other words, we adopt the pragmatic view that CAB regulatory policy is or can be exogenous.

As developed more fully later in this chapter, our justification for taking this approach rests primarily on three propositions:

1. Price competition plays a decidedly minor role in carrier marketing strategy; instead, carriers tend to view prices as given and compete (or rival) in nonprice (quality) dimensions.

2. The Board possesses statutory power to control entry and has exercised that power in a stringent and complex fashion.

3. While the Board can limit some aspects of competition in service

---

1. An example of this approach is the study of William A. Jordan, who portrays the industry and its regulator as engaged in a legalized, though imperfect, cartel. See his *Airline Regulation in America: Effects and Imperfections* (Johns Hopkins Press, 1970).

2. Some limited discussion of regulatory agency behavior is contained in Chapter 9.

quality, it cannot, by law, limit capacity in individual markets;[3] since flight frequency and timing are among the most important aspects of service quality, the carriers are in essence unrestrained in quality competition.

While the historical evidence on these propositions is not without exception, the conclusions we draw are consistent with the thorough examinations of industry behavior by previous investigators.[4]

In its simplest form, our model of airline industry behavior says that in any given market, and thus in the aggregate, whenever actual load factor rises above the break-even level and excess profits are earned,[5] carriers will commence scheduling additional capacity. This has the effect of driving the actual load factor back down toward break-even. On the other hand, if the actual load factor falls below break-even, carriers will curtail capacity; this, in turn, raises actual load factors toward break-even. Thus, over time, actual market load factors will tend to gravitate toward break-even levels, where the break-even load is determined by two parameters: (a) the structure and level of airline capacity costs and traffic costs, and (b) the fares approved and enforced by the Board. Thus, in market equilibrium the level of per-passenger cost is determined by the fare chosen. If the fare is lowered or raised, then per-passenger costs will fall or rise correspondingly. This simple dynamic, which until recently all but escaped the regulator's notice,[6] proves to be a very useful aid in developing and assessing policies that affect airline economic efficiency.

Characteristics of Market Rivalry

Although the statutory framework of regulation gives the CAB the power to set rates, it does not, in itself, preclude supervised price competition among the air carriers. The mechanism by which the Board supervises ratemaking, however, would seem in itself to deter price competition

3. Under section 412 of the Federal Aviation Act, the Board can approve, and on occasion has approved, intercarrier agreements to self-regulate capacity. See Chapter 7 and the appendix at the end of the book.

4. Except as noted in the text, these propositions are consistent with the descriptions of Richard E. Caves, *Air Transport and Its Regulators: An Industry Study* (Harvard University Press, 1962); Paul W. Cherington, *Airline Price Policy: A Study of Domestic Airline Passenger Fares* (Harvard University, Graduate School of Business Administration, 1958); George C. Eads, *The Local Service Airline Experiment* (Brookings Institution, 1972), and Jordan, *Airline Regulation in America.*

5. Note that by the term "break-even" we imply a cost level that includes a normal profit.

6. See Chapter 8.

and enhance any incipient tendency of the carriers to agree not to compete on the basis of price. Proposed changes in tariffs must be filed with the Board at least thirty days before their intended introduction. The Board must then determine if the proposed changes are lawful, and in doing so chooses one of four courses of action. It can (a) let the changes go into effect, thus implicitly finding them lawful, (b) let the changes go into effect but schedule an investigation which ultimately will resolve the issue of lawfulness, (c) suspend the changes and initiate an investigation to resolve the issue, or (d) find the changes unlawful per se. Significant changes in price are seldom granted without an investigation. Fare increases are likely to be challenged by the Board, whereas fare decreases are likely to be challenged by other carriers and subjected to litigation.

Thus, the process of changing fares, with the consequent exposure of a carrier's strategies to protest by other portions of the industry, serves to dissuade carriers from competing with each other on the basis of price. The issue of price rivalry might then be considered in two parts: (a) whether price competition could, or would be likely to, exist if not discouraged by Board policy, and (b) whether the rulings of the Board have in effect discouraged any incipient manifestations of price competition.

Examination of the record indicates that during the last three decades most significant attempts to change rates, rather than being instances of price competition, were attempts by the industry or the Board to bring realized profits into line with the Board's estimated "fair" or "reasonable" return on investment. That is, the important cases have involved across-the-board fare adjustments with the avowed purpose of adjusting the industry's profits. To some degree, the structure of these changes was a matter of dispute among the carriers, reflecting the different nature of their operations, but as such were principally a question of the apportionment of relief. The cases in which competitive price reductions were sanctioned principally reflect the interests of the airline industry as a whole against competing modes of transport, such as buses or automobiles. Thus, coach service and fares have been established, as well as a multiplicity of promotional fares. The Board manifested an interest in each of these developments, however, in seeing that the proposed reductions were not principally "diversionary," that is, "too competitive."[7] Moreover, examination of the

---

7. Most of these cases went before the Board when the industry was still on subsidy, or only recently removed from it. Thus, the Board's apparent behavior as an enforcer of joint profit-maximizing (cartel) strategies should perhaps be viewed in light of its avowed goal of removing the industry from subsidy.

regulatory history provides numerous examples of the regulator's denying incipient, competitive price reductions.

The pattern of rates themselves, moreover, strongly disputes the notion that price competition exists to any meaningful degree. For example, fares have a spatial uniformity that one would not expect, given the characteristics that affect costs in various markets. Also, the pattern of fares over time does not reflect fully the peak-load fluctuations that one might expect, given the seasonal nature of demand.

The most striking evidence of the absence of price competition, however, is the significant difference between fares in the California intrastate markets and those for trips of similar distance in interstate markets. Air carriers operating wholly within a state are not subject to CAB regulation, and in California specialized carriers have served the major intrastate markets with vigorous price competition for at least two decades. As reported by William Jordan, the regulation of air transportation on these routes by the California Public Utilities Commission has set only upper limits on fares, and this, in conjunction with free entry and exit, has served to encourage price competition.[8] Some comparisons between fares in major California intrastate markets and fares in eastern markets under CAB regulation are reported in Table 4-1.[9]

Thus, although the framework of CAB regulation does not prohibit price competition per se, the institutional rigidities associated with changing price, coupled with the pattern of the Board's decisions, would seem not to encourage it. Moreover, since there are so few carriers in each market, it is consistent with typical oligopoly behavior that the airlines prefer to avoid price competition, realizing that most price cuts will be met, generally to their mutual detriment. The price innovations that have occurred, such as price discrimination, follow the pattern of market enhancement and revenue maximization that typically are in the carriers' joint interest. As summarized by Paul Cherington in his thorough study of industry price behavior: "There is substantial evidence that many carriers would like to

8. Jordan, *Airline Regulation in America*. On September 17, 1965, however, the CPUC was given authority over intrastate air carrier entry, exit, and service. Ibid., p. 2.

9. We elaborate in Chapter 5 that, unlike Jordan, we do not believe that a price difference by itself represents either technical or allocative inefficiency. As postulated in this chapter, the higher-fare markets will be characterized by a lower average load factor (more excess capacity) and hence a higher standard of service. Deviations from the optimal price-quality combination is, however, a question of efficiency, as discussed later.

Table 4-1. Comparison of Air Fares in California Intrastate Markets with Fares in Similar East Coast Interstate Markets, July 1970

Market	Distance (miles)	Annual passengers[a]	Coach fare[b] (dollars)	Fare per mile (cents)
California				
Los Angeles– San Francisco	340	3,023,341	16.20	4.76
San Diego– San Francisco	449	359,025	22.63	5.04
San Diego– Los Angeles	109	637,447	7.97	7.31
East Coast				
Boston–New York	186	1,985,680	21.60	11.61
Boston–Washington	413	435,920	35.64	8.63
New York– Washington	228	1,663,850	23.76	10.42

Sources: William A. Jordan, *Airline Regulation in America: Effects and Imperfections* (Johns Hopkins Press, 1970), p. 105; and *Official Airline Guide: Quick Reference, North American Edition* (Reuben H. Donnelly, July 1, 1970).

a. On-line origin-and-destination passengers, 1965. These data show where passengers originate and terminate their journeys on individual carriers. Passengers using two or more carriers are counted in two or more city-pairs—one for each carrier.

b. Including tax.

regard price as one of the 'knowns' in an extremely complex formula, and that pricing action is often kept as a 'last resort' solution to a difficult problem."[10]

Essentially, therefore, airline firms rival each other primarily in nonprice, quality dimensions. Since basic outputs are so homogeneous, each firm tries to establish its identity through assorted gimmicks, some innovations, and extensive advertising. Such forms of service rivalry include aircraft type, interior design, seat width and pitch, meals, snacks, liquor, movie availability, computerized reservations, stewardesses' uniforms, and advertising image. Two aspects of this kind of activity are worth noting. First, it is usually not regulated by the Board, at least within broad limits. Second— and most important—all types of service rivalry are means of encouraging passenger traffic. Accordingly, they tend to be highly, positively correlated with the excess capacity rivalry discussed immediately below.

Of greatest importance in nonprice rivalry is the tendency of firms to compete on scheduling and capacity. More frequent flights and more capacity can increase air traffic, both by inducing additional travel and by diverting travelers from competing modes. While a monopoly carrier could thus

10. Cherington, *Airline Price Policy*, p. 457.

expect to enhance demand by increasing the frequency of scheduled flights, the effect anticipated by a single carrier in a competitive market may be far greater. That is, if a carrier unilaterally increases its schedule frequency, it can expect to divert passengers from other air carriers, if the other carriers do not match the increase. The mechanism by which this aspect of competitive behavior leads to a market equilibrium is described below.[11]

Equilibrium with Nonprice Competition

Even though entry by firms into specific markets is strongly constrained, nonprice competition tends to raise or lower average cost per passenger carried so that in equilibrium it is equal to price. That is, nonprice or quality rivalry in competitive markets tends to eliminate excess profits or "monopoly rents,"[12] which would perhaps be expected, given an absence of price competition in conjunction with blocked entry; such rivalry also tends to eliminate losses where the average cost of a standard service rises above price.[13]

11. This is not to say that at any particular point in time equilibrium necessarily obtains (that is, the market may be in disequilibrium, but be moving toward equilibrium).

12. Monopoly rents, or "excess profits," are a return on investment in excess of the opportunity cost on capital.

13. This basic description of airline competitive behavior, emphasizing the importance of scheduling and the achievement of equilibrium through adjustment in average cost via capacity offered, has been developed recently and independently by a number of economists. The earliest contributions include: Arthur De Vany, "The Economics of Quality Competition: Theory and Evidence on Airline Flight Scheduling" (University of California, Los Angeles, Department of Economics, c. 1969; processed); George W. Douglas, "A Study of Airline Efficiency" (1969; processed); James C. Miller III, "Scheduling and Airline Efficiency" (Ph.D. dissertation, University of Virginia, 1969), pp. 164–79; Mahlon R. Straszheim, "Pricing International Air Service: Oligopoly Models and the Role of State Influence" (paper delivered at the International Symposium on Transportation Pricing, 1969; processed); and Joseph V. Yance, "Nonprice Competition in Jet Aircraft Capacity," *Journal of Industrial Economics*, Vol. 21 (November 1972), pp. 55–71. Later contributions and/or those of related interest include: Christopher Barnekov, "Airlines in the United States: Effects of Regulation by the Federal Government" (1972; processed); George C. Eads, "Competition in the Domestic Trunk Airline Industry: Too Much or Too Little?" in Almarin Phillips (ed.), *Competition and Regulation* (Brookings Institution, 1974); Anthony H. Milward, "Wasted Seats in Air Transport: An Examination of the Importance of Load Factor," *Institute of Transport Journal* (May 1966), pp. 345–62; and Lawrence J. White, "Quality Variation When Prices Are Regulated," *Bell Journal of Economics and Management Science*, Vol. 3 (Autumn 1972), pp. 425–36.

While even the largest markets contain only a small number of firms in direct competition, vigorous nonprice competition seems to be pervasive. Since the markets are oligopolistic, a theoretical description of equilibrium can be determinate only if specific assumptions are made about the participants' reaction to their rivals' strategies. Nevertheless, the equilibrium achieved in competitive markets seems to conform with a pattern of non-price behavior hypothesized by George Stigler,[14] which in application to the airline industry is somewhat similar to the duopoly model of Cournot.[15] While the analysis can take as its output measure either passengers or capacity,[16] we shall, by analogy, follow Stigler in focusing on the unit actually sold.[17]

We assume that the quantity of air service demanded in a specific market is related to the price and to an index of service quality[18] which is an increasing function of the total number of seats offered in the market. Since demand is seasonal and unpredictable and since output is lumpy and cannot be stored, the system operates with a certain amount of excess capacity. Changes in the level of this excess capacity affect the convenience of the service. An increase in capacity caused by an additional flight scheduled means that flight departures overall can be more closely matched to desired departure times; moreover, as total capacity increases, the probability of not obtaining a seat on the preferred flight is reduced. This relationship between capacity offered and service quality allows us to make market demand a function of the regulated price and the number of seats offered.[19] Analogously, each firm's demand is a function of the regulated price and the number of seats it offers.[20] In either case, if price is lowered and capacity

14. George J. Stigler, "Price and Non-Price Competition," *Journal of Political Economy,* Vol. 76 (January–February 1968), pp. 149–54.

15. See Straszheim, "Pricing International Air Service."

16. An example of using capacity as the output measure is Yance, "Nonprice Competition," pp. 66–68.

17. A *complete* description of airline market equilibrium would be exceedingly complex if the orthodox conventions of price theory were to be followed. That is, each firm produces output in numerous city-pair markets, and the interdependence of production across these markets would tend to result in there being, in essence, many joint products. Moreover, production occurs in discrete, "lumpy" units. Nevertheless, it is instructive to ignore these characteristics and describe the hypothetical market in isolation (that is, assuming independence of production across markets).

18. $Q = Q(P_0, X)$, where Q = passenger traffic, P_0 = exogenously determined price, and X = index of service quality.

19. $Q = Q(P_0, S)$, where S = market seats.

20. $Q_i = Q_i(P_0, S_i)$, where Q_i = firm i's passenger traffic, and S_i = firm i's seats offered.

does not change, then total traffic will increase. Or, if capacity is increased while fares are held constant, traffic will likewise increase.[21]

The firm's total cost is a function of the number of passengers carried and the number of seats offered.[22] For simplicity, and consistent with the findings of Chapter 2, we will assume constant returns to scale.[23]

Profit maximization may be described for the market in two ways. Following Stigler, we can equate the marginal cost of attracting and carrying an additional passenger with the marginal revenue of carrying an additional passenger (which is equal to the price, since the price is fixed). Alternatively, we could equate the marginal cost of providing an additional unit of capacity with the marginal revenue which would be derived therefrom. In the former case, we recognize that the marginal cost of carrying an additional passenger is given by the unit cost of passenger service plus the cost of the additional capacity required to attract and carry an additional passenger.[24]

Equilibrium would occur in a monopoly market of one carrier with a regulated price as follows. Since there are no other carriers from which traffic may be diverted, the marginal cost of attracting and carrying an additional passenger rises steeply as the market becomes saturated with capacity.[25] Profit per passenger in excess of a normal return on investment is given by the difference between the carrier's average cost per passenger, which is much lower than its marginal cost, and the regulated fare.

Next, consider the equilibrium of this market if two or more carriers were to compete with capacity rivalry. A qualitative difference is clear at the outset. If each carrier believes that marginal changes in its own capacity will not be matched by its rivals, it could expect to gain more passengers

21. We should expect that for any given price, the number of passengers carried increases as capacity offered increases, but at a diminishing rate, reaching some plateau (or asymptotic value) as the market becomes saturated with capacity. See William A. Gunn, "Airline System Stimulation," *Operations Research*, Vol. 12 (March–April 1964), p. 209.

22. Total cost is also related to other aspects of service quality, such as meals and seat width. To simplify the exposition, however, we will assume these characteristics are held constant. (Alternatively, view the cost of a seat as including the cost of concomitant increases in other quality aspects.)

23. Thus, the firm's total cost function may be written, $TC_i = cQ_i + kS_i$, where c is per-passenger traffic cost, and k is per-seat capacity cost (see discussion in Chapter 2).

24. Expressed algebraically, the necessary condition for profit maximization is $MC_L = c + k[1/(\partial Q_i/\partial S_i)] = P_0$.

25. In the monopoly case, marginal cost is given by $MC = c + k[1/(\partial Q/\partial S)]$, whereas average cost is given by $AC = c + k[1/(Q/S)]$.

from an added unit of capacity than would a monopolist. That is, the individual carrier can expect not only to induce new travelers into the air market, but to divert some passengers from the flights of other carriers.

We may now describe an extreme-case equilibrium that might be reached in a two-carrier market. Assume that the market is shared equally and that both carriers offer the same levels of capacity. If each firm perceives that any changes in its capacity will be matched by its rival, each will offer precisely one-half the capacity offered by the monopolist, and the market equilibrium output and total excess profit will be the same as in the monopoly case.

However, as noted above, if each carrier believes that its capacity changes will not be matched, its perceived marginal cost of attracting and carrying additional passengers will be lower than in the example described above. At the monopoly (or joint profit maximizing) equilibrium, each carrier would wish to increase output, since its perceived marginal cost is less than the marginal revenue (the regulated fare). Contrary to their expectations, however, both carriers expand capacity, causing the average cost of both to rise, since the diversion effects are self-canceling. Equilibrium is reached when the perceived marginal cost equals price. It may be observed, then, that the level and existence of excess profits depend on the difference between average cost and perceived marginal cost. This difference, in turn, depends on the slope and position of the perceived marginal cost curve, which rests on the assumed response of the market rivals.

Moreover, to the extent that firms believe that they can improve their market share by increasing capacity, we would expect to find this effect greater (and thus the slope of the perceived marginal cost lower), the greater the number of carriers in the market. Thus, we would expect the level of excess profits in equilibrium to diminish as the number of firms increased. Where the number of firms is very large, each believes that its average load factor is given and would not be affected by marginal changes in its own capacity. Hence, its perceived marginal cost is equal to its average cost, and the market equilibrium would have zero excess profits.[26]

An issue of considerable interest for the description of market equilibrium, therefore, is how firms expect market shares to respond to capacity competition. We might expect a priori that with all firms charging the same price, each (homogeneous) flight would attract an equal number of passengers and that each individual firm's market share would equal the rela-

26. For more detail, see the appendix to this chapter.

tive share of total capacity offered in the market.[27] Several recent studies suggest, however, that the market share of a firm may be related nonlinearly to its capacity share. In a cross-section study of airline markets, Gilles Renard found that the relationships between market shares and capacity shares tend to fit S-shaped curves, which suggests that a carrier which dominates a market will have a higher average load factor than will the carriers it dominates. The implication is that by increasing capacity, and thus market share, a carrier can increase profits.[28] Moreover, testimony by representatives of the industry in the Domestic Passenger Fare Investigation indicates that airline managements tend to believe that this effect is valid.[29] The hypothesis is straightforward: given the lack of information on all schedules, customers tend to call the airline with the greatest number of flights. Thus, the carrier with a larger share of total capacity receives a greater than proportional amount of traffic; conversely, the carrier with a small share of total capacity receives an even smaller share of total traffic.

The existence of such a nonlinear relationship between capacity share and market share has interesting implications for market equilibrium. While in a linear-shares market with constant returns to scale different-sized firms may coexist in equilibrium, all earning excess profits, in the market in which shares are given by an S curve, an equilibrium in which all firms earn excess profits would normally involve identical-sized firms sharing the market equally. Also, if at equilibrium all firms are of equal size, the perceived marginal change in an individual firm's quantity demanded caused by an increase in its capacity is significantly greater than where the market shares relationship is proportional. This implies that the perceived marginal cost curve will have a smaller slope than would otherwise be the case, and that in equilibrium excess profits will be lower because of this effect.

Moreover, if firms persist in such myopic behavior, it is conceivable that under certain conditions scheduling competition could yield a short-run deficit equilibrium. This might occur if the market shares relationship

27. Firm i's share $= F_i/F$, where $F_i =$ firm i's flight capacity, and $F =$ total (market) flight capacity.

28. Gilles Renard, "Competition in Air Transportation: An Econometric Approach" (M.S. thesis, Massachusetts Institute of Technology, 1970); and William E. Fruhan, Jr., *The Fight for Competitive Advantage: A Study of the United States Domestic Trunk Air Carriers* (Harvard University, Graduate School of Business Administration, 1972), Chap. 5.

29. See CAB Docket 21866-6, Exhibit TW-6011; and Testimony of National Economic Research Associates, Inc., CAB Docket 21866-9, Exhibit TW 9-T-B.

diverged significantly from the proportional one, such that when quality competition had completely eliminated excess profits the firm's perception of the marginal cost of attracting and carrying an additional passenger by a unilateral increase in capacity was less than the average cost. This would occur if the perception of the marginal gain in traffic resulting from a unit increase in capacity were greater than its average load factor.[30] This hypothesis was first set forth and tested by Joseph V. Yance, who concluded that with existing estimates of the market shares relationship and elasticity of market demand with respect to capacity offered, such an equilibrium would be limited to markets with two or more competitors and a total daily schedule of three or fewer flights.[31] Significant markets served by few flights and by more than one carrier are fairly rare.[32]

The model and its variants described above are developed more explicitly in the appendix to this chapter. The basic implications, however, are simple. The existence of nonprice competition among carriers tends to eliminate excess profits in nonmonopoly markets, because average cost is bid up or down by changes in capacity. Put another way, in the trunk airlines costs are price-determined, rather than price-determining, as in unregulated, competitive markets.

Since a substantial portion of an airline's costs are associated with the production of available capacity, as noted in Chapter 2, the profit rate of a carrier is rather conveniently summarized by comparing its *average load factor* (number of passenger-miles divided by number of seat-miles) with its *break-even load factor* (the ratio of passenger-miles to seat-miles at which total revenues would equal total costs, including a normal profit). The implication of the model presented here, then, is that average load factors will approach break-even load factors where nonprice competition is reasonably strong.

Consider first a situation in which prevailing load factors are above break-even. Carriers perceive marginal cost below price and thus expand output. Expansion in output by any carrier lowers market average load factor (otherwise scheduling would increase indefinitely), and this process

30. That is, if $\partial Q_i/\partial S_i > Q_i/S_i$.

31. Joseph V. Yance, "The Possibility of Loss-Producing Equilibria in Air Carrier Markets" (Boston University, Department of Economics, 1971; processed).

32. We wish to emphasize that for the character of market equilibrium the important thing is not whether the S-shaped relation actually exists, but whether carrier management thinks it exists. If they proceed under this assumption, then excess profits in any few-carriers market will be less than if carrier management perceives a proportional market-share relation.

of schedule augmentation continues until the market average load factor falls to approximately the break-even point at which each carrier perceives that marginal cost and average cost equals price. On the other hand, if prevailing market load factors are below break-even, then individual carriers will perceive marginal cost in excess of price and will wish to contract output. Market average load factor increases and output declines, and the process of schedule contraction continues until market average load factor approximates break-even.

Given this industry behavior dynamic, it should be apparent that the regulator can control the equilibrium of the market, including the average load factor and implicitly the quality of service, by controlling the price level and structure.

The Pattern of Industry Equilibrium

We now turn to an examination of the pattern of equilibrium in airline markets and appraise its consistency with the patterns implied by the theory developed above.

The industry realized an average return over the period 1955–70 of approximately 6.5 percent, indicating that even in the absence of price competition and with relatively few firms in each market, significant excess profits were not earned.[33]

The industry responds rather sensitively to the business cycle, as well as to other exogenous impacts. An examination of the time series of the industry's actual and break-even average load factors reveals a pattern which is consistent with the hypothesis of competitive dynamics and market equilibrium described above.[34] For example, Figure 4-1 compares graphi-

33. U.S. Civil Aeronautics Board, *Handbook of Airline Statistics, 1971 Edition,* p. 391, and relevant preceding editions. These rates of return are based on the Board's definition of return, net profit before interest but after taxes, as a percent of equity plus long-term debt. Many measurement problems exist with such an imputation, and the reported figures may overestimate or underestimate the true return. The point we wish to make is that even allowing for considerable downward bias in the reported rates, there would not appear to be significant rents being earned if the regulated carriers' costs are taken as a measure of efficient costs.

34. In testing the model described in the previous section we must distinguish between a long-run equilibrium (such as zero excess profits), and a market disequilibrium situation, where the relevant issue is whether the market is moving toward the long-run equilibrium hypothesized (for instance, do actual load factors tend to gravitate toward break-even?).

cally the time series of actual and break-even load factors over the period
1949–68. (Break-even load factor in the figure does not include a profit
element.) Note the tendency of actual load factors to track the break-even
load factors when the latter have changed through productivity increases,
fare changes, and so on. During the period 1949–52, the introduction of
coach fares caused the average yield to decline slightly, and when coupled
with only modest increases in productivity and rising factor prices, the result was a rise in the break-even load factor. The growth in actual load
factor reflects this change in break-even, but it also reflects constraints on
capacity increases caused by the Korean war. In 1952, a flat $1 per
ticket increase was granted by the Board, and, as the airlines introduced
denser coach seating, break-even load factors leveled off at around 58
percent for the next several years. The realized load factors moved rapidly

**Figure 4-1. Actual and Break-even Passenger Load Factors,
Major U.S. Airlines, 1949–68**

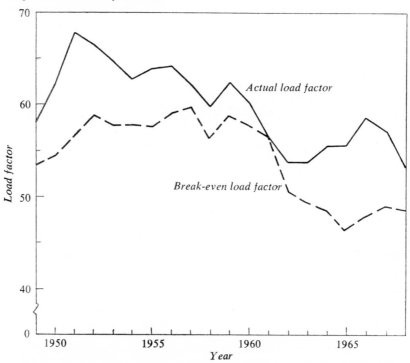

Source: Air Transport Association of America, "Major U.S. Airlines: Economic Review and Financial
Outlook, 1969–1973" (June 1969; processed), Slide 16.
a. Scheduled service only; data adjusted for strikes.

in this period toward the break-even level, as the wartime constraints which retarded fleet acquisition were lifted.

The next movement of significance occurred in the 1959–65 period, when the introduction of turbojet aircraft into air carrier fleets brought about a dramatic increase in productivity. The cost of capacity flown in jets, for example, was approximately 30 percent less than that of the piston aircraft they replaced. Fares during this period were increased across the board by approximately $1 per ticket plus 4 percent in 1958, $1 plus 2.5 percent in 1960, and 3 percent in 1962. This remarkable combination of increases in productivity and rising fares caused break-even load factors to drop sharply, from about 58 percent in 1959 to approximately 47 percent in 1965. Rapid increases in capacity occurred as the carriers reequipped their fleets, and the average load factor tracked the break-even level, as expected.

The period 1964–66 saw temporary increases in the profit margin, caused principally by a burgeoning demand reflecting the general economic boom. The carriers' subsequent acquisitions of capacity, along with rising factor costs not offset by gains in productivity, steadily narrowed the margin between actual and break-even load factors. In 1970, owing primarily to an unanticipated decline in traffic growth caused by the recession and a cessation in the secular fall in the real level of fares, the actual load factor for the industry fell sufficiently below break-even that the carriers as a whole incurred losses for the year. However, as would be predicted by the model, capacity growth was later held in line while load factors again rose above break-even.[35]

Another pattern in the equilibrium of the industry further corroborates the hypothesis of equilibrium under quality competition. As noted in Chapter 2, strong economies exist with respect to the length of flight. For example, the cost per passenger-mile on a typical four-engine jet transport is approximately 28 percent lower for a trip of 2,000 miles than for a trip of 600 miles, ceteris paribus. The structure of air fares, however, has not fully reflected these relative costs. A CAB staff study performed in 1967, for example, found the fare "taper" with respect to distance to be not as great as the average cost taper.[36] Moreover, even when adjusted for the relative

35. For the twelve months ending March 1973, actual passenger load factor was 52.3 percent as compared with a break-even passenger load factor of 49.4 percent (this for the domestic operations of the trunk airlines and Pan American World Airways). Civil Aeronautics Board, *Quarterly Airline Industry Economic Report,* Vol. 6-1 (May 30, 1973), p. 7.

36. Civil Aeronautics Board, Bureau of Economics, Rates Division, "A Study of the Domestic Passenger Air Fare Structure" (1968; processed), p. 142. For graphical illustration of fare (or cost) taper, see Figure 6-3 below.

volume of discounted traffic from promotional fares, the taper of average yield remained less than, but closer to, that of average costs.[37]

Observers have long noted (or perhaps suspected, since specific market load factor data have been held confidential) that the supposedly lucrative transcontinental markets had significantly lower load factors than average, and thus perhaps were not so lucrative after all. A wide sample of cross-section observations of load factors in various markets did become available with the recent Domestic Passenger Fare Investigation (DPFI), and an analysis of these indicates the pattern hypothesized. Average load factors are lower in transcontinental markets, for two reasons. First, these are large markets, and therefore have several firms in competition. Second, the lower cost per passenger relative to average yield means that the break-even load factor is lower at long distances. Thus, we would expect the scheduling form of nonprice competition to make the equilibrium average load factor lower in these long-distance markets, ceteris paribus.[38]

The DPFI load factor data were analyzed using multiple regression analysis. The results for 1969 are reported below.[39] (The curves shown later in Figure 6-4, obtained from the second regression, graphically illustrate the hypothesized effect.)

(1) $ALF = 0.588 - 2.11 \times 10^{-5}D + 7.62 \times 10^{-7}N - 7.06 \times 10^{-2}C$
$\qquad$ (1.4) $\qquad$ (9.1) $\qquad$ (6.5)
$\qquad$ $R^2 = 0.213$; degrees of freedom $= 347$.

(2) $ALF = 0.257 - 0.019 \ln D + 0.073 \ln N - 1.46 \ln C,$
$\qquad$ (1.8) $\qquad$ (7.1) $\qquad$ (5.5)
$\qquad$ $R^2 = 0.144$; degrees of freedom $= 347$.

where

ALF = market average load factor (total passengers divided by total seats)
D = market distance (miles)
N = average number of daily passengers in market
C = number of carriers in market

and the numbers in parentheses are the t-statistics.

37. This fare structure developed historically from a uniform mileage charge (irrespective of distance) that prevailed in the 1940s through various arbitrary amendments, such as constant dollar increases per ticket (see previous discussion).

38. Other forms of nonprice competition, such as advertising and meals, would not be directly reflected in the actual versus break-even load factor margin. However, we maintain that scheduled capacity is the dominant form of nonprice competition in terms of cost, and further, as explained earlier, we would expect other forms of nonprice competition to be positively related to the extent of capacity competition.

39. Based on data in CAB Docket 21866-6, Exhibit BE-6501 (July 6, 1970).

Note that the strongest influence on the market average load factor (*ALF*) is the number of firms, or, in general, the level of competitiveness. Moreover, the inverse relationship between load factor and market distance reflects the fact that the break-even load factor falls as distance increases.[40]

A final bit of corroborating evidence is Yance's study of commercial jet aircraft introduction during the late 1950s and early 1960s.[41] Developing and utilizing a model very similar to ours, Yance demonstrates that carrier management made rational decisions to add jet capacity, based on jet unit costs and expected marginal revenue generated by diverted passengers plus net new traffic. The explanatory power of his equations and the consistency of his results lend strong credence to the validity of the approach taken here.

A Theory of Regulatory Control

In spite of the complexity caused by the interdependence of production, and possibly demand, across markets and the lumpy characteristic of capacity, we suggest here that the market equilibrium responds predictably to the exogenously determined fare level and structure. Hence, if the industry is to be regulated, it does not appear that pervasive and extensive direct regulation is required to control effectively the important aspects of industry equilibrium. Rather, the regulator can affect the nature of equilibrium by manipulating the price level and structure, and by controlling the number of firms in specific markets.

The rate of profit (in the economic sense of excess profits) in the equilibrium of a market is not principally determined by the fare level but rather by the number of firms sharing the market. Accordingly, the regulator should recognize that control over entry rather than price is the principal control variable over industry profit rates. Second, and most important for subsequent analysis, the fare level and structure, instead of determining or controlling profit rates, should be viewed principally as determining the characteristics of the equilibrium, in particular, the relative level of excess capacity and the associated level of service quality.

---

40. As noted above, however, the equilibrium model described previously ignores the discrete nature of capacity and the interdependence of the various markets served. Hence, it is not surprising that although the relationships hypothesized are statistically significant, the model explains only approximately 20 percent of the total variation in observed load factors.

41. Yance, "Nonprice Competition."

The per-passenger cost curve illustrated in Figure 2-1 could be visualized as the "opportunity locus" facing the regulator. This could be viewed as applying to a single market or, more broadly, to the overall industry. What we observe in this locus is the fact that fair, or market, rates of return on investment can exist at many different fare levels. While the range is constrained at an upper and a lower level, principally by demand, price approximately equals average cost in equilibrium at any price within this range.[42] The relevance of this for efficiency will be discussed in Chapters 5 and 6.

As was suggested in the previous narrative of recent industry history, there is the potential that a neglect of the interrelationships among fares, load factors, and profits can set up a dynamic between the industry and its regulator that causes instability. Such a pattern can now be described more explicitly. Suppose we observe an opportunity locus (or equivalently, an industry "reaction" curve) such as R in Figure 4-2. The location of this curve is predicated on the costs of production and the market rate of return (or cost of capital) as perceived by the firms. Suppose, for example, that this market reaction curve does not coincide with the "official" opportunity locus perceived by the regulator R^*. This could occur, for example, if the CAB-defined reasonable rate of return exceeded the cost of capital as perceived by the carriers, or if the accounting conventions employed by the CAB had a consistent downward bias in measuring the carriers' earnings.

In such a case, one could imagine a "ratchet effect" of regulation and reaction, in which price increases, thought by the CAB as necessary to raise profits, only resulted in a new equilibrium with greater levels of excess capacity.[43] For example, if starting from industry equilibrium the Board raises price in an attempt to assure carriers a reasonable return on investment, the result will be an immediate reduction in break-even load factor, a subsequent expansion in capacity, and a fall in industry load factor. If subsequently the Board persists in its attempt to assure the carriers a reasonable return, the result will be a continual spiral in price and further increases in excess capacity.

42. Alternatively, for any price within this range, nonprice competition will result in approximately zero excess profits.

43. Even in the absence of divergent perceptions, a similar way to explain recent history is that the carriers have an innate expansionary bias, and since the CAB may be counted on to rationalize excess capacity with higher fares, the discipline of the market is forestalled and the relative level of excess capacity tends to creep ever upward.

Figure 4-2. Ratchet Effect on Rate of Return for Airlines When Reasonable Rate Differs from Normal Rate

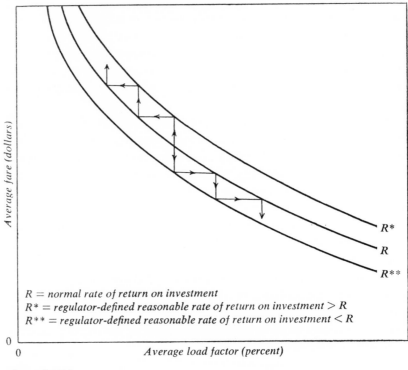

R = normal rate of return on investment
R* = regulator-defined reasonable rate of return on investment > R
R** = regulator-defined reasonable rate of return on investment < R

Source: See text.

The ratchet effect would also work, but in the reverse direction, if the Board's computed reasonable rate of return R^{**} were less than the industry's cost of capital R (see Figure 4-2). Starting at equilibrium, an attempt by the Board to lower return on investment to reasonable rate R^{**} by forcing price down will result in an immediate rise in break-even load factor, a subsequent contraction in industry capacity, and a rise in market load factor. Further attempts to lower industry profits by reducing price will only reduce industry capacity, raise average load factor, and reduce service quality.

Summary

The CAB regulates the domestic trunk carriers with a number of controls, the most important being the entry of firms into city-pair markets and the prices charged for services. However, the Board is prohibited by law from regulating directly the capacity offered by a carrier in any market it is authorized to serve. Carriers tend to accept price as given and compete on the basis of service quality, primarily the amount of excess capacity. Since only a small minority of significant markets are served by a single carrier and since informal collusion over scheduling tends to be difficult and cumbersome, nonprice competition tends to dissipate carrier excess profits. This imperfect cartel model of nonprice competition comports generally with available empirical evidence.

The relevance of this analysis for the regulator is that a broad range of prices is consistent with more or less normal carrier profits. Moreover, attempts to regulate precisely carrier return on investment through adjustments in price will prove futile, the much more important control variable being the number of carriers in a market. Finally, since price affects capacity and other dimensions of service quality, the Board must constantly confront the issue: Which combination of price and service quality is most in the public interest? A way of dealing with this question is described in Chapter 6.

Appendix: Specification of the Model

Equilibrium in a market with n firms

Market demand is given by

$$(3) \qquad Q = Q(P_0, S),$$

where P_0 is the given price, and S is total (market) seat capacity. Firm i's demand is given by

$$(4) \qquad Q_i = \lambda_i Q.$$

Total costs of firm i are

$$(5) \qquad TC_i = cQ_i + kS_i,$$

where c is per-passenger traffic cost, k is per-seat capacity cost, and S_i is firm i's capacity. Profits of firm i are thus

$$(6) \qquad \Pi_i = P_0 Q_i - cQ_i - kS_i,$$

or

$$(7) \qquad \Pi_i = P_0 \lambda_i Q - c\lambda_i Q - kS_i.$$

At equilibrium (first-order profit-maximizing conditions),

(8) $\partial\Pi_i/\partial S_i = P_0[Q(\partial\lambda_i/\partial S_i) + \lambda_i(\partial Q/\partial S)]$
$$- c[Q(\partial\lambda_i/\partial S_i) + \lambda_i(\partial Q/\partial S)] - k = 0,$$

or

(9) $P_0 = c + k\{1/[Q(\partial\lambda_i/\partial S_i) + \lambda_i(\partial Q/\partial S)]\} = MC.$

Average cost per passenger carried is given by

(10) $AC = (cQ_i + kS_i)/Q_i = c + k(S_i/Q_i).$

Proportional market shares case

Let $Q_i/Q = S_i/S = \lambda_i$. Then

(11) $\partial\lambda_i/\partial S_i = 1/S - S_i/S^2.$

If at equilibrium, $S_i/S = S_j/S = 1/n$, where j represents other firms in the market, and n is the total number of firms, then equation (9) may be written:

(12) $MC = c + k/[Q/S + (dQ/dS - Q/S)/n] = P_0.$

The profit margin per passenger is then

(13) $P_0 - AC = k/[Q/S + (dQ/dS - Q/S)/n] - k/(Q/S).$

Since $dQ/dS < Q/S$, $(P_0 - AC) > 0$, or $P_0 > AC$. However, from equation (13), $(P_0 - AC)$ approaches zero as n grows larger.

Nonproportional market shares case

Let the firm's relative capacity share be defined as

(14) $S_i = S'_i/S.$

Let the firm's relative market share be given by

(15) $Q_i/Q = S'_i{}^\alpha/\Sigma S'_j{}^\alpha,$

where

$$j = 1, \ldots, n$$
$$\alpha \geq 1.$$

Equation (9) now becomes

(16) $MC = c + k/\{\alpha[Q/S + (dQ/dS - Q/S)/n]\}.$

Profit margin per passenger thus becomes

(17) $P_0 - AC = k/\{\alpha[Q/S + (dQ/dS - Q/S)/n]\} - k/(Q/S),$

and is less than the margin given by equation (13).

Existence of a loss equilibrium

Following Yance,[44] let market demand be

(18) $$Q = ZS^e,$$

where Z is some constant, and e is the capacity elasticity of demand; that is, $e = (\partial Q/\partial S)(S/Q)$. Let the demand faced by firm i be given by

(19) $$Q_i = (S_i^\alpha/\Sigma S_j^\alpha) \cdot ZS^e.$$

The marginal cost of attracting and carrying an additional passenger for firm i is thus

(20) $$MC_i = c + k(\partial Q_i/\partial S_i)^{-1}.$$

By symmetry, assume that $S_j/S = 1/n, j = 1, \ldots, n$. Then

(21) $$Q_i = (S_i/S)^\alpha/(n/n^\alpha)(ZS^e) = (S_i/S)^\alpha(n^{\alpha-1})(ZS^e),$$

and

(22) $$\partial Q_i/\partial S_i = \alpha(S_i/S)^{\alpha-1}(1/S - S_i/S^2)(n^{\alpha-1})(ZS^e)$$
$$+ (S_i/S)^\alpha(n^{\alpha-1})(ZeS^{e-1}).$$

Since at equilibrium, $S_i/S = 1/n$,

(23) $$\partial Q_i/\partial S_i = \alpha(n - 1/n)(ZS^{e-1}) + (n^{-1})(ZeS^{e-1})$$
$$= ZS^{e-1}[\alpha(1 - 1/n) - e/n].$$

Average cost per passenger is given by

(24) $$AC = k(S_i/Q_i) + c.$$

Since $Q_i/S_i = Q/S$,

(25) $$AC = c + k(S/ZS^e) = c + kZ^{-1}S^{1-e}.$$

Excess profit exists so long as $(MC - AC) > 0$:

(26) $$MC - AC = Z^{-1}S^{1-e}\{[\alpha(1 - 1/n) + e/n]^{-1} - 1\},$$

which reduces to

(27) $$MC - AC > 0 \quad \text{if, and only if,} \quad \alpha(n - 1) + e < n.$$

Effect of regulated price on total capacity

Where n is large, industry profit is zero:

(28) $$\Pi = PQ - cQ - kS = 0,$$

44. Yance, "The Possibility of Loss-Producing Equilibria in Air Carrier Markets."

where P, price, is now a variable. Equation (28) may be differentiated implicitly to yield:

(29) $dS/dP = \{Q[1 + e_d(1 - c/P)]\}/[k - (\partial Q/\partial S)(P - c)]$,

where e_d is the price elasticity of demand [that is, $e_d = (\partial Q/\partial P)(P/Q)$]. Since $\partial Q/\partial S < Q/S$, and by reference to equation (28),

(30) $dS/dP < 0$ if, and only if, $e_d(1 - c/P) < -1$.

Otherwise, $dS/dP \geq 0$.[45]

45. Empirically, this sign is too close to call. From Table 2-1 we find that the ratio c/P ranges between 0.201 and 0.236, depending on the amount of overhead costs included in c. Thus, $dS/dP = 0$ for some value $-1.36 \leq e_d \leq -1.25$. Empirical estimates of e_d often fall within this range (see, for example, Table 3-4).

CHAPTER FIVE

Characteristics of an Efficient Airline Market

THIS CHAPTER describes in qualitative terms some of the major characteristics of an efficient airline market. It is best regarded as a theoretical orientation and introduction to the primarily quantitative assessment of industry performance presented in the succeeding two chapters. In two respects, however, the scope of this chapter is broader than those which follow. First, whereas subsequent chapters focus on Civil Aeronautics Board regulation of the industry, this chapter describes some efficiency characteristics that are not under the direct or indirect control of the Board. Second, it is often easy to posit a theoretical solution to an economic problem but typically more difficult to assess actual results in terms of the derived ideal. This chapter bears little restraint in the identification of ideal solutions, whereas subsequent chapters are limited in addressing those market characteristics more easily assessed.[1]

---

1. Even in this chapter we shall deal with efficiency within the industry and shall ignore considerations of "real externalities," "public goods," and the "economics of the second-best." The airlines do create certain negative externalities (such as smoke and noise pollution) and possibly even positive externalities. In truly efficient airline markets, prices would have to reflect these marginal costs and benefits.

A related externality issue is the economist's concept of a public good. (See Paul A. Samuelson, "The Pure Theory of Public Expenditure," *Review of Economics and Statistics,* Vol. 36 [November 1954], pp. 387–89.) As in any alleged case of public goods, the real question is whether public benefits would accrue from the airlines' operating differently from what emerges from the interplay of private market forces. If so, then the efficient solution is to induce changes in service quantity or quality, or both, depending on the relevant costs and benefits. In theory, the efficient solution is where real marginal cost equals the private plus public demand price. Alleged cases of airline public goods include the civil air fleet's contribution to national defense, such as supplying troop transports in time of war, and the economic development of sparsely populated regions.

Finally, in order to perform a "partial analysis" of the airlines, we ignore the fact that other industries may not be characterized by economic efficiency. If this

Preliminary Remark

As mentioned in the introduction and as will be discussed more fully later in this chapter, economic efficiency in airline markets requires that given services be produced at lowest total cost, that the optimal amounts (rates) of services be produced and consumed, and that those services be of optimal quality. Under these conditions, there is no other feasible means of production, no other combinations of quantities and qualities of outputs, and no other distribution of these outputs which would make actual and potential producers and consumers better off. This is our justification for presuming in the analysis that economic efficiency is the overriding policy objective. Of course we do not maintain that economic efficiency is inherently superior to other policy objectives. The extent to which other policy goals (such as equity, promotion of aviation, national defense) should be considered, we leave for others to determine. It is hoped that our focus on economic efficiency will imply something about the opportunity costs of pursuing such "noneconomic" objectives. If so, then one can conjecture that policy decisions will be more "enlightened" because of more complete information. In short, an analysis which focuses on economic efficiency is useful in that it expands our understanding of the industry, it establishes a benchmark for judging industry and regulator performance, and further it provides information on the technical trade-offs between economic efficiency and other policy objectives, thus making it easier for policymakers to sort out the ramifications of (and decide upon) alternative actions.

Efficiency in the Provision of Air Service of Given Quality

Minimizing the production cost of the air service, whatever its quality, is a necessary condition for economic efficiency. Even under regulation,

---

assumption does not hold, then the appropriate analytical framework is the "economics of the second best." We note, however, that according to Meyer and Straszheim, the allocative efficiency costs that arise from not considering second-best problems in the pricing and allocation of transportation resources is probably very small. John R. Meyer and Mahlon R. Straszheim, *Pricing and Project Evaluation,* Vol. 1 of John R. Meyer (ed.), *Techniques of Transport Planning* (Brookings Institution, 1971), p. 79.

of course, air carriers have profit incentives to lower production costs, increase quality, or both. As discussed in the first appendix to this chapter, a firm which does not achieve the lowest feasible cost level for the given service quality is said to be technically inefficient.

Regulatory policies may significantly affect the level of technical efficiency. First, the probability of a firm's achieving technical efficiency is greater the more competitive the market. Conversely, actions by the regulator or by the industry itself to reduce actual and potential competition may be expected to diminish technical efficiency, ceteris paribus. Minimum or maximum restraints on the number of firms in an industry may also affect the level of technical efficiency if there exist economies or diseconomies of scale. Finally, a market's index of technical efficiency will be adversely affected if firms that are more efficient than average are restrained from entering markets or if firms less efficient than average are restrained from leaving markets.

Allocative efficiency, which means achieving the optimal level (rate) of a given quality of service, is usually expressed in terms of conditions for optimal pricing. There are two basic conditions: (a) price equals marginal cost, and (b) price equals average cost.[2] Price reflects the marginal evaluation of extra output, whereas marginal cost reflects the opportunity cost of the resources used. If price exceeds marginal cost, then output is less than optimal (that is, consumers would value extra output more than the value of the additional resources used); on the other hand, if price is below marginal cost and markets are cleared, then output is excessive (that is, the value of resources saved by reducing output is greater than consumers' marginal evaluation of the output reduction).

The relationship between price and average cost is important inasmuch as if price equals marginal cost (and optimal quality obtains) the profit rate is a surrogate measure of optimal industry investment. That is, if profits are excessive (exceeding the opportunity cost on capital), then industry investment at that time is too small; if profits are below normal or negative, then industry investment is too large. Accordingly, if price equals

2. Of course, under certain well-known conditions pricing rules (a) and (b) may come into conflict: for example, the natural monopoly case where marginal cost is below average cost where the latter intercepts demand. But as we have shown in Chapter 2, the airlines are characterized by reasonably constant returns to scale, and this tends to be true of specific services as well as total output. Thus with few exceptions, there is no conflict between "marginal cost pricing" and "average cost pricing."

average cost, then, under the stated conditions, industry investment is at the optimal level.

Applying these pricing rules to airline service, we would first require that over the long run total revenues exceed total costs by a "normal profit," reflecting the opportunity cost on capital. In such manner, average price equals average (and weighted-average marginal) cost. (Average price, so defined, is referred to variously as "fare-level," or "yield.") It is also essential that over time industry investment respond to excessive or insufficient profits in the appropriate manner just described.

The efficient pricing rules must also be applied in individual markets: price must equal marginal and average cost for each type of service. An important implication is that cross-subsidization is inconsistent with economic efficiency. Thus, for example, industry and regulator efforts to offset losses from excessive service in short-haul markets with profits from constricted service in long-haul markets distort the allocation of resources and lead to an inefficient mix of outputs.

The application of the efficient pricing rules in specific instances is sometimes difficult, owing to imprecision in the measure of marginal and average costs. In the succeeding paragraphs we shall discuss a number of these cases.

First, given the inflexibilities of airline fleet acquisition (marginal cost of capacity rises quite rapidly in the short run), what is the marginal and average cost of airline resources when demand shifts in a way that had not been anticipated? Suppose, for example, there is an unanticipated surge in the demand for air travel. As in all cases, the real cost of the airline resource must be measured by its opportunity cost. A price which remains low, consistent with a normal return on accounting costs, will result in queues, or, as we shall see later, deteriorating service. Application of the pricing rules would require a rise in fares to ration demand or raise the quality of service. Such a price increase, leading to higher accounting profits, would also hasten the introduction of the capacity to meet this demand. On the other hand, visualize an unanticipated decline in demand. In such a case, the real cost of airline resources is low.[3] The point here is a classic distinction between economic costs and accounting costs. For efficiency to obtain, prices must reflect economic costs and by doing so hasten a convergence between economic and accounting costs.

3. For example, the real cost of using an airplane is approximated by its rental or lease value. In times of traffic decline, aircraft command very low prices. On this, see Stephen P. Sobotka and others, *Prices of Used Commercial Aircraft, 1959–1965* (Northwestern University, Transportation Center, 1959), Chap. 3.

A related example is the pricing of demand over the seasonal peaks described in Chapter 3. The greatest variations were in the daily cycles (Table 3-1). For convenience, let us think in terms of a peak period and an off-peak period. By definition, in the peak period the opportunity cost of airline resources is very high, and if the price is set below a market-clearing level, queues will form; the price that people in the queues would pay for service is, in turn, a measure of the real cost of the airline resources. In the off-peak period, the opportunity cost of airline resources is very low, measured by the price passengers at that time are willing to pay for their use. In such a case, efficiency dictates that price be equal to the marginal cost of those resources in scarce supply. This would not include, for example, the fully apportioned depreciation cost of a fixed station installation nor would it include the pro rata depreciation on aircraft.

The question of discount fares is another area where application of the efficient pricing rules requires an evaluation of opportunity costs. The idea behind discount fares is that by price discriminating (setting lower prices for youth than for older people, for example) the airlines may increase traffic.[4] This, arguably, leads to higher load factors, lower per-passenger costs, and thus higher carrier profits or lower average fares or both (that is, "everybody gains, no one loses"). However, keeping in mind three propositions from previous chapters, it is easy to show the inconsistency of this logic and how such pricing is inefficient. First, returns to scale for a given service quality are reasonably constant; therefore, increasing size per se will not lower average cost. Second, average load factor is an important measure of service quality; thus, an increase in average load factor lowers service quality. Third, carriers tend to adjust capacity in such manner that average price equals average cost; therefore, given time for adjustment, carriers will earn neither excess profits nor losses.

Given a steady-state equilibrium comporting with the model described in the previous chapter, the introduction of discount fares lowers average fare and thus raises break-even load factor. Over time, carriers will restrict capacity in order to obtain this higher break-even load factor. However, in the process normal-fare passengers realize a reduction in service quality. Consider now a steady-state equilibrium which includes discount fares. The price paid by the normal-fare passenger of course exceeds the marginal and average cost of a filled seat by an amount depending on the proportion

---

4. Presumably excess profits are not the main incentive, since the Board constrains carriers to a reasonable rate of return on investment. (Also see the discussion of the Board's implied regulatory objectives in Chapter 9 below.)

of discount passengers and the amount of their discount. The discount passenger, however, pays a price below the average and marginal cost of a filled seat. Thus, the pricing rules are violated in both markets.[5]

Another difficulty arises out of the fact that often different services use the same resource simultaneously. For example, the typical passenger aircraft accommodates first class passengers, coach passengers, and air freight. How do we apportion these costs and thus price output? First, we must distinguish between joint costs and common costs. Joint costs arise whenever two or more products or services can be produced only simultaneously and in fixed proportions. Common costs arise whenever two or more products or services that are produced together can also be produced separately or can be produced together but in different proportions. Since the bulkhead division between the first class and coach sections of the aircraft can easily be moved and seats rearranged, these are common products which share common costs. The most important scarce resource is cabin space, and thus the ratio of marginal and average first class passenger capacity costs to that of the coach passenger is approximated by the ratio of passengers per unit of floor space in the first class cabin to passengers per unit of floor space in the coach cabin.

In the short run, passenger space and belly-freight space in a passenger or combination aircraft are true joint products. (Capacity costs related to weight are common costs.) Given an aircraft of a certain configuration it is difficult to vary the relative amounts of cargo and passenger space. One option is to block off passenger space in the rear to accommodate freight, but even this is difficult to accomplish with existing aircraft, given requirements to protect passengers with a strong bulkhead and given the need to distribute loads evenly. However, in the long run belly and passenger space is a common product, since it is possible, within limits, to vary aircraft configuration. For example, on the new wide-bodied jets, galleys can be located either above deck or below deck. Passenger space may be contracted to place freight above deck. Going to the other extreme, there is the possibility of locating passengers below the deck. Finally, at the design stage of the aircraft, it is possible to vary, within limits, the relative proportions of above-deck and below-deck space.

Essentially, then, belly freight is a true joint product in the short run,

5. From another perspective, the marginal cost of a discount passenger's use of the filled seat is the marginal price that would have been paid by the normal passenger. Either way, there is a divergence between price and marginal (and average) cost.

becoming a common product in the longer run as new generations of combination aircraft are designed to replace existing ones. Application of the pricing rules in the short run is difficult, inasmuch as joint costs cannot be allocated without knowledge of demand. However, it would appear that to assign belly freight space a cost equal to the cost of carrying freight in all-freighter aircraft is a useful starting point, assigning remaining costs to passengers.[6]

Our discussion to this point has presumed the existence of scheduled service and stable rates without explaining why they come about. There are, of course, alternative schemes. For example, even with scheduled service, why not vary price instantaneously so as to fill the aircraft by the precise time of departure?[7] At the other extreme, why not charge a published rate and then depart whenever the plane became fully loaded? The reason for the convention of scheduled service at published rates is that information is not costless. Consumers plan consumption patterns based on information about alternatives, and this information itself is a scarce resource. Even though the passenger's ticket price is higher when neither of the above extremes is adopted, passengers are typically willing to pay some premium for the institution of published rates and scheduled service since it lowers their information costs. We may not conclude from this, however, that an efficient market would have only scheduled service, since a mix of services, possibly including contract-pricing and on-demand scheduling, may be optimal. However, we do note the existence of scheduled service and published rates almost universally in the unregulated commuter airline markets.

A related efficiency question has to do with the institution of costless reservations. Since there is no penalty for not showing up for the flight, some passengers will book passage on several flights to assure their having accommodations when the flight is finally selected. This tendency, in turn, leads carriers to overbook flights, relying on no-shows to yield enough extra seats. Occasionally, however, the number of reserved-seat passengers who show exceeds the flight's capacity. The Board now imposes fines on

6. See the second appendix to this chapter on the efficient pricing of freight.
7. This has been suggested by William Vickrey, "Responsive Pricing of Public Utility Services," *Bell Journal of Economics and Management Science*, Vol. 2 (Spring 1971), pp. 337–46. Vickrey's scheme would work as follows: Months before the flight the carrier would begin selling tickets at a price which it expected to fill the aircraft by departure time. If, over time, the demand for the flight appeared higher or lower than previously anticipated, then the rate would be adjusted upward or downward accordingly.

the airlines for this practice, but obviously, given the institution of free reservations, some overbooking is optimal.[8]

Optimal Service Quality

In a broadly defined market for a good or service, it is abundantly clear that consumers would prefer having more rather than fewer price-quality options, provided such increase in alternatives can be accomplished at little or no increase in the cost of the otherwise major alternative. However, in most markets economies of production and distribution tend to impose natural limits on the number of alternatives. In any event, it should be possible to identify an optimal number of price-quality options, provided sufficient information is known about consumer preferences and cost relationships.

As discussed in the previous chapter, although there is a broad range of feasible price-quality options, CAB regulation of prices tends to dictate a single option. Since this option is not subject to a market test of its optimality, one of the basic problems faced by the Board is determining whether this chosen price-quality combination is optimal. That is, in an industry where the price-quality option is regulated, economic efficiency requires not only technical efficiency and allocative efficiency, but efficiency in the choice of service quality.

The theoretical determination of optimal service quality may be described as follows. Whether for the individual or for the whole market, we may presume that a quality increase is desirable, ceteris paribus. Past some point, however, the extra value of increasing quality begins to fall. Thus, for a given unit cost of quality increase the individual (or group) values increased quality more than the commensurate increase in per-unit cost for some range. Past a certain point, however, greater quality is still desirable, but is of less value to the consumer than its cost. Such a point, together with its associated price, represents the optimal combination of price and quality. Of course, the optimal combination may differ among individuals. When, as in the airline industry, a single price-quality option

---

8. We conjecture that the optimal fine is one which causes the airlines to overbook just to the point that the opportunity cost of reserve-seat passengers left at the gate offsets the opportunity cost of extra passengers who could have been accommodated in seats made available by no-show reservation passengers.

is chosen for all consumers, there is, of course, the problem of weighting all these marginal evaluations for changes in quality.[9]

In the production and consumption of travel services, the optimal price-quality configuration is best analyzed in terms of the full-cost model, which includes not only ticket price but the value of time in transit. Applying this model, there are several efficiency characteristics of the choice of aircraft and its routing. First, as shown in Chapter 2 there are significant economies with respect to aircraft size. On the other hand, simply replacing small aircraft with large aircraft lowers actual load factor and for this reason raises average cost (and thus price paid by the passenger). A concomitant effect is that the lower average load factor increases the chance of getting a seat on the desired flight and thus it increases service quality. A more common approach is to increase aircraft size and simultaneously decrease schedule frequency, reducing achieved load factors only a marginal amount. The effect of this, however, is to increase the time between scheduled flights, and thereby to reduce service quality. It should be apparent that for any market of known characteristics, there exists an optimal aircraft size—one which minimizes the passengers' full cost of the trip.[10]

From this discussion we may draw some conclusions about the efficient choice of aircraft. First, ceteris paribus, larger aircraft are appropriate in denser markets, whereas smaller aircraft are appropriate in low density markets. This is because in high density markets, where frequency is high in any event, the increase in frequency delay is small in comparison with the reduction in cost attributed to the large aircraft. In smaller markets, the reduction in frequency delay caused by decreasing plane size outweighs the increase in per-passenger cost. Second, because of significant economies with respect to distance flown, ceteris paribus, the large aircraft are more appropriate in long-haul markets, whereas small aircraft are more appropriate in short-haul markets. The reasoning is similar. The per-passenger cost saving accruing from increased aircraft size is much larger for a long trip than for a short one. Thus, passengers will choose a greater frequency delay in long-haul markets than in short, in order to take advantage of the increased savings made possible by passenger trip consolidation. Third, ceteris paribus, larger aircraft are more appropriate in markets where the passengers' time value is low, whereas smaller aircraft are more appropriate where time value is high.

9. For a more analytic description of optimal quality-price determination, see the first appendix to this chapter on aspects of economic efficiency.
10. We might also consider a mix of aircraft.

The problem of minimizing passengers' full cost of travel is much more complicated when one considers the routing of aircraft as well as their selection. Two examples illustrate. First, a transcontinental trip can be flown either direct or with stops along the way. As opposed to the nonstop flight, the one-stop flight increases the transcontinental passenger's transit time and also increases his production cost to the airline. However, this flight increases the frequency of service to the midcontinent city from the coastal points, and also, in turn, means a greater frequency of transcontinental flights. Moreover, it would be possible to exchange a reduction in schedule delay cost for the lower per-passenger cost concomitant with larger aircraft. That is, the greater density along the two-section route would allow the introduction of larger aircraft. In theory, of course, there is a lowest-cost solution, but identifying it a priori is a practical impossibility.

A similar case concerns the proposals of Ronald E. Miller,[11] and Arthur S. De Vany and Eleanor H. Garges.[12] Essentially their recommendation, based on computer simulation of aircraft and passenger routings, is to move in the direction of an air system which utilizes smaller aircraft to feed from small and medium-sized airports into hub markets, and there to use large aircraft for inter-hub travel. A relevant example is whether under the proposed scheme a passenger traveling from Indianapolis to New York City would incur a lower full cost going via Chicago than under the present system of direct flights.

The major component of airline service quality is reflected in load factor, which is a surrogate measure for what we have termed schedule delay. Ceteris paribus, an increase in load factor increases the probability of not obtaining a seat on the flight of first choice, and also, for a given number of passengers, means fewer flights, spaced further apart. But while an increase in load factor increases schedule delay, it decreases per-passenger cost, and if the airlines behave as described in the previous chapter, then the increase in load factor also is reflected in a lower price paid by the passenger.

The analysis of optimal load factor is straightforward. Essentially the idea is to find where an increase in load factor would cause an increase in schedule delay which, given the travelers' evaluation of time, costs travelers

11. Ronald E. Miller, *Domestic Airline Efficiency: An Application of Linear Programming* (M.I.T. Press, 1963).

12. Arthur S. De Vany and Eleanor H. Garges, "A Forecast of Air Travel and Airport Use in 1980," *Transportation Research*, Vol. 6 (1972), pp. 1–18.

more than the associated savings in lower fares—and where at the same time a reduction in load factor would not entail decreases in schedule delay valued sufficiently to offset the associated increase in fare.[13]

We may draw some conclusions about the nature of this equilibrium and how it responds to important market characteristics. First, since delay cost is the product of time delay and the passenger's imputed value of time, then in markets where the value of time is especially high the optimal point will occur at a higher fare, lower load factor combination. Second, ceteris paribus, in a market of greater density, at each load factor level there is a higher cost of reducing incremental schedule delay and thus the optimal combination has a lower fare and a higher load factor. Finally, longer-distance markets will have a higher marginal value associated with each level of load factor (that is, the ticket price savings from a given increase in load factor is greater) and thus the optimal load factor is higher (so is the associated fare).[14]

Several other aspects of airline market efficiency might be noted. First, although the subject of airline safety is much too broad to receive adequate attention here, it is important to note that safety has its costs. Its benefit, of course, is a reduced probability of a serious or perhaps fatal accident. Depending on one's personal evaluation of human life and suffering, the optimal quality of service in the safety dimension is where the expected reduction in accident "costs" just equals the marginal cost of this (increased) safety provision.[15]

There is, finally, a plethora of additional quality dimensions, such as the speed of baggage claim, the elegance of on-board accommodations, the amount of personal attention granted by airline employees, and the noise level aboard the aircraft. From the individual passenger's viewpoint, the problem is basically one of trading off the marginal value of increased quality with the associated increase in cost. In other words, each passenger has an ideal mix of these service amenities he would pick to have available. In the aggregate, he is faced with little real differentiation among carriers, either in terms of quality level or in terms of mix. Since the level of expendi-

13. Also see further discussion in the next chapter.
14. These a priori conclusions are confirmed in the next chapter.
15. For an interesting discussion along these general lines, see T. C. Schelling, "The Life You Save May Be Your Own," in Samuel B. Chase, Jr. (ed.), *Problems in Public Expenditure Analysis* (Brookings Institution, 1968). Also see Richard J. Barber, "Economics of Air Safety," *Journal of Air Law and Commerce*, Vol. 34 (Summer 1968), pp. 431–33.

tures on these kinds of quality aspects appears to be very closely related to the capacity dimension of quality, we feel justified in focusing on the latter in subsequent analyses.

Conclusion

Efficiency in the provision of airline service requires that (a) services of given quality be produced at lowest feasible cost, (b) prices for such services be equal to relevant marginal and average costs, and (c) the optimal price-quality options be chosen. As we shall develop subsequently, profit incentives in the airlines appear to bring about a reasonable degree of technical efficiency (given the nature of institutional restraints), and opportunities for changing the quality of individual services in response to price result in a fair approximation of allocative efficiency. Thus, the major responsibility of the Board, and one which has great potential for error and thus social welfare cost, is in the choice of the optimal price-quality combinations.

Appendix: Aspects of Economic Efficiency

Technical Efficiency

One requirement for economic efficiency in any industry is "technical efficiency," and by that we mean achieving any rate of output of a given quality at lowest total cost (per time period). Given a production function of the form,

$$(1) \qquad X = f(a, b, \ldots, m),$$

and also given the prices paid for inputs $a, b, \ldots, m$, we may determine a function which gives the lowest feasible total cost for any rate of output:

$$(2) \qquad C = g(X).$$

An airline produces many outputs (service between several city pairs, different classes of service, and so on), and thus we may write the production function more generally (in implicit form) as

$$(3) \qquad h(X_1, X_2, \ldots, X_n, a, b, c, \ldots, m) = 0,$$

where $X_1, X_2, \ldots, X_n$ denote the various outputs. The technically efficient cost equation then becomes

$$(4) \qquad C = C(X_1, X_2, \ldots, X_n),$$

which gives us the lowest total cost for producing any combination (rates) of outputs $X_1, X_2, \ldots, X_n$. If the industry's total cost is greater than that given by (4), then it is said to be technically inefficient.

Allocative Efficiency

A second necessary condition for industry efficiency is "allocative efficiency." As generally used, the term refers to the optimal production (and consumption) rates of outputs of given quality, given the technically feasible lowest-cost relationship and given consumer demands for the outputs. Let us define the demand price for output X_i as

$$(5) \qquad P_i = P_i(X_i) \qquad i = 1, 2, \ldots, n,$$

and thus consumers' total evaluation for consumption X_i is the area under (5) from zero to X_i. Consumers surplus, CS, may be determined by netting out revenues paid:

$$(6) \qquad CS = \sum_{i=1}^{n} \left[\int_0^{X_i} P_i(X_i)dX_i - P_i(X_i)X_1 \right].$$

Producers surplus, PS, is simple (economic) profit:

$$(7) \qquad PS = \sum_{i=1}^{n} P_i(X_i)X_1 - C(X_1, X_2, \ldots, X_n).$$

Adding equations (6) and (7) we have total economic welfare, TW, and may maximize it to determine optimal rates of output:[16]

$$(8) \qquad TW = \sum_{i=1}^{n} \left[\int_0^{X_i} P_i(X_i)dX_i - C(X_1, X_2, \ldots, X_n) \right].$$

The first-order conditions for maximizing (8) are:[17]

$$(9) \qquad P_i(X_i) - \partial C/\partial X_i = 0 \qquad i = 1, 2, \ldots, n.$$

This merely states that the efficient output (and consumption) rates are those where the price (or marginal evaluation) of each output equals its marginal (production) cost.

16. Conceptually, there are difficulties with simply adding surpluses, since marginal utilities of income need not be constant, and one need not be neutral when it comes to income (re)distribution. Operationally, however, it is a useful approach to many policy problems.

17. We shall assume without further comment that second-order conditions are fulfilled.

Allocative Efficiency with Variable Quality

If quality is variable, then allocative efficiency pertains not only to the optimal rates of outputs, but to their optimal quality levels as well. Lowest total cost with variable quality may be written as

(10) $$C = C(X_1, X_2, \ldots, X_n, Q),$$

where Q is the (homogeneous) quality level, and where increasing quality, ceteris paribus, raises total cost:

(11) $$\partial C/\partial Q > 0.$$

Demand price for each output is given by

(12) $$P_i = P_i(X_i, Q) \qquad i = 1, 2, \ldots, n,$$

where

(13) $$\partial P_i/\partial Q > 0 \qquad i = 1, 2, \ldots, n.$$

With these new relationships, consumers surplus may be measured either as

(14) $$CS = \sum_{i=1}^{n} \left[\int_0^{X_i} P_i(X_i, Q)dX_i - P_i(X_i, Q)\cdot X_i \right],$$

or as

(15) $$CS = \sum_{i=1}^{n} \left[\int_0^Q X_i(P_i, Q)(\partial P_i/\partial Q)dQ - P_i(X_i, Q)\cdot X_i \right].$$

In either case, producers surplus is

(16) $$PS = \sum_{i=1}^{n} P_i(X_i, Q)\cdot X_i - C(X_1, X_2, \ldots, X_n, Q).$$

The first-order conditions for maximizing welfare are as follows:

(17) $$P_i(X_i, Q) = \partial C/\partial X_i \qquad i = 1, 2, \ldots, n.$$

(18) $$\sum_{i=1}^{n} X_i(\partial P_i/\partial Q) = \partial C/\partial Q.$$

Equation set (17) merely requires that individual demand prices equal individual output marginal costs. Equation (18) requires that the sum of individual demand marginal evaluations equal the marginal cost of quality.[18]

18. Some readers will note that viewed this way output (X) is a private good, whereas quality (Q) is in some ways a public good.

Whether total welfare is a single-peaked function of increasing quality in every

Quality in the Utility Function

The relevance of quality can be seen also with a simple model of individual utility maximization. Let the individual's utility be defined by

$$(19) \qquad\qquad U = U(X, Q, W),$$

where

X = quantity of composite good consumed
Q = quality of composite good
W = work expended.

Of course, $\partial U/\partial X > 0$, $\partial U/\partial Q > 0$, and $\partial U/\partial W < 0$. Let the individual's total cost of output be defined as

$$(20) \qquad\qquad C = C(X, Q),$$

where $\partial C/\partial X > 0$ and $\partial C/\partial Q > 0$. Finally, the individual's total income (for spending on output X) is the wage rate r times the work expended, W.

The problem resolves into maximizing:

$$(21) \qquad\qquad Z = U(X, Q, W) - \lambda[C(X, Q) - rW].$$

Finding the first-order conditions and simplifying, we have

$$(22) \qquad (\partial U/\partial X)/(\partial C/\partial X) = (\partial U/\partial Q)/(\partial C/\partial Q) = (\partial U/\partial W)/(-r),$$

and

$$(23) \qquad\qquad C(X, Q) - rW = 0.$$

Equation (23) is the budget constraint, and equation (22) means that the ratios of marginal utilities of output quantity, output quality, and work expended to their respective marginal costs are equal.

---

case cannot be ascertained a priori, although our empirical analysis in Chapter 6 strongly suggests that this is true for the quality of air service. Possible counter-examples come to mind. If restrained to one price-quality option, the U.S. domestic television set market would probably have two major peaks—one at the quality level of an inexpensive monochrome set, and another at a reasonably inexpensive color set. Arguably, restaurant service would peak at least twice—at an inexpensive franchise-burger level, and again at a more sophisticated restaurant level. Finally, one can imagine restraining automobiles to a single price-quality option and finding strong markets for both the compact car and the luxury sedan.

In fact, on a priori grounds any market where there appears to be dominant price-quality choices is likely to be multipeaked in welfare as the single option is varied. We might also visualize an industry's becoming government-regulated, with only one price-quality option available, and noting the division in public opinion over the optimal price-quality configuration.

Appendix: A Model for the Efficient Pricing of Freight in Combination Aircraft[19]

This appendix presents a model which derives certain necessary conditions for the efficient pricing of freight in combination aircraft. The reader should note that the model incorporates numerous simplifications of complex relationships and omits a number of empirically relevant variables.

Definitions and Notation

D_p = passenger demand for air travel

D_f = demand for air freight

X_p = passenger revenue ton-miles

X_{f1} = freight revenue ton-miles in combination aircraft

X_{f2} = freight revenue ton-miles in freighter aircraft

X_f = freight revenue ton-miles, total ($X_f = X_{f1} + X_{f2}$)

L_p = target (and actual) passenger load factor

L_{f1} = target (and actual) freight load factor in combination aircraft

L_{f2} = target (and actual) freight load factor in freighter aircraft

R = ratio of freighter (ton-mile) capacity to passenger (ton-mile) capacity in combination aircraft

C_p = average (and marginal) passenger traffic cost (per revenue ton-mile)

C_{f1} = average (and marginal) freight traffic cost (per revenue ton-mile) in combination aircraft

C_{f2} = average (and marginal) freight traffic cost (per revenue ton-mile) in freighter aircraft

C_a = average (and marginal) aircraft capacity cost (per available ton-mile) for either aircraft type.

Freight and Passenger Demands

The (weighted average) demand price for freight is a function of freight revenue ton-miles carried:

$$(24) \qquad D_f = D_f(X_f) = D_f(X_{f1} + X_{f2}),$$

19. This appendix is based on James C. Miller III, "The Optimal Pricing of Freight in Combination Aircraft," *Journal of Transport Economics and Policy*, Vol. 7 (September 1973), pp. 258–68.

and the freight demand curve is downward-sloping:

$$(25) \qquad \partial D_f / \partial X_f < 0.$$

In like manner, the (weighted average) demand price for passenger service is a function of passenger revenue ton-miles:

$$(26) \qquad D_p = D_p(X_p),$$

and the passenger demand curve is downward-sloping:

$$(27) \qquad \partial D_p / \partial X_p < 0.$$

Freight and Passenger Costs

Following the distinction made in Chapter 2, we may separate total cost for each type of service into two elements—traffic costs and capacity costs.[20] (In the case of freight service, traffic costs refer to expenses incurred in pickup and delivery, inventory, ticketing, insurance, and loading and unloading.) Thus, there are two cost functions, one for passengers and freight carried in combination aircraft, and the other for freight carried in freighter aircraft.[21] Total cost in combination aircraft is defined as follows:

$$(28) \qquad K_c = C_p X_p + C_{f1} X_{f1} + C_a(X_p/L_p + X_{f1}/L_{f1}).$$

That is, total cost is the sum of (a) passenger traffic cost times passenger revenue ton-miles, (b) freight traffic cost in combination aircraft times freight revenue ton-miles in combination aircraft, and (c) per-unit capacity cost times aircraft capacity needed to carry passengers and freight (at the desired or feasible load factor levels). Total cost in freighter aircraft is defined as

$$(29) \qquad K_2 = C_{f2} X_{f2} + C_a(X_f/L_{f2}).$$

20. Note from the set of definitions that we have assumed constant returns to scale (marginal cost equals average cost). Although we know of no studies which have addressed air freight economies directly, most airline cost analyses strongly suggest constant or barely significant increasing returns (see Chapter 2). The model could accommodate a different assumption regarding scale economies, and this might affect the general conclusions.

21. There is some evidence that freighter traffic costs are lower than those for freight in combination aircraft ($C_{f2} < C_{f1}$). This is consistent with common sense, since it is more difficult to raise freight into the belly of an aircraft than to place it directly into the fuselage; in addition, the greater space affords more flexibility in loading. (However, the move to containerization for belly freight on the wide-bodied jets may reduce or even reverse this cost differential.)

That is, freighter cost is the sum of traffic cost and capacity cost (at the desired or feasible load factor level).

Economic Welfare Function

Given these equations, we may define economic welfare as the sum of consumers and producers surpluses, then determine optimal pricing (and outputs) by maximizing the following equation:

$$(30) \quad W = \int_0^{X_p} D_p(X_p)dX_p + \int_0^{X_f} D_f(X_f)dX_f$$
$$- [C_pX_p + C_{f1}X_{f1} + C_a(X_p/L_p + X_{f1}/L_{f1})]$$
$$- [C_{f2}X_{f2} + C_a(X_{f2}/L_{f2})] - \lambda(RX_p/L_p - X_{f1}/L_{f1}).$$

The first two terms in the equation represent areas under the demand curves for passengers and freight respectively. The two bracketed terms are total costs for combination and freighter aircraft. The Lagrangian term (λ) relates freight capacity (in combination aircraft) to passenger capacity, by the ratio term, R.

Assume that the following parameters (in addition to C_p, C_{f1}, C_{f2}, and C_a) are constant: L_p, L_{f1}, L_{f2}, and R.[22] This leaves (30) as an equation with four independent variables: X_p, X_{f1}, X_{f2}, and λ. We may maximize economic welfare by taking partial derivatives with respect to each variable, setting equal to zero, and solving the resulting equations simultaneously:

$$(31) \quad \partial W/\partial X_p = D_p(X_p) - C_p - C_a/L_p - \lambda R/L_p = 0.$$
$$(32) \quad \partial W/\partial X_{f1} = D_f(X_f) - C_{f1} - C_a/L_{f1} + \lambda/L_{f1} = 0.$$
$$(33) \quad \partial W/\partial X_{f2} = D_f(X_f) - C_{f2} - C_a/L_{f2} = 0.$$
$$(34) \quad \partial W/\partial \lambda = RX_p/L_p - X_{f1}/L_{f1} = 0.$$

Implications of the Model

One important conclusion that can be drawn from this model is that the optimal level for freight rates is the average (and marginal) cost of carrying such freight in freighter aircraft. Rearranging equation (33), we have

$$(35) \quad D_f(X_f) = C_{f2} + C_a/L_{f2}.$$

22. This assumes that the ratio of passenger and freight capacity in combination aircraft cannot be changed. This is true for the short run, but not for the long run, as some changes in aircraft configuration are possible. (See Miller, "Optimal Pricing," pp. 262–63.) Note also that load factors are assumed to be exogenous variables. In a dynamic setting, load factors are endogenous, as discussed in Chapter 4.

The left side of equation (35) is the demand price for freight, whereas the right side is freighter cost (per unit of service).

Note also from equation (31) that optimal passenger fares differ from the sum of traffic cost and pro rata capacity cost by a factor of $(\lambda R/L_p)$. Parameters R and L_p are both positive, but the sign of λ is indeterminate at this point. Thus, optimal passenger fares may either exceed or be below pro rata (ton-mile) costs. Freight costs in combination aircraft differ from freight rates by an amount (λ/L_{f1}), and thus may either exceed or be below pro rata (combination aircraft) costs. Also note that if one divides equation (31) by equation (34) the resulting fraction suggests that if R were to increase (that is, if the proportion of combination-aircraft space allocated to freight were to increase), then the optimal ratio of passenger fares to freight rates would rise; if proportionately less space were allocated to freight, then optimally the ratio of passenger fares to freight rates would fall.

CHAPTER SIX

Market Performance under Regulation: Prices and Service Quality

IN THIS CHAPTER and the subsequent one we shall attempt to express in quantitative terms some of the major characteristics of efficient airline markets and, by implication, appraise the performance of the industry under CAB regulation. This chapter focuses on rate regulation and its derivative, quality regulation. A major prerequisite is the estimation of optimal fare-quality combinations, and to accomplish this we must first quantify the relationship between fare levels and excess capacity and then relate excess capacity to service convenience. While we do not have sufficient information on travelers' preferences for service convenience to determine efficient prices and optimal levels of service quality precisely,[1] we can identify with some confidence a fairly narrow range in which efficient fares are likely to be found.

Measuring Service Convenience

The most direct way of quantifying service convenience is by measuring the time required to gain service. That is, holding fare, speed, and other demand decision variables constant, if potential passengers were polled as to the exact time they would most prefer having their departure, or if there were scheduled departures with infinite capacity each minute of the day, we would observe some time pattern of demand, one probably much more peaked than that described in Table 3-1.[2] Actual markets, however,

1. See the discussion of time value estimates in Chapter 3 (especially Table 3-4).
2. Recall that the traffic data shown in Table 3-1 reflect supply restraints as well as demand.
On another matter, we do not mean to imply that arrival time is unimportant to

are characterized by a much lower rate of scheduling and capacity, implying a difference for most travelers between their preferred departure time and the scheduled departure closest to it. If these time differentials increased significantly, we would expect the number of air travelers to diminish, as passengers chose other modes such as the auto, other destinations, or even canceled the trip. This aspect of convenience can be quantified crudely by the inverse of schedule frequency, or more precisely by estimating the sum of all the time differentials or delays for potential travelers in the market. The latter technique is obviously preferable, since convenience depends not only on the number of flights scheduled, but on how they are scheduled and on the time pattern of demand that prevails in a market.

We shall define "frequency delay" as the expected differential, in minutes, per passenger between the most desired departure time and that of the closest scheduled departure.[3] For example, a traveler whose most desired departure time is 9:30 A.M. but who finds that the nearest scheduled departure time is 9:00 A.M. incurs a thirty-minute "delay." If, instead, the nearest departure time were 10:30 A.M., the traveler would experience a sixty-minute delay, and so forth.[4]

The frequency of flights, however, is not the only determinant of service convenience. If the most-preferred scheduled flight is filled, the traveler will have to take a later or earlier flight. Flights are occasionally booked up because of demand fluctuations, both seasonal and stochastic.[5] The stochastic phenomenon, which will be discussed first, is similar to a queuing process, and can be analyzed using Markov techniques (see the appendix to this chapter).

---

the potential passenger. We merely presume here that preferences regarding departure and arrival may be expressed in terms of a desired time of departure.

3. Expressed functionally for a specific market: $T_f = T_f(F)$, where $T_f =$ per-passenger expected frequency delay, and $F =$ schedule frequency. Expected frequency delay decreases with greater flight frequency, but equal increments of schedule frequency decrease expected frequency delay by successively smaller increments ($\partial T_f/\partial F < 0$, and $\partial^2 T_f/\partial F^2 > 0$).

4. We recognize that travelers' preferences regarding schedules may not be symmetric—some may prefer to take a later flight, even though an earlier flight is closer to their desired departure time. Moreover, a potential passenger's first (feasible) alternative choice need not be the closest scheduled flight, such as a businessman choosing a night flight if an early-morning flight the next day is not available. However, we believe that our method of measuring service convenience is reasonably accurate and provides a consistent estimate of the temporal synchronization of supply and demand.

5. We focus here on the stochastic aspect alone and treat the seasonal pattern of demand later in the chapter.

We define stochastic delay as the expected length of delay a potential passenger faces because of the chance that his most preferred scheduled departure will be booked up and he will have to select another and possibly even a third or fourth, and so on.[6] Characteristic of queuing processes, the length of the average delay is related to the degree of dispersion of the quantity demanded distribution facing each flight, the average level of quantity demanded, the average aircraft capacity, and the time intervals between flights. Hence, as the average number of passengers on each flight approaches the average capacity of the aircraft, the probability of not obtaining a seat grows large, and the expected delay grows long.

The summation of frequency and stochastic delays constitutes the expected difference between a potential traveler's preferred departure time and his actual departure time, not accounting for equipment delays. We denote this sum as expected schedule delay and utilize it as the basic raw measure of service inconvenience.[7]

The Costs of Service Convenience

Under suitable assumptions, expected schedule delay functions can be estimated. Using the frequency-delay model developed in the appendix to this chapter, we are able to describe frequency delay for one specific pattern of demand as a function of schedule frequency:

6. These delays exist even with the current system of free reservations. Although the passenger is not required to actually wait at the terminal, a booked flight will mean that some travelers must fly at nonpreferred times. Alternatively, we could measure this phenomenon by the length of advance notice required to request a seat on a flight with a given probability of obtaining it.

We represent the (expected value) stochastic delay per traveler as $T_s = T_s$ (N, F, S, σ), where N = average daily quantity demanded, F = daily flight frequency, S = average aircraft capacity, and σ = dispersion of quantity demanded distribution. As discussed above, we would expect the following set of inequalities to hold: $\partial T_s/\partial N > 0$, $\partial^2 T_s/\partial N^2 > 0$, $\partial T_s/\partial F < 0$, $\partial^2 T_s/\partial F^2 > 0$, $\partial T_s/\partial S < 0$, $\partial^2 T_s/\partial S^2 > 0$, $\partial T_s/\partial \sigma > 0$, and $\partial^2 T_s/\partial \sigma^2 > 0$.

7. Schedule delay is not the only type of delay impacting on overall service quality. Delays in departure, in receiving on-board services, in arrival, and in baggage claim are important. For example, the Board collects data on carrier arrival performance in major markets of over 200 miles, and for April 1972 the trunk carriers completed only 81.2 percent of such flights within fifteen minutes of scheduled arrival time. (*Aviation Week and Space Technology*, Vol. 97, July 10, 1972, p. 30.) For the time being, however, we shall treat these as exogenous and focus on schedule delay only.

$$(1) \qquad\qquad T_f = 92(F^{-0.456}),$$

where T_f is the average, or expected, frequency delay in minutes, and F is the daily flight frequency. The queuing model described in the appendix simulated an actual airline system over many configurations, and yielded estimates of stochastic delay which may be approximated as follows:

$$(2) \qquad\qquad T_s = 0.455(Y^{-0.645})(X^{-1.79})(I),$$
$$R^2 = 0.910.$$

where

T_s = expected stochastic delay in minutes

$Y = N_f/\sigma_f$ = average quantity demanded per flight divided by the distribution's standard deviation

$X = (S_f - N_f)/\sigma_f$ = relative excess capacity per flight, measured in units of standard deviation

I = average interval between flights in minutes.

Thus, total schedule delay per passenger is given by

$$(3) \qquad\quad T = 92(F^{-0.456}) + 0.455(Y^{-0.645})(X^{-1.79})(I).$$

For a specific market served by aircraft of uniform size, we can describe schedule delay and its components, frequency and stochastic delays, as a function of flight frequency, or its derivative, average load factor. Figure 6-1 illustrates these effects for a hypothetical market based on computations summarized in Table 6-1. (Note particularly the sensitivity of stochastic delay to the level of excess capacity.) Cost per passenger is also a function of average load factor (Table 6-1), and thus the regulator is faced with an "opportunity locus" representing feasible combinations of price and service quality measured in terms of expected schedule delay (Figure 6-2).

Optimal Fare-Quality Level, and Structure

To appraise the efficiency of the fare-quality combination selected by the regulator (or by the market, as the case may be) we must first identify the optimal, or efficient, combination. One approach would be to locate the point on the opportunity locus where the technological rate of substitution between fare level and quantity is equal to the subjective trade-off or rate of substitution of the representative traveler.[8] Alternatively, we

8. The existence of such a unique solution requires that the typical traveler's (tangential) indifference curve be *less* convex (relative to the origin) than the regulator's opportunity locus (Figure 6-2).

Figure 6-1. Frequency Delay, Stochastic Delay, and Schedule Delay as a Function of Average Load Factor, Hypothetical Market

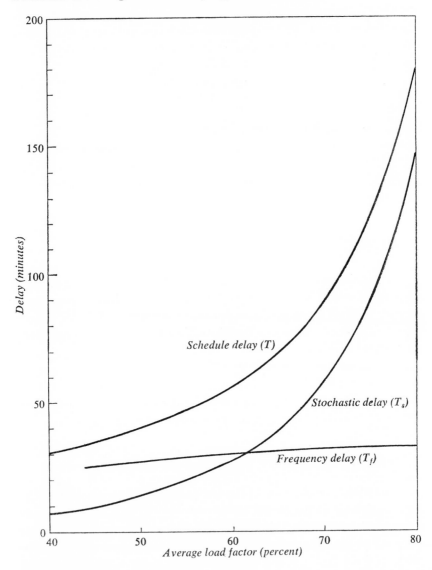

Source: Table 6-1.

Table 6-1. Expected Delays per Passenger, Hypothetical Market[a]

Average load factor (percent)	Delay (minutes per passenger)			Cost per passenger (dollars)
	Stochastic	Frequency	Schedule	
40	6.90	23.86	30.76	43.84
44	9.07	24.92	33.99	40.99
48	11.87	25.93	37.80	38.61
52	15.54	26.90	42.44	36.59
56	20.40	27.82	48.22	34.85
60	26.97	28.71	55.68	33.34
64	36.05	29.57	65.62	32.01
68	48.96	30.40	79.36	30.84
72	68.03	31.21	99.24	29.79
76	97.60	31.99	129.59	28.85
80	146.63	32.74	179.37	28.00

Source: Authors' calculations based on models outlined in appendixes to Chapters 2 and 6.

a. Distance of 600 miles, average passengers per day of 800, and utilizing three-engine turbo-fan jet aircraft.

b. Weighted average of coach and first class costs, including 12 percent reasonable return on investment.

could estimate the monetary valuation the representative air traveler places on avoiding schedule delays[9] and seek that combination of fares and delays which minimizes his total trip cost. For reasons of data unavailability, we adopt the second approach but note from the outset that imputations of the value of schedule-delay time must be applied with caution. The reason, as explained in Chapter 3, is that schedule delay does not necessarily cause time to be actually expended, or wasted. In terms of a rank ordering we would expect passengers to ascribe a higher value to time en route, since its use is generally less flexible than schedule delay.

Ideally, we would measure the valuation of schedule delay as the ratio of demand price sensitivity to demand schedule-delay sensitivity.[10] But not having information on demand elasticity with respect to scheduling delay, we must rely on various proxy measures. As discussed in Chapter 3, De Vany's estimate of revealed value of time in air travel was $7.28 per hour, based on a comparison of price elasticity and demand elasticity with respect to time en route (Table 3-4). The Brown-Watkins imputations were $11.97 for first class passengers, and $8.09 for coach class travelers. Of course, as mentioned before, the traditional approach to measuring value of time in travel is to assume that it is equal to the passenger's opportunity cost,

9. The slope of the tangency point under the first approach is the monetary valuation being estimated.

10. That is, $\rho = (\partial N / \partial T) / (\partial N / \partial P)$. See Chapter 3.

Figure 6-2. Relation of Average Cost per Air Passenger to Expected
Schedule Delay, Hypothetical Market

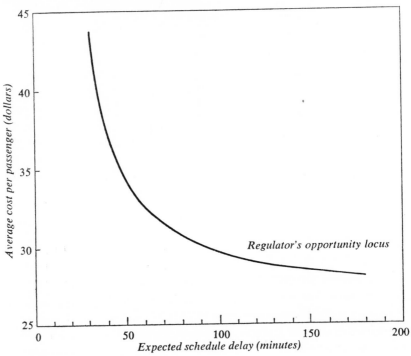

Source: Table 6-1.

approximated by his wage rate. For example, the study by the Institute for
Defense Analyses (IDA) concluded that in 1957 the mean average hourly
earnings of passengers were $6.20 (expressed in 1960 dollars).[11] The same
study also found that during the 1959–63 transition period approximately
74 percent of domestic air travelers chose the time savings of jet aircraft
over piston aircraft at a surcharge of approximately $3.40 per hour.
Finally, the IDA study showed that in 1954 air travelers had been willing
to pay a surcharge of $5.28 (in 1960 prices) an hour saved over ground
transport. Since these are all measures of en route time valuation, they
would appear to set upper limits on the valuation of schedule delay. To
sum up, while we cannot measure time value for the representative passen-

11. Norman J. Asher and others, "Demand Analysis for Air Travel by Supersonic Transport (Arlington, Va.: Institute for Defense Analyses, 1966; processed),
Vol. 2, pp. 34, 38, 51.

ger with great precision, we can, nevertheless, posit a range of time values and hence derive a range in which optimal fares would probably be found.

Our approach to optimal load factor is to minimize the total trip cost. That is, we compare the reduction in average cost per passenger enabled by an increase of the average load factor by a given increment with the imputed value of the additional schedule delay incurred because of the incremental increase in average load factor. Where these two are equal, the passenger minimizes his total trip cost. In other words, the least-cost equilibrium is determined by the intersection of the two equations: (a) marginal cost reduction, and (b) marginal delay cost, both of which are functions of average load factor.

As would be expected, the optimal average load factor increases with trip length and decreases with the value of delay time. Moreover, the optimal load factor also is related to the level or density of the market's demand. This occurs because at a given average load factor, the daily flight frequency in a dense market is proportionately higher, and the interval between flights is less. Hence, while a reduction in relative excess capacity in any market increases the probability of being delayed, the intervals of delay are less, the denser the market.

Although we have no precise estimates of the price travelers would be willing to pay in order to avoid units of schedule delay (or conversely, how much increase in schedule delay they would be willing to encounter for a given reduction in fare), it is instructive to observe the level and pattern of optimal load factors and associated prices consistent with assumed values of delay. In Table 6-2 we report our estimates of optimal load factors and associated fares, by distance and by market density, based on valuations of time of $10 per hour and $5 per hour.

A striking conclusion from our analysis is that the existing overall fare level is much higher than the one consistent with maximizing economic efficiency. This can be seen in Figure 6-3, which compares the Board-approved fare-mileage formula for 1971 with that estimated to be optimal using the methodology just described. Table 6-3 also shows this discrepancy by comparing optimal fares with existing fares and recording the ratios of actual to optimal fares.

Another issue is the structure of load factors. For example, Figure 6-4 shows the range of optimal load factors for routes of various distances (dashed lines) and compares this pattern with that which has prevailed in the regulated market (solid lines). As shown, the average load factors generated by the regulated market (that is, growing out of the structure of

Table 6-2. Optimal Average Load Factors (ALF) and Domestic Trunk Air Coach Fares as a Function of Market Distance and Density, and Value of Time[a]

Load factors in percent; fares in dollars; value of time in dollars per hour

Number of daily passengers and value of time	Flight distance (miles)													
	200		600		1,000		1,400		1,800		2,200		2,600	
	ALF	Fare	ALF	Fare	ALF	Fare	ALF	Fare	ALF	Fare	ALF	Fare	ALF	Fare
100 at $10	44	22.64	48	39.06	50	55.20	54	65.93	57	81.06	58	94.52	59	107.70
at $ 5	48	21.32	52	36.98	54	52.38	58	62.92	61	77.54	62	90.52	63	103.26
200 at $10	49	20.42	54	34.76	56	49.16	57	63.63	61	77.54	62	90.52	62	104.32
at $ 5	54	19.16	58	33.19	60	47.02	61	60.92	64	75.20	65	87.85	66	100.28
400 at $10	54	19.16	57	33.56	60	47.02	61	60.92	64	75.20	65	87.85	66	100.28
at $ 5	58	18.32	61	32.15	63	45.60	65	58.54	68	72.39	68	85.41	69	97.56
800 at $10	57	18.52	61	32.15	63	45.60	64	59.11	67	73.06	68	85.41	69	97.56
at $ 5	62	17.58	65	30.91	66	44.31	68	56.94	71	70.49	71	83.18	72	95.07
1,600 at $10	61	17.75	64	31.20	66	44.31	68	56.94	71	70.49	71	83.18	72	95.07
at $ 5	65	17.08	68	30.07	70	42.75	71	55.48	73	69.31	74	81.12	75	92.77
3,200 at $10	65	17.08	68	30.07	69	43.13	71	55.48	73	69.31	74	81.12	75	92.77
at $ 5	68	16.62	71	29.31	72	42.04	74	54.13	76	67.65	77	79.23	77	91.34
6,400 at $10	68	16.62	71	29.31	72	42.04	73	54.57	76	67.65	77	79.23	77	91.34
at $ 5	71	16.22	74	28.61	75	41.05	76	53.29	78	66.62	79	78.05	79	89.99

Source: Authors' calculations based on methodology outlined in appendixes to Chapters 2 and 6.
a. DC-8 aircraft were assigned to all routes in excess of 1,600 miles; DC-9 aircraft were assigned to markets of 100 daily passengers over the range 100–1,000 miles; B-727 aircraft were assigned to all remaining markets.

Figure 6-3. Optimal and Actual Yield per Mile of Domestic
Trunk Air Coach Fares, 1971

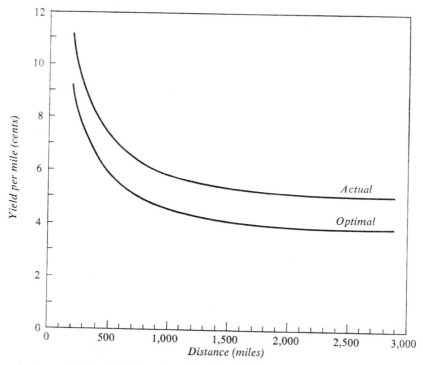

Sources: Actual fares—CAB Docket 21866-9, Exhibit DOT-S-1 (rev.); optimal fares—authors' calculations based on methodology outlined in appendixes to Chapters 2 and 6.

fares as related to distance) have been qualitatively perverse. That is, load factors on long routes have been significantly lower than on short routes, while the optimal pattern, whatever the value of delay (assuming that it is constant across markets), is just the reverse.[12]

In terms of the structure of average load factors with respect to market density, we do observe that the pattern of market equilibrium has been

12. Given the higher proportion of leisure (for instance, vacation) travel on long-distance flights, we might conclude that the valuation of schedule delay for the representative passenger would decrease with distance traveled. This would accentuate the characteristic revealed above, namely, that optimal load factors rise with greater distance. Since markets are characterized by both distance and density, the optimal load factor in a long-haul, low-density market is not so easily identified. Such instances require market-by-market analysis. However, of the top ten markets in terms of market density, four are in excess of 1,000 miles. See U.S. Civil Aeronautics Board, *Handbook of Airline Statistics, 1971 Edition* (1972), p. 409.

Table 6-3. Estimated Optimal Domestic Trunk Air Coach Fares and Actual Fares, Selected Markets, 1971

City-pair market	Distance (miles)	Daily traffic	Optimal coach fare, $5 an hour time value (dollars)	Optimal coach fare, $10 an hour time value (dollars)	Published coach fare (dollars)	Adjusted yield[a] (dollars)	Ratio of adjusted yield to optimal fares	
							$5 an hour time value	$10 an hour time value
Baltimore–New York	180	2,000	16.82	17.99	24.00	20.85	1.24	1.16
Huntsville–Memphis	184	170	20.63	21.90	23.00	19.97	0.97	0.91
Chicago–St. Louis	256	2,600	18.67	19.38	28.00	24.23	1.30	1.25
Chicago–Philadelphia	675	2,000	32.29	33.48	55.00	46.63	1.44	1.39
New York–Miami	1,092	5,500	44.65	45.77	83.00	69.95	1.57	1.53
Denver–New York	1,627	700	64.99	67.36	113.00	93.05	1.43	1.38
Los Angeles–New York	2,453	3,200	86.88	88.25	163.00	134.21	1.54	1.52
San Francisco–Washington	2,431	600	92.10	94.67	155.00	127.63	1.39	1.35

Sources: Distance and passenger data are from direct testimony in CAB, Bureau of Economics, CAB Docket 21866-6, Exhibit BE-6501 (July 6, 1970). Published fare is from *Official Airline Guide: Quick Reference, North American Edition* (Reuben H. Donnelley, July 1, 1971). The other calculations are based on the methodology outlined in the appendixes to Chapters 2 and 6.

a. Adjusted for incidence of discount fares (see CAB Docket 21866-9, Exhibit BC-6006).

Figure 6-4. Optimal Average Load Factors as a Function of Domestic Trunk Air Market Distance, by Value of Time, and Actual Average Load Factors, by Number of Carriers[a]

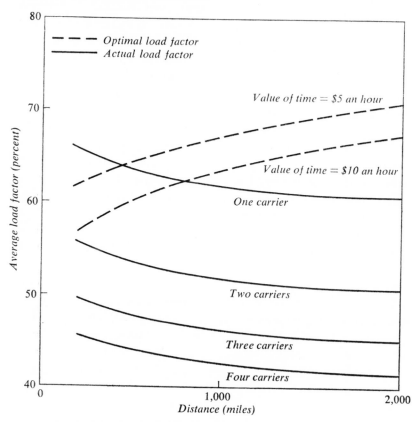

Sources: Dashed lines—Table 6-2; solid lines—Chapter 4, equation (2).
a. Assumes a daily average of 800 passengers.

consistent qualitatively with the structure of optimal fares. Cross-section regressions (1) and (2) shown in Chapter 4 indicate that load factors tend to rise with market density. The same is true of optimal load factors (Table 6-2). However, it is not possible to compare directly this existing structure with the optimal one, since the underlying pattern is so inefficient with respect to optimal load factors as a function of market distance.

To return to the question of overall levels, it must be concluded that existing load factors lie significantly below those defined by delay values of less than $10 an hour. This would imply that unless the representative passenger is willing to pay considerably in excess of $10 per hour to avoid schedule delay, existing fares are too high in general and the consequent load factors are too low. Of course, major markets differ in important characteristics other than distance and density, and since we have only limited information on the value passengers attach to schedule delay, there can be errors in this assessment. Empirical evidence does question severely the efficiency of the price-quality level and structure emerging under regulation. If nothing else, the severity of the assumptions needed to make the existing outcome an optimal one stretches credibility.

Until recently,[13] the price-quality option has been regulator-chosen, with little apparent regard for the trade-offs between price and quality. A major necessary condition for the perpetuation of such a system is that the market has been given only limited opportunity to select for itself the preferred option, in effect having only one option. Obviously, there is need to structure the regulated market so that different combinations of fare and service can and will be offered. This pertains not only to a determination of the optimal combination, but also to the optimal structure of available price-quality options.

If the market is defined very broadly to include all types of air transportation, we do observe limited differentiation of service quality and price. As mentioned in Chapter 3, at one end of the scale is the exceedingly high price paid by corporations for personal transportation in executive jets, which reduce schedule delay to a minimum. At the other extreme charter flights offer the lowest possible prices, with commensurate increases in schedule delay. The scheduled air transportation system occupies some intermediate range. An appropriate question to investigate, then, is whether within the framework of scheduled transportation the common aspect of service quality described here cannot be further differentiated, thereby conforming even more closely to the diverse preferences of the traveling public with regard to schedule delay.

Within limits, this could be accomplished. Stochastic delays, which are the principal component of schedule delays, could be differentiated by many techniques. Already the regulated market has devised at least three: (a) the sale of standby passage at a discount, (b) the leisure class marketing device of Eastern Air Lines, and (c) the demand scheduling fares proposed by TWA. Standby discounts are a legitimate way to price certainty, which, as we have seen, is an integral component of the industry's costs. As previ-

13. See Chapter 8.

ously practiced, however, standby fares are further restricted by the class of traveler (for example, youth, military) and thus do not serve to their potential. Eastern's leisure class program essentially is a device for reducing the penalty for overbooking. Under this system a passenger may purchase a leisure class ticket at the full price, and if through overbooking and a less than expected rate of no-shows the flight is actually full, the traveler receives free passage on the next flight having an empty seat.[14] Thus, on a probabilistic basis the traveler pays a lower fare for a lower-quality service. The proposed demand scheduling scheme is still another means of differentiating price-quality options; under this program the passenger makes a reservation at least ninety days in advance and submits a $20 nonrefundable deposit within fifteen days of the date of the reservation. The reservation is for the day of departure, and not for any particular flight. Immediately after full payment is received, the carrier notifies the passenger of the actual flight. For this lower quality of service, the passenger receives a discount ranging between 16 and 37 percent, depending on season.

Another aspect of fare differentials that indirectly relates to differences in expected schedule delay is that first class sections commonly operate at much lower average load factors than coach. Hence, a person may occasionally avoid delay by booking first class passage if no coach class seats are available.[15] This differentiation could be more purposefully pursued, however, by the simple expedient of selling a given quota of tickets per flight at different fares, with no accompanying distinctions in other service aspects such as seat width and meals. The lower-priced tickets would indeed be relatively scarce, but the system would constitute an explicit set of choices with regard to the possibility of schedule delays versus the prices paid by the travelers. Experience in marketing air travel by this or similar techniques would enable the system to develop a pattern of price-quality options more directly responsive to the structure of traveler preferences.[16]

Finally, we should mention William Vickrey's proposal to vary price over time so that aircraft seats are rationed off just prior to departure.[17] Such a system would eliminate stochastic delay or, more accurately, would

14. This is in contrast to the penalty faced by the carrier for "bumping" a "standard" passenger, which in some cases requires free passage plus cash compensation.

15. Typically an airline will offer to place such a passenger's name on the coach "waiting list."

16. Almost any modification that involves the selling of "priorities" would require abandoning the current practice of free (no deposit) reservations.

17. William Vickrey, "Responsive Pricing of Public Utility Services," *Bell Journal of Economics and Management Science*, Vol. 2 (Spring 1971), pp. 337–46.

reflect in price the marginal passenger's valuation of avoiding a certain delay. It is notable that at present Board policy prevents carriers from employing such a scheme. Moreover, the Board prohibits block purchasing of tickets, thereby preventing the entry of a private agent. The Board does allow carriers to contract with travel agents for charter services at per-seat prices below scheduled fares, but only under very strict conditions which clearly separate this market from the scheduled market.

Peak Load Pricing

As discussed in Chapter 3, strong fluctuations in the demand for air travel occur over a daily cycle, a weekly cycle, and an annual cycle (Tables 3-1, 3-2, and 3-3). As described in Chapter 5, efficient pricing would require lower prices during off-peak periods, and higher prices in peak periods, such that average price through all periods equals average and marginal cost at the mean (optimal) quality level.

In the absence of market tests, the determination of an optimum structure of peak and off-peak pricing is difficult since it involves the measurement of resource opportunity costs. Moreover, data on daily traffic peaking, which presumably is somewhat less peaked than demand, given supply restraints, may convey false impressions regarding the variance of loads on resources. For example, unless the daily time structure of traffic is the same for every market to and from a given city, the variance of loads on the fixed (ground) installation will be less than the variance in a single market. Second, especially in view of the multiple time zones, peak demands on aircraft will be less than traffic peaking—unless markets all have the same daily time pattern of demand, time-zone adjusted. Finally, there are times during each twenty-four-hour period when aircraft must be serviced and inspected, when ground facilities must be cleaned, and so on. A similar, but of course less significant, bias applies to the traffic peaking data describing weekly and annual cycles.[18]

Probably the most reasonable approach to comparing peak and off-peak production costs is to examine carrier scheduling practices during peak and off-peak periods. Applying the model of nonprice competition set forth in Chapter 4, we would expect carriers to adjust capacity in each period so that total revenue generated in that period offsets that period's resource

18. For example, aircraft have to be overhauled, and ground installations occasionally require remodeling.

opportunity cost. In other words, firms break even in each period and thus reveal the implicit value placed on resources. Utilizing this indirect measure of cost, we can thus attempt a crude estimate of the differential between the optimal peak and off-peak fare, abstracting from considerations of quality and assuming zero temporal cross-elasticity of demand (that is, that changing the ratio of peak to off-peak fares does not affect the time pattern of demand).

In the Domestic Passenger Fare Investigation, carriers submitted flight-departure load factor data by time-of-day, day-of-week, and selected-month for their three highest load factor markets.[19] These data were portrayed in Tables 3-1, 3-2, and 3-3. As shown in Table 3-1, the ratio of daily peak to off-peak load factors is in the neighborhood of 1.4 (counting 9:00 A.M. through 7:00 P.M. as peak, the rest as off-peak). From Table 3-2 we have a peak to off-peak load factor ratio of approximately 1.1 (counting Fridays and Sundays as peaks, the rest as off-peak). From Table 3-3, we have a ratio of approximately 1.2 (counting August as peak, the others as off-peak).

These figures suggest optimal discounts from the peak fare on the order of 40 percent for time of day, 10 percent for day of week, and 20 percent for the month. However, three, possibly offsetting, biases should be noted. First, the sample bias (high load factor markets) presumably narrows the ratio of peak to off-peak load factors and thus would tend to understate the cost ratio. Second, standby and various reserved-seat discounts tend to be used relatively more in the off-peak periods and thus average yield is perhaps a bit lower during the off-peaks, implying an even lower opportunity cost of off-peak resources.

On the other hand, any increase in the peak to off-peak price ratio can be expected to alter the time structure of demand in the direction of smoothing out the peaks. This implies that as one increases the actual price ratio the perceived optimal ratio would diminish. (However, this does not invalidate a comparison of existing discounts with imputed optimal ones, since off-peak load factors presently include the yield-deflating effects of existing off-peak discounts.)

In contrast with the suggested efficient fare differentials, the industry has employed peak-load pricing to only a very limited extent. The only wide-

19. The sample included all flights for these markets during the months of February and November 1969. Similar information, but in aggregate form only, was provided for May and August 1969.

spread true peak-load pricing device is variously termed "night-coach," "early-bird," and "owly-bird"—essentially a 20 percent discount for travel between 10:00 P.M. and 7:00 A.M. Other types of discounts are widely available, but are utilized as a means of increasing total travel through price discrimination, not for the purpose of peak-load pricing. (Typical discriminatory discounts which have existed are shown in Table 6-4.) At present, some of these fares are unavailable, or blacked out during peak periods, but on the whole it is uncertain whether such blackouts significantly affect differences in average yield between the peak and off-peak periods. All this would imply that the industry falls short of efficient use of peak-load pricing.

Another view of the peak-load question is to focus on the peak and off-peak price-quality options. Except in cases such as noted above, the passenger is faced with the same price in both periods, with better service quality during the off-peak periods including lower load factors and thus less stochastic delay, less congestion, and more on-board attention by airline personnel. We might pose the question, "Would peak-load passengers be willing to pay a relatively higher fare to increase service quality and would off-peak passengers be willing to accept some service quality deterioration to obtain a lower off-peak fare?" If the answer to either aspect is affirmative, then the ratio of peak to off-peak fares is too small. Casual empiricism would support affirmative answers in both cases. Of course the questions could be answered with more precision by minimizing passengers' total cost, including schedule delay, through the various time periods. Unfortunately, requisite data are not now available.

Table 6-4. Authorized Discount Air Fares, September 1969
Percent

Fare type	Discount from regular ticket price
Youth standby[a]	40
Youth reservation[a]	20
Family plan[b]	
Children 12–21	33⅓
Children 2–11	50
Discover America[c]	20

Source: CAB Order 69-9-68 (Sept. 12, 1969), p. 8.
a. Passenger must be less than twenty-one years of age.
b. Passenger must be accompanied by a full-fare paying adult.
c. Return trip must be at least seven days subsequent to initial departure.

Other Aspects of Price and Quality Structure

Cross-Subsidization

In the past, the Board has actively promoted a policy of cross-subsidization, that is, encouraging carriers to use profits in some markets to offset losses in others. At first the effort was directed toward getting the trunk carriers off subsidy. That being accomplished in the 1950s, the present rationale is to assure adequate service in markets which allegedly the carriers would prefer to abandon. Despite grand pronouncements from the Board and even lip service from the carriers, it is our conclusion that most trunk airline markets are characterized by little actual cross-subsidization.

The most notable attempt at cross-subsidization is the purported use of long-haul profits to subsidize short-haul losses. Short-haul markets are alleged to be very price elastic because of competition from other modes, and thus price must be depressed below average cost in order to sustain the market. On the other hand, long-haul markets are allegedly less price elastic, making it possible to maintain fares above average costs without losing substantial traffic. Ideally, prices are adjusted to make such losses and profits precisely offsetting. However, in view of our previous discussions we would expect carriers to adjust service quality in such manner as to realize normal returns insofar as practical in each market. As indicated in Figure 6-4, such behavior is, in fact, observed: load factors tend to decline with distance, thus "twisting" the average cost curve to match the average fare curve (see Chapter 4, regressions [1] and [2], and Figure 6-3).[20]

Discount Fares

A similar analysis would apply to other attempts at cross-subsidization, provided there is sufficient leeway for carriers to vary quality and thus adjust average cost to price. One major exception to quality flexibility, and one area where there has been significant cross-subsidization, is in the discount-fare markets. When, during the mid-1960s, industry profits sprinted upward and the Board applied pressure for lower fares, the carriers responded with a variety of discount tariffs directed toward limited,

20. An additional piece of evidence is that there appears to be no correlation between carrier profitability and average stage length.

allegedly more price-elastic markets (see Table 6-4). The Board approved these initiatives and until recently[21] has actively encouraged their use. Quite plainly, however, discounts cross-subsidize from normal-fare passengers to the discount passenger, given the quality of service.[22] An alternative view (which amounts to the same thing) is that without discounts the normal-fare passenger would receive a higher quality of service.[23] Either way, there is cross-subsidy, and economic welfare losses stem from this inefficient structure of prices.[24]

Charter Restrictions

Air charters (either by trunk carriers or by supplemental carriers[25]) are one way in which air transportation can be differentiated in terms of the price-quality combination. Since charters are designed to realize as fully as possible the economies of high utilization, their average cost per passenger approaches the minimum level. As of this date, charter fares have not been regulated by the CAB, and lively price competition has elicited low fares commensurate with the low unit costs. While charter service is demonstrably less convenient for the vast majority of air travelers, in some long-distance markets, particularly international flights, the charters' price advantage has led to an increasing share of the market. The trunk carriers have feared this encroachment and the CAB has provided significant protection. An example is the well-known affinity rule, whereby a charter may be booked only by members of one (or under certain circumstances more than one) bona fide organization.

The carriers argue the necessity of protecting scheduled service with the claim that unrestrained charters would ultimately cause the demise of regularly scheduled flights in many markets. We strongly doubt this result. Since the principle of the charter is the booking of full planeloads of

21. See Chapter 8 below.

22. That is, with minor exceptions, discount and normal-fare passengers receive the same quality of service. Yet one group pays a fare in excess of average cost, whereas the other group pays less than average cost. With zero (economic) profits, the profits from normal-fare passengers make up precisely the losses from discount passengers.

23. That is, if discount fares were eliminated, the system would operate with lower average load factors and thus less stochastic delay, less crowding, and so forth.

24. A possible exception might be noted. In very low-density markets the reduction in schedule delay stemming from the traffic-stimulating aspect of discriminatory discount fares conceivably could outweigh for the normal-fare payer the excess he pays over average cost.

25. See appendix at the end of the book.

travelers to a common destination at a common time, such a service would certainly not be achievable in most markets of light and medium density. Moreover, air charters do not necessarily have a natural cost advantage over the flights of scheduled carriers since they must fly many empty back-hauls and front-haul, delivery flights.

The emergence of air charters is really a manifestation of the inefficiently high costs and fares which have resulted from CAB regulation. If the fares of regularly scheduled flights were optimally set to minimize the full cost of air travel, the competitive edge possessed by charters would largely disappear. For example, in those few CAB-regulated markets where fares approach the lower levels we have estimated as being optimal—the East Coast–Puerto Rico and West Coast–Hawaii markets—there is no appreciable charter activity. In an efficient market the role of charters would be somewhat diminished; they would continue serving affinity group travel, but no restrictions would be necessary to limit them to this market.

Congestion Pricing

For efficiency, air fares should reflect congestion costs. As pointed out by a number of economists,[26] the airport and airway congestion problem is basically one of excess amounts demanded, caused by the provision of these services to the industry at only nominal charges. The implications of this became dramatically clear in 1968, when congestion delays at many major airports reached two or more hours.[27] While additional investment in the airport and airway systems may be justified, decisions on such investment will not be very efficient unless prices are used to allocate these scarce resources.

A determination of appropriate charges requires an estimation of the marginal costs of resource use. In an airport at capacity, for example, the cost of an additional landing is primarily the external cost imposed on

26. See, for example, Alan Carlin and R. E. Park, "Marginal Cost Pricing of Airport Runway Capacity," *American Economic Review*, Vol. 60 (June 1970), pp. 310–19; and Joseph V. Yance, "Analysis of Delays at Washington National Airport" (U.S. Department of Transportation, Office of Economics and Systems Analyses, 1968; processed). Also see Ross D. Eckert, *Airports and Congestion: A Problem of Misplaced Subsidies* (Washington: American Enterprise Institute for Public Policy Research, 1972), and the contributions he lists therein (pp. 66–67, note 1) by A. S. De Vany and E. H. Garges, P. Feldman, M. E. Levine, J. D. Likens, J. C. Miller III, J. R. Minasian and R. D. Eckert, and Yance.

27. This problem was resolved through intercarrier agreements to limit capacity during peak hours. See discussion in the next chapter.

others whose landings are thereby delayed. Such congestion delays have been estimated by economists and show generally very high marginal congestion costs during peak periods of the day.[28] The efficient utilization of an airport requires, then, a user fee based on the level of congestion prevailing at the time of use. The appropriate fee may be negligible during slack periods, but may be many times the prevailing rate during peak periods.

The major welfare gains from imposing peak-load congestion pricing result from shifting, or smoothing, the time profile of demand so that less capacity is required for a given traffic, or more use can be made of a given capacity. Hence, congestion fees can be fully successful only if they are added pro rata to the ticket price. Moreover, it is essential that these fees be collected from the airlines.[29] Accordingly, the installation of user fees would result in profits at many airports. This is appropriate, however, as in many cases it would reflect the very high opportunity costs of the resources dedicated to that use.[30] Moreover, such revenue provides a measure of the benefits that would accrue from additional public investments in the airport-airway system. Although the actual pricing of airports and airway services is beyond the purview of the CAB, being a responsibility of the Federal Aviation Administration and local authorities, the Board's cooperation in structuring fares to include these costs would be required, should such measures be taken.[31]

Joint and Common Products

In addition to passenger services, the airlines also market freight services, about 60 percent of which are produced in combination aircraft, where

28. See especially Carlin and Park's study of Kennedy International Airport before the imposition of quotas (*The Efficient Use of Airport Runway Capacity in a Time of Scarcity,* RM-5817, RAND Corporation, 1969). Of course congestion delays are airport-specific as well as time-specific. In a slightly different form, Yance has estimated congestion delays for Washington National Airport (see "Analysis of Delays at Washington National Airport").

29. Increasing fares without collecting fees from the airlines could, in fact, exacerbate the congestion problem. See the appendix to Chapter 4.

30. National Airport in Washington, D.C., is but one example.

31. Under provisions of the Airport and Airway Development Act of 1970 and the Airport and Airway Revenue Act of 1970, the secretary of transportation is charged with conducting a study to determine the appropriate allocation and recovery of the cost of the airport and airway system. The first installment of this report was submitted to Congress in September 1973. U.S. Department of Transportation, *Airport and Airway Cost Allocation Study, Pt. 1 Report: Determination, Allocation and Recovery of System Costs* (DOT, 1973).

freight, mail, and baggage are carried in the aircraft's belly.[32] In the short run, belly-freight capacity is a joint product with passenger capacity, since the aircraft's configuration can be changed only at great cost. Whereas in perfectly competitive markets the prices of joint products would be determined by relative demands, in air service they are controlled by the Board. Essentially, the policy has been one of setting freight rates at the average and marginal costs of producing such services in all-cargo air freighters. This is seen to be a necessary condition for protecting the financial viability of the two all-cargo airlines.[33]

In carrying out this pricing policy the Board has formally interpreted belly-freight as a by-product of passenger service and has used the revenue offset method of cost allocation. The rationale is that the flight is scheduled for passengers, not for freight (ignoring the fact that like all joint products with sale value, their revenues affect output decisions just as do revenues from the sale of primary products). Viewed this way, revenues from the sale of belly capacity serve to offset the cost of passenger service.

Despite the illogical rationale of this pricing policy, it would appear to be an efficient one, at least in the short run.[34] The reason is that freighter costs are the relevant opportunity costs for carrying freight in combination aircraft. In the longer run, however, passengers and belly-freight are common products and their relative prices should reflect their relative marginal production costs, measured by their marginal rates of substitution.

The choice of a pricing rule is important not only from the standpoint of optimal rates of passengers and freight traffic, but relative passenger-freight rates can affect the configuration of new aircraft. Over the long run, load factors in both sections will tend toward break-even, costs being allocated in accord with what carriers perceive as the marginal trade-off between passenger capacity and cargo space. If freight rates were to rise

32. Scheduled air freight revenues in domestic service totaled $543.8 million for the year ending September 30, 1972—about 6.4 percent of total operating revenues. U.S. Civil Aeronautics Board, *Air Carrier Financial Statistics* (September 1972), p. 1.

33. A Board publication explains: "A basic consideration in ratemaking is that the rates should cover the costs of service, including a reasonable profit element. In air transportation, where airfreight is carried in the cargo compartments of passenger aircraft as well as in all-cargo aircraft, it is generally considered that the costs which must be covered are those of an all-cargo aircraft operation. This approach is usually followed since the allocation of costs in a combination aircraft is difficult, and the maximum development of an air cargo industry requires the operation of all-cargo aircraft whose costs must be met." U.S. Civil Aeronautics Board, *An Introduction to Airfreight Rates* (no date), p. 5.

34. See the second appendix to Chapter 5.

relative to passenger fares, break-even load factors in the belly compartment would fall relative to those in the passenger compartment. Since the demand for air freight is generally conceded to be relatively more price elastic than the demand for passenger service, and since the ratio of freight traffic cost to capacity cost is not significantly different from that of passengers, we would expect the carriers to require relatively less cargo space in new aircraft. If freight rates were to fall relative to passenger fares, then cargo space would increase relative to passenger space.

Thus far, the Board has officially ignored these long-run implications of its belly-freight pricing policy. In the Domestic Passenger Fare Investigation it concluded that for the time being at least it would continue to utilize the revenue-offset method of cost allocation and regulate belly-freight rates of the level of marginal and average freighter costs.[35] The Board did say that it would defer judgment on various joint-product methods of cost allocation until completion of the Domestic Air Freight Rate Investigation and other air freight cases. However, given the stakes in preserving competitive balance between passenger and all-cargo carriers, it is doubtful that the Board will adopt efficient pricing policies if the results appear likely to impair either class of carrier.

First class and coach service are appropriately termed common products since their relative space can be varied quite easily by moving the bulkhead and changing a few seats. From information summarized by the Board in the Domestic Passenger Fare Investigation we can infer the per-passenger cost differential is on the order of 50 to 60 percent, depending on the route, fully adjusted for differences in load factor.[36] On the other hand, in recent years the Board has regulated the differential at 30 percent. There is an apparent contradiction here, for if our zero-profit model of nonprice competition applied consistently we would expect carriers to adjust the relative proportions of service so that the average cost differential was equal to the fare differential. However, in choosing the optimal bulkhead location what is of importance is trading off opportunity costs of floor space. When coach load factors are relatively low, the opportunity cost of displaced coach floor space is relatively small, resulting in a tendency of allocated costs to overestimate carrier-perceived costs. Whether the rents being earned are different for these two sections is difficult to determine, but if so

35. See CAB Orders 71-4-59 and 71-4-60 (April 9, 1971), pp. 44, 45, and 72-8-50 (Aug. 10, 1972), pp. 23–28.

36. The principal differences pertain to the aircraft floor space, food services, and stewardess services. See CAB Order 74-3-82 (March 18, 1974), pp. 129–35.

this represents a case of successful price discrimination made possible by Board enforcement of the pricing structure.[37]

Conclusion

There is strong evidence that the overall level of airline fares is inefficient in that it leads to a price-quality combination higher than that consistent with minimizing the traveler's total cost of transport. Moreover, there is also evidence that the structure of fares is inefficient in at least four important dimensions. First, minimization of traveler transport cost would require that load factors rise with market distance, whereas now they fall with distance. Second, inefficient use is made of peak-load pricing, leading to a nonoptimal structure of price-quality options that does not reflect daily, weekly, and seasonal variations in demand. Third, discount fares result in cross-subsidization among passengers and violate the efficient pricing rules.[38] Finally, the absence of a market mechanism in rationing airport and airway facilities leads to inefficient use of these resources. With the possible exception of the latter, all of these inefficiencies may be ascribed to deficiencies in CAB regulatory policy.

Appendix: Estimation of Schedule Delays

Frequency Delay

The average difference between a passenger's preferred departure time and the closest scheduled departure time can be estimated by simulation. First, the daily time pattern of demand must be measured for the specific market (for example, Table 3-1). Then, for any number of daily flights one can determine a schedule of departures which either (a) minimizes the sum of delays or (b) equalizes the number of passengers per flight. (Either approach, of course, ignores the interdependence of markets—that is, the demand for one flight is a function of the timing of adjoining flights.) In application we followed the latter course as being a better approximation of the market equilibrium reached under regulation (see Chapter 5). Daily

---

37. In the Domestic Passenger Fare Investigation the carriers almost uniformly opposed increasing the first class versus coach fare differential.

38. Certain discount fares are now being eliminated. See Chapter 8.

Table 6-5. One-Step Transition Matrix of Stochastic Delay—the Probability of Not Obtaining a Seat on a Flight

State (queue length) at T_0[a]	State (queue length) at $T_0 + 1$[a]										
	0.13N	0.40N	0.67N	0.93N	1.20N	1.47N	1.73N	2.00N	2.27N	2.53N	3.07N
0.13N	0.049	0.100	0.158	0.194	0.187	0.141	0.084	0.039	0.014	0.004	0.028
0.40N	0.049	0.100	0.158	0.194	0.187	0.141	0.084	0.039	0.014	0.004	0.028
0.67N	0.049	0.100	0.158	0.194	0.187	0.141	0.084	0.039	0.014	0.004	0.028
0.93N	0.049	0.100	0.158	0.194	0.187	0.141	0.084	0.039	0.014	0.004	0.028
1.20N	0.049	0.100	0.158	0.194	0.187	0.141	0.084	0.039	0.014	0.004	0.028
1.47N	0	0.049	0.100	0.158	0.194	0.187	0.141	0.084	0.039	0.014	0.032
1.73N	0	0	0.049	0.100	0.158	0.194	0.187	0.141	0.084	0.039	0.046
2.00N	0	0	0	0.049	0.100	0.158	0.194	0.187	0.141	0.084	0.085
2.27N	0	0	0	0	0.049	0.100	0.158	0.194	0.187	0.141	0.169
2.53N	0	0	0	0	0	0.049	0.100	0.158	0.194	0.187	0.310
3.07N	0	0	0	0	0	0	0.049	0.100	0.158	0.194	0.497

Source: Derived by authors (see text), using relative capacity, X, of 0.575, and a value of 2.0 for Y, the ratio of flight-demand mean to its standard deviation. N represents the mean demand per flight period. The matrix is condensed for expository purposes; the computations were made using a 33 × 33 matrix.

a. T_0 = fixed time.

flight frequency, F, was varied in the hypothetical market cited below,[39] yielding estimates of per-passenger frequency delay:

$$(1) \qquad T_f = 92(F^{-0.456}).$$
$$R^2 = 0.497.$$

Of course, the frequency delay function will vary with the time distribution of the specific market studied, and the assumptions made here regarding market independence and scheduling practices may not hold in practice. However, these parameters affect primarily the level of the delay function, whereas the relevant aspect for optimal load factor analysis is the change in frequency delay resulting from a given change in daily frequency. For various reasons more confidence might be placed in this latter aspect.

Stochastic Delay

The stochastic delay phenomenon is similar to a queuing process and can be described as a Markov process, with certain simplifying assumptions. From the Domestic Passenger Fare Investigation, data are available on daily passenger traffic in selected markets during February and November 1969. These data were found to be consistent with a Poisson process with the sample variance linearly related to the sample mean by $\mathrm{Var}(n) = 16.978\bar{n}$. We could thus assume that the distribution of demand arising within any time interval, t, would be Poisson, with $\sigma_n \simeq 4.12\bar{n}^{1/2}$. This allows us to define a Markov process, in which the state of the system is described by Q, the number of (potential) passengers drawn from the demand distribution for that flight *plus* those passengers who were unable to obtain seats on previous flights. The transition matrix is defined by the parameters of the demand distribution facing each flight and the aircraft size, S. The process can be generalized, moreover, by expressing these parameters in two summary measures—relative capacity,

$$(2) \qquad X = (S - N_f)/\sigma_f,$$

and the ratio of flight-demand mean to its standard deviation,

$$(3) \qquad Y = N_f/\sigma_f.$$

A typical one-step transition matrix for an arbitrary value of relative capacity (X) is reproduced as Table 6-5. Each element, $\pi_{i,j}$, of this matrix is the conditional probability that the system (the queue length) will be in

39. James C. Miller III, "A Time-of-Day Model for Aircraft Scheduling," *Transportation Science*, Vol. 6 (August 1972), p. 233.

state j at time $t_0 + 1$ if it was in state i at time t_0. The first row of the steady state matrix for this system can be interpreted as the probability (or relative frequency) of finding the system in any state j. We computed these probability distributions for each of 360 values of the demand and capacity parameters. An example of one distribution is given in Table 6-6. One can then derive from this distribution the probability of the queue's length being less than the capacity of one flight, S (no delay); the probability that $S < Q \leq 2S$ (one-period delay); the probability that $2S < Q \leq 3S$ (two-period delay), and so forth. The results are closely approximated by the expression:

(4) $$T_S = 0.455(Y^{-0.645})(X^{-1.79})(I),$$
$$R^2 = 0.951.$$

where I is the average interval between flights.

This model of stochastic delay could be tested only indirectly. Given the probability distribution of the queue length and the flight capacity S, one can forecast a distribution of flight load factors, N_f/S. Load factor data are available for selected markets, and these can be compared with those forecast. Table 6-7 provides such a comparison. The forecast distributions do provide a reasonable approximation of the actual distributions in those cases where the model (constrained to a single aircraft type) is applicable. There appears to be a consistent discrepancy, however, between the observed relative frequencies and forecast probabilities in cases of high load factors (and, implicitly, high delays). This result could arise from two sources: (a) that the observed distribution itself is biased as a representation of the actual demands and delays or (b) that the model itself is biased. A

Table 6-6. Steady State Probabilities of Stochastic Delay

State[a]	Probability
0.13N	0.0195
0.40N	0.0447
0.67N	0.0774
0.93N	0.1061
1.20N	0.1188
1.47N	0.1120
1.73N	0.0930
2.00N	0.0724
2.27N	0.0562
2.53N	0.0456
3.07N	0.2544

Source: Computed from Table 6-5.
a. N represents the mean demand per flight period.

Table 6-7. Observed and Forecast Distributions of Air Flight Load
Factors, Selected Markets, February and November 1969

Market, month, and range of average load factors	Observed relative frequency	Forecast probability[a]
Atlanta–Boston		
February		$X = 0.844$
0.00–0.59	0.125	0.237
0.60–0.79	0.216	0.157
0.80–0.89	0.148	0.080
0.90–1.00	0.511	0.526
November		$X = 1.18$
0.00–0.59	0.358	0.361
0.60–0.79	0.236	0.223
0.80–0.89	0.044	0.097
0.90–1.00	0.226	0.318
Charlotte–New York		
February		$X = 1.49$
0.00–0.59	0.522	0.452
0.60–0.79	0.282	0.232
0.80–0.89	0.151	0.087
0.90–1.00	0.045	0.226
November		$X = 1.0$
0.00–0.59	0.355	0.324
0.60–0.79	0.263	0.194
0.80–0.89	0.140	0.088
0.90–1.00	0.242	0.394
Los Angeles–Pittsburgh		
November		$X = 2.01$
0.00–0.59	0.651	0.598
0.60–0.79	0.238	0.219
0.80–0.89	0.046	0.059
0.90–1.00	0.064	0.123
St. Louis–San Francisco[b]		
November (daily)		$X = 0.82$
0.00–0.59	0.167	0.236
0.60–0.79	0.298	0.158
0.80–0.89	0.210	0.080
0.90–1.00	0.325	0.525
November (weekday)		$X = 1.31$
0.00–0.59	0.167	0.405
0.60–0.79	0.298	0.214
0.80–0.89	0.210	0.086
0.90–1.00	0.325	0.294

Source: Derived by authors from data in Tables 6-5 and 6-6.
a. X = relative capacity.
b. Two forecasts were computed for St. Louis–San Francisco: the first with X estimated from all daily observations of passengers carried, and the second from weekday data only. Observations of the frequency distributions were not, however, disaggregated.

possible source of the former bias could follow from the airlines' policy of granting free reservations. It is well known that potential passengers frequently obtain multiple reservations, and this can lead to the subsequent rejection of last-minute reservations for a filled flight which ultimately leaves with many empty seats. The airlines attempt to dampen this effect by overbooking, but the asymmetry of the costs facing the airlines in this attempt dissuades them from completely eliminating this bias. The model itself probably does have a positive bias in the estimation of high load factors and delays, which might be traced to the assumption of independence of the demands for the individual flights. Since the dispersion of demand for the individual flight is derived from the observed dispersion of the total daily demand by the relation, $\sigma_F = F^{-1/2}\sigma_D$, were there a positive correlation of demands between flights, the dispersion would be overestimated, and the probability of delays and high load factors would have a positive bias.

CHAPTER SEVEN

Other Aspects of Market Performance

IN ADDITION to regulating the price, and thus the quality, of commercial air service, the Civil Aeronautics Board regulates carrier access to new markets and sets constraints on route abandonments. The Board also has the power to disapprove mergers between air carriers and to regulate overt carrier collusion. This chapter attempts an indirect assessment of airline market performance in these nonprice areas. The principal theme is that by setting policies which would restrain the market equilibrium from an otherwise presumably efficient one,[1] the Board imposes economic efficiency costs, primarily in terms of decreased technical efficiency—that is, higher cost for a given output. Having few good standards against which to measure this loss, we are forced at times into indirect measures based on casual empiricism and introspection.

Entry

The Federal Aviation Act requires Board approval before a carrier may institute commercial interstate air service. As a matter of procedure, the carrier proposing the service must obtain from the Board a "certificate of public convenience and necessity," which describes in detail the routings authorized. To some degree, the certificate also obligates the carrier to provide a minimal service as described in the certificate. In such manner the Board regulates entry of operating airlines into and exit from air travel markets. A derivative of this power is that the Board thus regulates the entry of new air carriers into the industry.

1. We shall conjecture about the efficiency of an unregulated market in Chapter 9.

Entry of New Carriers[2]

The Board has never allowed the entry of a new trunk carrier. The Civil Aeronautics Act of 1938 made provision for giving existing carriers "grandfather" rights on the routes they were serving. Accordingly, sixteen carriers made formal application and were established as trunks. Because of various mergers, the number had dwindled to ten by 1974.

While the Board has not allowed a new trunk carrier to enter the market, it has authorized additional carrier groups or "classes" of carriers. As Table 7-1 shows, the local service airlines were authorized on an experi-

Table 7-1. Certificated Air Carrier Groups and Dates of Authorization by the Civil Aeronautics Board

Carrier group	Date first authorized
Trunk	August 22, 1938
Local service	November 5, 1943 (experimental);
	June 1, 1955 (permanent)
Supplemental	October 9, 1962 (interim);
	March 11, 1966 (permanent)
All-cargo	July 29, 1949
Commuter	February 20, 1952

Source: U.S. Civil Aeronautics Board, *Handbook of Airline Statistics, 1971 Edition* (1972), Pt. 8.

mental basis in 1943 and permanently a dozen years later. Essentially, these carriers were designated to provide service on a subsidy basis to low-density, primarily rural areas and, in addition, to serve as feeders to trunk-carrier hub markets. In 1949, the all-cargo carriers were authorized, and later, in 1952, the Board established an exempt class of carriers—the air taxi operators, some of which later established scheduled service and became known as commuter airlines. The supplemental air carriers were certificated on an interim basis in 1962 and permanently in 1966.

Table 7-2 shows the relative size of today's average air carrier in comparison with the typical trunk carrier in 1938. In all cases but commuter airlines, today's typical carrier is larger in size, measured by revenue ton-miles, than the 1938 trunk carrier. In an important sense, then, the Board has allowed entry of numerous air carriers as large as the original trunks.

2. For a more comprehensive treatment of the history and issues surrounding new carrier entry, see Lucile S. Keyes, *Federal Control of Entry into Air Transportation* (Harvard University Press, 1951); also see her article, "A Reconsideration of Federal Control of Entry into Air Transportation," *Journal of Air Law and Commerce*, Vol. 22 (Spring 1955), pp. 192–202.

Table 7-2. Comparison of Domestic Revenue Ton-Miles, Air Trunk Carriers, 1938, with Carrier Groups, 1970

Carrier group and year	Total revenue ton-miles (millions)	Number of carriers at end of year	Revenue ton-miles per carrier (millions)
1938			
Trunk	55.3	16	3.5
1970			
Trunk[a]	12,288.7	11	1,117.2
Local service[b]	851.5	9	94.6
Supplemental	390.9	13	30.1
All-cargo	301.5	2	150.8
Commuter	47.1	179	0.3

Sources: Table A-2 and CAB, *Handbook of Airline Statistics, 1971*, p. 12.
a. Excludes Pan American World Airways, which is not certificated domestically but engages in some domestic traffic in connection with its international operations.
b. The certificate of Air West, Inc., was transferred to Hughes Air Corporation d/b/a Air West, effective April 3, 1970. Revenue data include the Air West operations.

However, the new carriers do not generally approach comparability with today's trunks.[3] Moreover, in most cases the emergence of the new carrier group was characterized by recalcitrance on the part of the Board, and even where entry was allowed, pains were taken to protect the trunk-carrier "club" from outside competition. Between the grandfather era and the end of the Second World War, the Board rejected new entrants mostly on grounds that they failed to meet conditions of adequacy. For various reasons, proposed trunk operators were judged inexperienced, unsafe, or lacking in required resources. After the war, however, conditions changed markedly. The influx of veteran pilots and the mounting surplus of aircraft made rejection of entrants on these grounds feeble at best. Consequently, the Board yielded to pressure and created a new class of carriers, carefully segregating their operations from those of the trunk airlines. These "local service carriers" thus became an experiment to determine whether air service to the smaller communities could be provided at a reasonable cost to the government through mail subsidy; at the same time, of course, the local service carriers would help the trunks by feeding them traffic and taking over some of their low-density markets.

But even these local carriers were not assured of permanency. The first local service carrier was granted a certificate on November 5, 1943; the majority were certificated in 1946 and shortly thereafter. In 1950 the first

3. The merger of Mohawk with Allegheny in April 1972 created a local service carrier which begins to rival the smaller trunks in size.

temporary local service certificate was renewed—again on a temporary basis. In the end it required congressional action, in the form of Public Law 38 of May 19, 1955, to force the Board to grant permanent operating authority to this new class of carrier.[4]

Other would-be carriers fared far worse. With a reservoir of trained pilots and inexpensive aircraft, many operators began (illegal) interstate operations, only to be squashed by CAB crackdowns on their activities. The Board did establish a category of noncertificated "irregular carriers" which were permitted to operate as long as no attempt was made to engage in scheduled service. This was in 1947. Later, in 1949, the Board certificated four all-cargo carriers which were not authorized to carry passengers. In 1952, largely by default,[5] the Board exempted a special class of operators from economic regulation—those that flew aircraft having no more than 12,500 pounds gross takeoff weight, such as air taxis. Finally, in 1962, the Board was forced by Congress to upgrade "qualified" irregular route carriers, classing them as "supplementals" and giving them authority to engage in unlimited domestic charter (nonscheduled) service.[6]

In all of this one is struck by the fact that the Board has unswervingly protected the grandfather trunk carriers from new sources of competition. Only in the local service experiment did the trunks stand to lose much, and even then the markets were potential, not actual.[7] Moreover, by limiting irregular carriers to nonscheduled service, all-cargo carriers to freight only, commuter carriers to very small and costly aircraft, and supplementals to charter operations, the Board clearly intended to place constraints on the ability of these new groups to compete with the trunk carriers.

Besides carefully designing entry of these new carrier groups to protect the trunk carriers, the Board on several occasions has specifically denied

4. U.S. Civil Aeronautics Board, *Handbook of Airline Statistics, 1971 Edition* (1972), Pt. 8.

5. The Board, faced with responsibility for regulating the interstate air taxis, decided merely to grant them an exemption under section 416(b) of the Federal Aviation Act. At that time aircraft technology was in a stage of development where the 12,500-pound gross takeoff weight limit was presumed to rule out exempt-carrier competition with trunks and local service carriers. Over time, however, efficient, specialized aircraft have been developed for this market, resulting in a plethora of commuter airlines which provide short-haul scheduled air service, often at competitive rates.

6. The governing statute was Public Law 87-528, enacted on July 10, 1962.

7. Many of the trunks objected to the local service experiment, stating that they were the best equipped to provide the service. However, it is doubtful that the trunks would have initiated such service.

independent attempts to enter trunk-line air service.[8] An example is the application of World Airways, a supplemental, to provide direct, nonstop, transcontinental scheduled service between Oakland/San Francisco and Ontario/Long Beach on the one hand, and New York/Newark and Washington/Baltimore on the other. In 1967 World made this service proposal to the Board and promised substantial fare reductions.[9] The Board refused to act upon the petition and through a technicality years later dismissed it from the docket as being "stale."

The Board's protection of the trunk carriers has not, of course, been perfect. As shown below, the trunk lines face head-to-head competition from local service carriers on many routes. Sometimes even commuter airlines compete on trunk routes. Also, the supplemental carriers and the all-cargo carriers drain away business. However, CAB entry protection has been sufficient to enable the grandfather carriers to retain about nine-tenths of total domestic air service, despite a 250-fold increase in total traffic since 1938.[10] While one could speculate on the proposition that without entry controls the grandfather trunks would still dominate, it is difficult to imagine their retaining this level of industry share without direct regulatory intervention.

Entry into City-Pair Markets

The Board's policy toward the entry of existing trunk carriers into new city-pair competition has been much more liberal than its policy toward the entry of new firms. Whereas in the early 1950s the typical trunk carrier generated about one-half its traffic in monopoly markets, monopoly traffic is less than 25 percent today.[11] (See Table 7-3.)

This increase in city-pair competition means that the Board has certificated new entry at a pace greater than the creation of additional monopoly routes. With a secularly growing demand for air travel there is a good deal of pressure on the Board to certificate new service. A typical scenario is

8. For a passionate and well-reasoned plea for a more liberal entry policy, see Hardy K. Maclay and William C. Burt, "Entry of New Carriers into Domestic Trunkline Air Transportation," *Journal of Air Law and Commerce,* Vol. 22 (Spring 1955), pp. 131–56.

9. "Motion of World Airways, Inc. for Expedited Hearing," CAB Docket 18468 (Oct. 9, 1967).

10. See Appendix Tables A-1 and A-2.

11. Even so, total monopoly traffic is larger than ever today because of the secular growth in air traffic.

Table 7-3. Percentage Share of Revenue Passenger-Miles in Competitive Markets, by Carrier, Selected Years, 1955–71[a]

Carrier	1955	1960	1965	1969	1970	1971[b]
American Airlines	58.6	77.2	80.7	83.0	83.0	83.4
Eastern Air Lines	46.3	73.7	76.9	74.2	76.6	76.2
Trans World Airlines	62.9	78.8	82.2	87.3	91.1	89.3
United Air Lines	61.3	71.0	67.8	69.3	67.5	67.1
Big four share	n.a.	n.a.	76.2	77.2	77.8	77.4
Braniff Airways	32.4	50.2	42.6	65.7	66.0	64.3
Continental Air Lines	12.5	65.2	72.4	76.3	79.4	79.8
Delta Air Lines	37.9	58.9	60.0	58.2	67.9	69.3
National Airlines	80.2	78.0	68.8	72.9	89.1	85.4
Northeast Airlines[c]	8.7	79.9	81.8	87.2	88.9	87.2
Northwest Airlines	59.3	73.9	61.6	60.6	63.5	82.9
Western Air Lines	54.4	53.4	53.5	54.7	73.4	72.3
Other trunks' share	n.a.	n.a.	61.5	67.3	73.7	75.9
All trunks	55.6[d]	72.2[d]	71.7	74.0	76.5	76.6

Sources: 1955 and 1960—Richard J. Barber, "Airline Mergers, Monopoly, and the CAB," *Journal of Air Law and Commerce*, Vol. 28 (Summer 1961–62), p. 213; 1965 and 1971—data provided to authors by CAB, Bureau of Operating Rights; 1969 and 1970—CAB Docket 23852, Exhibits BOR-16, 17 (Feb. 1, 1972).
n.a. Not available.
a. A market is considered competitive if no one carrier has over 90 percent of the traffic in that market.
b. Fiscal year.
c. Northeast merged with Delta on August 1, 1972.
d. Weighted average; includes data for Capital, which merged with United in 1961, not shown in table (49.2 in 1955, and 70.5 in 1960).

that a growing city-pair market graduates successively from connecting service to single-plane service; from single-plane to nonstop service; and then on to competitive service. Since some new monopoly service goes to trunk carriers, the authorization of additional competition in trunk markets has had to be more than offsetting.

Over the last decade, trunk carriers have lost monopoly traffic in a number of ways. First, the Board has authorized additional carriers to serve monopoly markets and has allowed them to compete directly with the incumbent carriers with nonstop service. Second, in many cases where a competing carrier served a market indirectly, and thus was at a disadvantage, the Board has authorized direct, nonstop service. Third, in many monopoly markets the Board has allowed a local service carrier to replace a trunk carrier. Finally, in some cases the Board has certificated an aggressive carrier to serve a multi-carrier market, where for some reason one carrier dominated with more than 90 percent of the traffic.

The trend of successive route awards was accelerated during the latter part of the 1960s. For example, the trunk carriers' route miles operated grew by 70 percent over the period 1966–70. The big four trunks grew relatively less than the other trunks: 37 percent versus 98 percent.[12] The chief gainers were Braniff, Continental, Northeast, and Western.[13] Actually, these figures underestimate the extent of new entry over the period. There are two reasons. First, as trunk carriers were adding new routes and points served, they transferred some of their lesser markets to local service carriers. Second, whenever a carrier with previously indirect service was authorized to serve directly, route-miles operated might actually decline. Unfortunately, no good aggregate measures of market entry exist. From the information available, however, it would appear that, compared with previous policy, the Board was fairly liberal in approving entry into city-pair competition among existing trunk carriers over the last part of the 1960s.[14]

Even if the Board has imposed fewer restraints on trunk-carrier entry into new city-pair competition in the last several years, this is not to say that entry has been governed solely by economic forces. Under a regime of free entry, a carrier would enter a market whenever it saw an opportunity to make a profit. In addition to the prospective entrant's desire to provide service, however, the CAB applies additional standards. First, the entrant must be "fit, willing, and able." In cases involving the simultaneous petition of more than one carrier, the petitioners often attempt to outdo each other in proving the sincerity of their intentions and in some cases go to the extreme of purchasing aircraft and "getting ready" just to show their eminent qualifications. Second, the Board must establish a need for the proposed service, or more accurately, determine that "the public convenience and necessity" require it.[15] Where there is an incumbent carrier, this often boils down to an administrative decision as to which carrier is more capable of meeting the public's needs—the incumbent alone or one or more of the petitioners in conjunction with, or instead of, the incumbent. Finally, the Board is reluctant to certificate entry when, in its view, the likely effect would be to impair financially and significantly either the incumbent or the

12. CAB, *Handbook of Airline Statistics, 1971,* p. 404.

13. During this period Braniff, Continental, and Western acquired operating authority to Hawaii.

14. For example, an unpublished industry document lists thirty route award cases decided over the period May 7, 1969, to July 6, 1970; in these decisions new nonstop service was awarded in 120 markets. "Summary of Presentation on Behalf of Domestic Trunk Carriers" (no date; processed), App. 2.

15. Both quotations are in section 401d(2) of the Federal Aviation Act of 1958.

potential entrants. As opposed to a regime of free entry, clearly these are important restraints.[16]

On the other hand, the Board does recognize that additional competition will mean improved service. For example, over the years the Board has considered abnormally high load factors in monopoly markets as an indication that additional service is needed. However, in keeping with the model outlined in Chapter 4, the Board views the advantages of competition almost exclusively in terms of service adequacy, neglecting the possibility that competition might lead to lower prices if not restrained otherwise by Board policy. In fact, one detects a consistent Board resistance to consider the proposed fares of the petitioning carrier as relevant to the decision.[17] Actually, since there is great concern for the financial viability of incumbent carriers in a market, a carrier treads dangerously if it proposes fare-cutting. Perhaps this is one explanation of why World Airways' transcontinental proposal was dismissed from the docket.[18]

16. In a major recent case, the Board summed up its philosophy toward entry (in the context of a then-existing severe traffic slowdown) as follows: "It will be observed that our decisions in these two cases will not give rise to multiple competition [that is, more than two carriers] in any market. . . . Although our decision in each instance has been based primarily on the evidence shown of record as to the needs and potentialities of each market, we have nevertheless also been influenced by our belief that at this time—in view of the nationwide slowdown in air traffic growth and the financial pinch in which a number of carriers currently find themselves—new multiple competition should be authorized only in markets which . . . are clearly large enough to support such competition without inflicting seriously harmful losses on any carrier, and only where the relevant public convenience and necessity factors clearly call for such multiple awards. Current economic conditions in the industry do not in our opinion justify a denial of the benefits of competition to markets . . . which have heretofore suffered the disadvantages which so frequently accompany monopoly service; but . . . the authorization of multiple competition at a time of economic stringency such as this calls in our judgment for both a clear showing of feasibility and a substantial justification in terms of public benefits to be received." CAB Order 70-7-24 (July 6, 1970), pp. 4, 5.

17. In one of the very few exceptions to that rule, the Board's opinion in the Service to Puerto Rico Case contained the following statement, reproduced from Chief Examiner Francis W. Brown's recommended decision: "Clearly, no route should be judged solely on the fare representations of competing applicants since a decision on such a basis would in effect constitute a return to the unsatisfactory bidding system which preceded the Civil Aeronautics Act. Nevertheless, it must be recognized that the Puerto Rican Market is probably more responsive to low-cost service than any other U.S. market." *Civil Aeronautics Board Reports,* Vol. 26 (October 1957–June 1958), p. 151.

18. World proposed to lower the transcontinental air fare from $145.10 to $79.00 ("Motion of World Airways," Docket 18468, pp. 7, 14).

The Board also erects procedural barriers to entry.[19] First, a minor one: in fiscal year 1970, the Board collected $920,200 in licensing fees from carriers which entered new markets.[20] Second, and much more important, a petitioning carrier stands to incur enormous expenses associated with litigating route cases. Not only are there legal fees, but the preparation of exhibits and expert testimony drains away resources that could be productively employed elsewhere. Finally, there is the uncertainty over the regulatory lag. The time interval between original petition and final decision is difficult to predict, and accordingly plans for eventual market participation are difficult to formalize. In all of this, of course, there is only the prospect of obtaining approval and thus costs must be inflated by the inverse of one's subjective probability of a successful outcome.[21] Moreover, in cases involving additional competition, seldom does the incumbent carrier act passively. To protect its monopoly or oligopoly position the incumbent carrier will actively oppose new entry, and it, too, must absorb the consequent expenses associated with litigation.

On occasion the Board has utilized route policy to achieve other objectives. For example, over the latter part of the 1960s, the Board attempted to reduce local service carrier subsidy needs by authorizing local carriers to compete in longer and allegedly more profitable routes, often alongside trunk carriers. The idea was to use profits on the longer routes to offset losses at subsidy-eligible points. The program, however, has generally failed. Not only did such profits fail to materialize, but subsidy needs have increased.[22] In a similar vein, the Board often has granted monopoly

19. For a description of the institutional process through which carriers obtain route awards, see William K. Jones, "Licensing of Domestic Air Transportation," Pt. 1, in *Journal of Air Law and Commerce,* Vol. 30 (Spring 1964), pp. 113–72, and Pt. 2, in ibid., Vol. 31 (Spring 1965), pp. 89–125.

20. *Civil Aeronautics Board Reports to Congress, Fiscal Year 1970,* p. 73.

21. It is partly because of such litigation costs (and partly to exploit more fully monopoly opportunities and slow down the rate of competitive route awards) that in 1973 several carriers suggested that the Board establish a policy of approving the sale and transfer of operating authority among carriers. See Laurence Doty, "Proposed Route Swap Tests CAB Policy," *Aviation Week and Space Technology,* Vol. 98 (April 16, 1973), pp. 28, 29.

22. See George C. Eads, *The Local Service Airline Experiment* (Brookings Institution, 1972), pp. 169–76.

Local service carrier subsidy needs grew from $34.3 million in fiscal year 1970 to $62.8 million in fiscal year 1972. See U.S. Civil Aeronautics Board, "Subsidy for United States Certificated Air Carriers" (August 1972; processed), App. 7. Subsidy needs for 1973 are set at $65.5 million. See CAB Order 73-10-1 (Oct. 1, 1973), App. A.

routes to that carrier among the applicants which appeared to be in the greatest need of financial support. This program has partially succeeded, but in one case—the granting of the Miami–Los Angeles route to Northeast—it failed to have the anticipated effect of buoying the firm; moreover, as if to deny the implicit value of the award granted, when another carrier, Northwest, proposed to merge with Northeast and thus bail it out of difficulty, the Board conditioned its approval on the nontransfer of the Miami–Los Angeles route; because of this, Northwest backed out of the agreement. Finally, a more laudable goal has been the Board's limited attempts to rationalize route structures by making marginal changes in operating authority where the effect would be to lower carrier costs of providing service.[23]

A different sort of criticism of the route award mechanism has been raised by William E. Fruhan, Jr.[24] In his study of competition among the domestic trunks, Fruhan likened route award proceedings to the "prisoner's dilemma," where persons suspected of a crime are induced to inform on each other to their mutual detriment. In essence, Fruhan's argument is that carriers as a group lose by engaging in route proceedings, but individually they would lose more if they did not. For example, carriers often realize that for a time at least they will incur losses in new markets, yet if they fail to act—to get their share of new routes—they will find themselves foreclosed from new opportunities, with gradually encroaching competition on their own territory.

A variant of this thesis is that to secure the option of profitable service at some later date, carriers are prompted to enter markets prematurely, suffering losses until traffic can support a minimal level of operations. If entry were unrestrained, there would be no incentive to "buy in," and carriers would inaugurate new service at a more propitious time.

It would appear, therefore, that control of entry has had its costs. The trunk carriers have been protected from new entrants and thus, arguably, more technically efficient carriers have been denied access to markets and air passengers have incurred forgone opportunities. Industry costs have also been raised by regulator-imposed restraints on aircraft routings and points served. Finally, the route certification procedure leads to inflated

23. For example, removing a circuitous routing restriction when direct service would be lower in cost as well as higher in quality.

24. William E. Fruhan, Jr., *The Fight for Competitive Advantage: A Study of the United States Domestic Trunk Air Carriers* (Harvard University, Graduate School of Business Administration, 1972), Chap. 4.

costs of litigation and wasteful attempts to "buy in" new routes with conspicuous demonstrations of service qualification. The extent of these losses is almost impossible to determine. However, from what information is available one may rationally conclude that they are indeed significant.

Exit

In a rapidly growing industry, where competition is carefully controlled and regulation is administered to protect the financial viability of individual firms, one would not expect to observe a high incidence of exit via bankruptcy. Indeed, although the number of trunk carriers has shrunk from sixteen to ten, in each of these cases exit has been the result of merger (see Table 7-4).[25]

Among the other groups of certificated carriers, there have been a few cases of bankruptcy and several instances of the Board's forcing exit by refusing to renew or canceling a certificate. Of the twenty-six cases of certificate termination to the end of 1970, in nine cases the carrier's certificate was canceled by the Board because of noncompliance with the certificate's stated provisions, usually not meeting schedules; in eight cases a temporary certificate was allowed to expire even though the carrier wished to have it renewed; in six cases the carrier sought to abandon the certificated service; in two cases the certificates were transferred to another line; and in the one other case the certificate "ceased to be effective."[26] Three of the cases of nonrenewal were local service carriers (Florida Airways, 1949; Mid-West Airlines, 1952; and E. W. Wiggins Airways, 1953). The rest were smaller, less significant carriers, including helicopter, cargo, and commuter carriers.

To recapitulate, all of the trunk carriers that have left airline service have done so by merging with another trunk line. Local service carriers also have merged, but three were forced to exit by CAB refusal to renew operating authority. In several other, less important cases exit was at the carrier's request.[27]

Besides exit from service altogether, there is the question of exit from

25. In some of these cases (for example, United's acquisition of Capital and Delta's acquisition of Northeast), bankruptcy probably would have resulted had some merger partner not been found.

26. CAB, *Handbook of Airline Statistics, 1971,* p. 533.

27. Jordan reports that in two cases California intrastate carriers were forced to suspend service when the Federal Aviation Administration withdrew their commercial operator certificates (in one case due to alleged safety violations and in another due to the carrier's failure to meet minimum financial standards as required under

individual routes. Over the last decade, the trunk carriers have turned over a number of their lower-density points to local service carriers. At first, when the locals operated with decidedly inferior equipment, local communities hotly protested. However, as the local carriers acquired jet aircraft, beginning in 1965, there was less opposition. Taking this evolution one step further, in the last few years the local service carriers have begun to turn over their least profitable markets to commuter carriers, many times under a contractual arrangement whereby the local carrier guarantees the commuter a minimum operating revenue.[28] By most standards this scheme has been successful—both in reducing the required subsidy and in improving the level of service, primarily increased frequency and thus decreased frequency delay.[29]

All in all, exit from city-pair service has not proved difficult for the domestic trunks. For local service carriers it continues to be a vexing problem. Whatever the case, exit restraint is inefficient from an economic standpoint, and there is little economic justification for its continuation. If a market fails to be profitable, this simply means that the users of the service (including the public sector which sometimes provides subsidy) value it less than the resources used. In some cases, of course, service could be provided at a profit, but only with a more efficient carrier, a different fare-service configuration, or both.[30] By controlling fares and preventing exit, the Board violates the efficient pricing rules and withholds from the market the efficient price-quality combination.

Mergers

Since 1938, there have been six mergers between trunk carriers: Braniff–Mid-Continent (1952), Western-Inland (1952), Delta–Chicago and South-

---

FAA regulations). William A. Jordan, *Airline Regulation in America: Effects and Imperfections* (Johns Hopkins Press, 1970), pp. 21, 22.

28. The first such transfer occurred in late 1967, when Henson Aviation replaced Allegheny Airlines at Hagerstown, Maryland.

29. See U.S. Civil Aeronautics Board, Bureau of Operating Rights, "Service to Small Communities, Part II: Small Aircraft and Small Communities . . . A History and Economic Analysis" (March 1972; processed), Apps. F, G, H. During fiscal year 1970, the Board approved transfer of eleven local service points and eight trunk carrier points to commuter carriers. *Civil Aeronautics Board Reports to Congress, Fiscal Year 1970*, pp. 8, 9.

30. The success of commuter airlines in replacing local service carriers at many points attests to the opportunities for subsidy-free, profitable operations at a more frequent service configuration, though sometimes at higher prices.

Table 7-4. Successful and Unsuccessful Mergers Involving Domestic Trunk Air Carriers, 1938–73

Year	Number of trunk carriers[a]	Comments
1938	16	
1939	16	
1940	16	United*-Western* merger denied
1941	16	Transcontinental and Western Air* absorbed Marquette
1942	16	
1943	16	
1944	16	
1945	16	Northeast* absorbed Mayflower; American* absorbed American Export
1946	16	Braniff*-Frontier merger denied; American*–Mid-Continent* merger denied
1947	16	Capital*-Northeast* merger denied
1948	16	
1949	16	
1950	16	Mid-Continent*–Parks merger denied
1951	16	Continental*-Midwest merger withdrawn
1952	16	Northwest*-Capital* merger dismissed; Braniff* absorbed Mid-Continent*; Western* absorbed Inland*
1953	14	Delta* absorbed Chicago and Southern*
1954	13	Eastern*-Colonial*-National* merger denied
1955	13	Continental* absorbed Pioneer; Delta*-Northeast* merger withdrawn
1956	13	Eastern* absorbed Colonial*
1957	12	
1958	12	
1959	12	
1960	12	
1961	12	United* absorbed Capital*
1962	11	Continental*-National* merger withdrawn
1963	11	Pan American–TWA* merger withdrawn; American*-Eastern* merger disapproved
1964	11	
1965	11	
1966	11	
1967	11	Eastern* absorbed Mackey; Braniff* absorbed Pan American–Grace; Western* absorbed Pacific Northern
1968	11	
1969	11	

Table 7-4 (*continued*)

Year	Number of trunk carriers[a]	Comments
1970	11	American* absorbed Trans Caribbean; Northeast*-Northwest* merger approved, subsequently terminated by Northwest*
1971	11	
1972	11	Delta* absorbed Northeast*; American*-Western* merger denied; Northwest*-National* merger dismissed; Eastern*-Caribair merger disapproved, but pending
1973	10	Acquisition of Caribair by Eastern* approved

Sources: CAB, *Handbook of Airline Statistics, 1971*, pp. 9, 479–95, 531, 532; and various Board orders.
a. Any airline that operated for any portion of a year is counted for that year. Figures do not include Pan American (see Table 7-2, note a).
* Indicates trunk carrier.

ern (1953), Eastern-Colonial (1956), United-Capital (1961), and Delta-Northeast (1972). Table 7-4 lists these mergers and all other successful and unsuccessful mergers involving trunk carriers for the period 1938 through 1973. As shown in the table, in nineteen of its thirty-six years of existence the Board has faced a decision involving a merger of a trunk carrier.

The Board's policy toward mergers has vacillated over the years.[31] From 1938 through most of the 1940s, the Board maintained a strongly procompetitive stance, and even though it allowed trunks to absorb three minor carriers, in no case did it approve a merger among trunks. From early in the 1950s until about 1956, the Board swung to the other extreme, actively campaigning for mergers and approving several having important anticompetitive effects. Beginning in 1956 and lasting until recently, the Board has resisted trunk-line merger attempts, approving only one (United-Capital), and that on grounds of rescuing a "failing firm" (Capital). This was in spite of much carrier zeal for mergers in the early 1960s. During the last few years, the Board has expressed a slightly more liberal attitude, approving mergers between Northwest and Northeast in 1970,[32] between Allegheny and Mohawk (two local service carriers) in

31. For a summary of the history of CAB policy toward airline mergers, see Lucile S. Keyes, "Notes on the History of Federal Regulation of Airline Mergers," *Journal of Air Law and Commerce*, Vol. 37 (Summer 1971), pp. 357–87.
32. CAB Orders 70-12-162 and 70-12-163 (Dec. 22, 1970), p. 2. As written into the original agreement, Northwest had the option of backing out of the merger in

1972,[33] and between Delta and Northeast, also in 1972.[34] However, in its most significant recent case (in terms of impact on overall industry concentration), the Board disapproved a merger between American and Western in 1972,[35] and subsequently a purported "defensive" merger between Northwest and National was dismissed when National withdrew from the agreement in 1972.[36]

The statutory passage governing airline mergers states that the Board must approve the merger unless it finds it "will not be consistent with the public interest."[37] But, it must not approve a proposed merger if it would "result in creating a monopoly or monopolies and thereby restrain competition or jeopardize another air carrier not a party to the ... merger."[38] In addition to these rather broad standards, the Board is also obligated to consider section 7 of the Clayton Act.[39]

The Board often bases its decisions on rather subjective interpretations of even more subjective statutory standards. To identify the Board's implicit criteria is risky at best,[40] but one government-sponsored report listed the following as among those considerations the Board finds the most relevant: (a) efficiency and economy and reduction or elimination of subsidies; (b) integrated air service and service improvement; (c) preservation of competition; (d) prevention of traffic diversion; (e) rescue of a failing airline; and (f) reasonableness of the purchase price.[41]

In 1971, the Department of Transportation in consultation with the

---

the event the Board failed to approve the transfer of Northeast's potentially lucrative Los Angeles–Miami route. With Board disapproval of this transfer, Northwest exercised its option and the agreement was terminated.

33. See CAB Orders 72-4-31 and 72-4-32 (March 28, 1972).

34. CAB Orders 72-5-73 and 72-5-74 (April 24, 1972).

35. CAB Orders 72-7-91 and 72-7-92 (June 13, 1972).

36. See CAB Order 72-12-92 (Dec. 20, 1972).

37. Federal Aviation Act of 1958, sec. 408(b) (72 Stat. 767).

38. Ibid.

39. See the appendix at the end of the book.

40. According to Barber, "The Board's opinions simply do not opine. Rather they recite any of a number of objectives that are deemed desirable, announce that the instant decision promises their fulfillment, and add the old caveat that the facts of each case govern. This result is to leave the reader with very little guidance for the future and with only a vague understanding of what explains the Board's conclusion." Richard J. Barber, "Airline Mergers, Monopoly, and the CAB," *Journal of Air Law and Commerce,* Vol. 28 (Summer 1961–62), p. 210.

41. Arthur D. Little, Inc., "Working Papers on Air and Surface Transportation Policy and Regulation," prepared for the Joint DOT-NASA Civil Aviation Research and Development Policy Study, Vol. 1 (1971; processed), pp. 91, 92.

Department of Justice released a set of criteria to be used by executive-branch agencies in judging the desirability of domestic airline mergers. They are as follows:

A. A merger should not result in either the elimination of effective competition, or an excessive market share for the surviving firm, in significant city-pair, regional or national markets for airline services.

B. A merger should not result in undue concentration within the air carrier industry.

C. A merger should not be likely to lead to extensive reactions and defensive merger proposals by competitive carriers so that the end result will be a restructuring of the industry and excessive concentration in a few firms.

D. A merger should not result in substantial foreclosure of competition for interchange traffic or other excessive injury to other carriers.

E. A merger should bring about substantial operational, service, or organizational benefits for the surviving firm so that the public will receive significant benefits such as greater efficiency and better service, and the size of the airline resulting from the merger should not be such as to produce significant diseconomies.

F. In the case of a merger of a relatively effective carrier and one that is marginal, or in the case of two marginal carriers, the resulting benefits of the surviving firm should be corrective of the original difficulty of the weaker merger partner. Alternative solutions to the problems of a marginal merging carrier should be shown to be considerably less effective than merger.

G. The protection afforded labor in the merging firms should be in accordance with the present policies of the Board.[42]

Even though these criteria are defined a bit more carefully in the rest of the document, they still are somewhat unclear and ambiguous, perhaps purposely so.[43] An illustration is that in the most important merger case in recent years—American-Western—the Department of Transportation supported the merger, and, ostensibly following the same set of criteria, the Justice Department opposed it.[44]

We shall attempt now to view airline mergers from the standpoint of economic efficiency. On the cost side, it is often alleged that mergers result in substantial savings because of economies of scale. Chapter 2 looked at this question and concluded that the airlines' long-run cost function (at

42. U.S. Department of Transportation, "Executive Branch Criteria for Domestic Airline Merger Proposals" (Aug. 31, 1971; processed), p. 3.

43. The department's statement admonished the reader that "the criteria are meant to be looked at as a whole. There is not any one criterion of overriding significance." Ibid.

44. See Briefs of Departments of Transportation and Justice to Hearing Examiner William J. Madden in CAB Docket 22916, "American-Western Merger Case" (Aug. 31, 1971).

least over the relevant range of output) has the characteristic of constant returns to scale. This is not to say that any particular merger could not result in cost savings (or even cost increases). No one knows for sure. However, the best estimate is that size alone has no significant effect on the average and marginal costs of providing scheduled air service.[45]

If cost savings are unlikely, what motivates carriers to merge? Broadly speaking, there are two reasons. On the one hand, merger is a means for an aggressive carrier to acquire new routes it otherwise could not hope to obtain as cheaply through the long and tortuous conventional route-award procedure.[46] Such an expansion may afford any of several opportunities for a carrier. First, an efficient carrier management may feel that it can run the acquired firm at greater technical efficiency and thereby raise profits. Second, a carrier may gain a marketing advantage over its competitors. For example, where before merger the two firms had to interline passengers, now service can be direct or at least without plane changes; this may divert traffic from competing carriers. Third, an expansion-type merger might be used defensively, to head off or block a merger between the acquired firm and some other competitor, and thus prevent having traffic diverted away.[47]

Mergers of this route-expanding variety, where competition is not eliminated in any significant city-pair markets, are, as a general rule, relatively innocuous. There may be gains in technical efficiency in the form of reduced waste either because of management replacement or because the merger allows a more efficient routing pattern. The quality of service, too, stands to gain from increased single-plane service, and this is to the public's advantage. Potentially offsetting these gains are four arguments against such mergers. If there are marketing gains, then the merger may put competing carriers at a financial disadvantage and, depending on severity, may possibly impair the competitor's ability to provide service elsewhere.[48] Moreover a merger forecloses potential competition. The

45. William A. Jordan has speculated that domestic interstate air service could be provided by over 200 separate airlines and still not encounter significant diseconomies of small size. See Jordan, *Airline Regulation in America*, p. 27.

46. See ibid., pp. 15–23; and "Testimony of William A. Jordan," CAB Docket 22916, Exhibit DJ-RT-1 (March 29, 1971), pp. 6–10.

47. A carrier's concern for diverted traffic depends on a comparison of expected revenues and costs.

48. While there may be wealth transfers in such instances, cases of the public's suffering because of this unfair competition are extremely difficult to document. A similar point can be raised in cases of bankruptcy (as a counterargument to the alleged necessity of bailing out a failing firm): although assets are written down

relevant question then is whether the Board would be less likely to certificate new competition for a carrier because one of its prospective competitors has been absorbed. In addition, to the degree the merger partners face the same set of competitors in their respective markets, the easier it may be to orchestrate collusion with these carriers after merger. Finally, ceteris paribus, the greater the number of firms in an industry the more likely it is to be characterized by economic efficiency. In the airline industry there are few firms and little price competition; presumably, one would want to preserve conditions making price competition more likely and reducing the tendency to act in concert. Moreover, in the past some of the smaller carriers have been the most innovative and aggressive.[49] Reducing the number of carriers cuts down on the number and diversity of such sources of experimentation. Obviously these considerations become progressively more important the more concentrated the industry becomes.

Of more concern is the second reason for merger, the elimination or reduction of competition in city-pair markets to improve prospects for higher profits through service deterioration, higher fares, or both. Traditionally such parallel mergers have been seriously questioned by the Board and, with few exceptions, disapproved. One such exception involved the markets in which competition was completely eliminated by the United-Capital merger of 1961. A CAB staff study reviewing that experience found what one would have predicted from the behavioral model described in Chapter 4.[50] Briefly, the conclusions are as follows: (a) traffic grew at a lower-than-average rate after the merger whereas before 1961 it was higher than average, (b) frequency of service was lower after the merger, but rebounded after the Board's decision in late 1964 to certificate new competition, (c) jet equipment was introduced into these markets at a slower pace than in comparable competitive markets, and (d) coach service grew

---

and/or change hands, usually this does not much affect the way such resources are actually utilized.

49. See Richard E. Caves, *Air Transport and Its Regulators: An Industry Study* (Harvard University Press, 1962), pp. 425–27; Jessie Markham, "An Economic Study of the Competitive Effects of the Proposed American Airlines, Inc., Eastern Airlines, Inc. Merger," CAB Docket 13355, Exhibit JI-1 (1962), pp. 2, 3; and "Rebuttal Testimony of Richard J. Barber," CAB Docket 23852, Exhibit CO-T-4-R (Jan. 10, 1972), pp. 27–29.

50. See Max H. Burstein, "Restoring Competition in the Cleveland–New York, Chicago–Cleveland, Detroit–Philadelphia, and Cleveland–Philadelphia Airline Markets: A Study of Traffic, Fares, and Quality of Service before and after the Capital-United Merger, and the CAB Action to Restore Competition in These Markets, 1959–1967" (CAB, Bureau of Economics, June 1970; processed).

less rapidly in these markets than in others as a way of keeping the average fare high.

In evaluating airline mergers, it must be understood that CAB policy toward entry plays a crucial role. If entry were free, carriers would have little if any incentive to merge. They could expand without the need of buying out another firm; marketing advantages over competitors would be seriously deflated; and opportunities for monopoly gain through parallel merger would have to be discounted. Free entry would also deflate the major arguments against merger. Since the economic barriers to new-carrier entry are very low, one would expect a plethora of specialized and conventional carriers to enter city-pair service and provide effective alternatives to the industry giants. Also, no carrier could expect to exploit monopoly markets created through parallel merger, since excess profits, high fares, or poor service would all attract new competition.

In summary, mergers seldom result in significant cost savings, and thus any improvements in the financial picture of the merger partners can be attributed primarily to monopoly gains (higher prices, poorer service, or both) or outright traffic transfer from competing carriers. In neither case is economic efficiency enhanced. If, however, the Board had a much more liberal policy toward entry into city-pair competition *and* entry of new trunk carriers, then airline mergers would be much less important from the standpoint of public policy.

Collusion

In almost any industry, firms stand to gain higher profits by keeping others out, by controlling prices, outputs, or both, and by regulating other forms of nonprice competition. The airline industry is no exception, the only distinction being that CAB regulation complicates and, on balance, appears to facilitate this effort. However, as will become apparent below, it is our judgment that while strikingly anticompetitive actions are approved (and sometimes sponsored) by the CAB, this campaign remains so "imperfect," to use Jordan's adjective,[51] that trunk airline profits would have fared just about as well without it.

Collusion among carriers can be either legal (Board-sanctioned) or

---

51. *Airline Regulation in America.* Jordan describes the CAB as presiding over an "imperfect cartel" (p. 227).

extra-legal (arising out of either illegal agreement or explicit parallel action). For several reasons, legal collusion in the airlines is more important and pervasive than extra-legal collusion. First, the Board has been accommodating to most anticompetitive programs, thus obviating the need for (and risks attendant on) extra-legal collusion. Second, the Board uses its powers to enforce many of its anticompetitive policies, especially fare and entry regulations, making formal collusion preferred to extra-legal. Finally, the areas not covered by CAB-endorsed collusion are such that extra-legal collusion is extremely difficult to arrange and enforce.

Ways in which the CAB accommodates rate and entry control for the industry were described previously. This section focuses on other forms of collusion. Its major theme is that with few, but notable, exceptions, trunk-carrier collusion fails to have any significant impact on profits; instead, it leads to decreased technical efficiency and nonoptimal price-quality options.

CAB Approval of Formal Carrier Agreements

By law, the Board may approve any multi-carrier agreement relating to "pooling or apportioning earnings, losses, traffic, service, or equipment, or relating to the establishment of transportation rates, fares, charges, or classifications, or for preserving and improving safety, economy, and efficiency of operation, or for controlling, regulating, preventing, or otherwise eliminating destructive, oppressive, or wasteful competition, or for regulating stops, schedules, and character of service, or for other cooperative working arrangements,"[52] which it does not find to be adverse to the public interest.[53] Such approval carries with it exemption from the antitrust laws.

There are literally thousands of such agreements on file at any one time, and since 1967 the Board has reviewed over one thousand proposals each year.[54] For the most part these are innocuous, being approved as a matter of course by CAB staff under powers delegated by the Board.[55] They relate to such matters as joint or subcontracted passenger servicing at low-density points, spare parts, inventory pooling, maintenance subcontracting, standards for ticketing and payment for interline services, and equipment interchanges. Others, however, are much more important to economic efficiency, at least potentially so, and some of these are discussed below.

52. Section 412(a) of the Federal Aviation Act of 1958.
53. Section 412(b) of the Federal Aviation Act.
54. *Civil Aeronautics Board Reports to Congress, Fiscal Year 1970,* p. 12; *1969,* p. 11; *1968,* p. 16; *1967,* p. 55; *1966,* p. 43.
55. Part 385 of the Board's Economic Regulations.

Capacity Limitation Agreements[56]

By far the most important, precedent-setting legal collusive arrangement of recent years is the capacity reduction agreement among American, United, and TWA approved by the Board on August 19, 1971. As discussed in Chapter 4, scheduling additional capacity is the most important dimension of nonprice competition. The Federal Aviation Act expressly prohibits the Board from controlling carrier schedules.[57] However, the Board can approve an agreement among carriers for industry "self-regulation."

During the height of the 1970–71 traffic slowdown, American, United, and TWA filed an agreement with the Board which would have reduced seat-mile capacity in the neighborhood of 10–15 percent in fifteen long-haul markets served only by these three carriers.[58] Amid considerable controversy, which included opposition by the Justice Department and some trunk carriers, the Board rejected the agreement because the carriers had not previously obtained CAB approval (more specifically, antitrust immunity) for discussions and because of other shortcomings of the proposed agreement.[59] However, the Board did state that it would entertain proposals to discuss new agreements and granted permission to TWA on March 11, 1971, making provision for CAB staff monitoring of all capacity discussion meetings.[60] Subsequently, on August 19, 1971, the Board formally approved an agreement among the three carriers which would decrease the number of flights in four long-haul markets by 6.1 to 38.0 percent, depending on market and season—a move designed to raise load factors from then-existing levels of 26–36 percent to off-peak and peak levels of 50 percent and 60 percent respectively.[61]

---

56. On such agreements see also William A. Jordan, "Airline Capacity Agreements: Correcting a Regulatory Imperfection," *Journal of Air Law and Commerce,* Vol. 39 (Spring 1973), and George Eads, "Airline Capacity Limitation Controls: Public Vice or Public Virtue?" in American Economic Association, *Papers and Proceedings of the Eighty-sixth Annual Meeting, 1973* (*American Economic Review,* Vol. 64, May 1974), pp. 365–71.

57. Federal Aviation Act of 1958, sec. 401e (72 Stat. 755).

58. "Joint Statement of American Airlines, Inc., Trans World Airlines, Inc., and United Airlines, Inc. in Support of the Agreement," CAB Docket 22525 (Aug. 28, 1970).

59. See CAB Order 70-11-35 (Nov. 6, 1970).

60. CAB Order 71-3-71 (March 11, 1971).

61. CAB Order 71-8-91 (Aug. 19, 1971). The four city-pair markets are New York/Newark–Los Angeles, New York/Newark–San Francisco, Chicago–San Francisco, and Washington/Baltimore–Los Angeles.

Building on this initial, precedent-setting decision, the Board later approved the following: (a) an agreement between Aloha Airlines and Hawaiian Airlines to limit capacity in inter-island competition,[62] (b) an agreement among American, Eastern, and Pan American to limit capacity in the New York/Newark–San Juan market, bringing load factors up to 65 percent and 75 percent, depending on season,[63] (c) a renewal of the initial three-carrier agreement,[64] and (d) an extension of the New York/Newark–San Juan agreement, this time with target load factors of 70 and 75 percent.[65] Our discussion here relates primarily to the three-carrier domestic agreement.

The effects of the agreement are straightforward and predictable. First, by definition, as capacity has been reduced, schedule frequencies have dropped and load factors have risen. Thus, schedule delay has increased and service quality has diminished.[66] Second, traffic appears to have grown more slowly in these markets than in similar markets.[67] Third, carrier profits have risen substantially over the routes in question.[68]

From an economic efficiency standpoint, there is something to say for the agreement from an extremely short-run, "second-best" perspective. If optimal load factors for these markets are considerably higher than those actually obtaining, then the value of this excess capacity to consumers is less than its cost. Conceivably the additional profits generated by the capacity restrictions could more than offset the commensurate loss to consumers, actual and potential. On the other hand, approval of such a collusive arrangement sets a dangerous precedent and in the long run clearly will operate to the detriment of economic efficiency. First, the carrot of profits and the stick of losses give carriers incentives to match capacity plans with growth in passenger demand. If there exists the prospect that the Board will obligingly bail out the industry with capacity agreements, then carriers will have less incentive to make correct decisions.[69] Second, as explained in

62. CAB Order 71-12-143 (Dec. 30, 1971). Certain inter-island capacity agreements predate this order.

63. CAB Order 72-6-70 (June 16, 1972).

64. CAB Order 72-11-6 (Nov. 2, 1972).

65. CAB Order 72-11-7 (Nov. 2, 1972).

66. Note that this contradicts the Board's assertion that the proposed agreement "will not have an adverse impact on the quality and quantity of service available to the public." (CAB Order 71-8-91, p. 5.)

67. CAB Order 72-11-6, p. 4.

68. See ibid., p. 3, and James P. Woolsey, "Capacity Limitation Plan Faces New Test," *Aviation Week and Space Technology*, Vol. 96 (Feb. 7, 1972), pp. 24, 25.

69. Of course, since foresight is not perfect, sometimes carriers will earn abnormal (accounting) profits, sometimes abnormal (accounting) losses in short-run

the previous chapter, the existence of low load factors is an indication that the fare is too high, that is, the break-even load factor is too low. With a fare taper which is less than the cost taper, low load factors in long-haul markets are to be expected (see Chapter 4, regressions [1] and [2], and Figure 6-4). The appropriate remedy for an excessively low load factor is a fare decrease, not a direct control over capacity.

As justification for their agreement, the three carriers argued that the temptation for carriers to add additional capacity in order to increase market share is too great, and thus carrier system capacity and resulting load factors are beyond the control of individual carrier management. Accordingly, the industry is characterized by a hopeless spiral of excess capacity, the only solution being multilateral control, monitored by the Board.[70]

However, as borne out empirically in Chapter 4, the airlines do not appear to behave in this unstable way.[71] First, as shown in Chapter 4, any chronic excess capacity is due to the Board's setting too high a fare; if over a period of time there is a spiral of excess capacity, this reveals that the Board is too responsive to the carriers' petitions for fare increases. Second, as for the possibility of a market loss equilibrium mentioned in Chapter 4 (a prospect, incidentally, frequently raised by the carriers), it suggests very peculiar behavior on the part of carrier management. That is, on the one hand carriers assert that they are operating efficiently yet on the other reveal themselves to be so myopic as to fall into the loss-equilibrium trap. Another way of saying this is that a foresighted manager will simply get out of, or avoid getting into, a loss equilibrium market. Of course, to take the problem seriously we must presume that the necessary conditions for a loss equilibrium are widespread. Such is not the case. In fact, the set of markets where, under even the most extreme assumptions, a loss equilib-

---

equilibrium, even when capacity decisions are based on profit motives and are made in "good faith."

70. See "Application of Trans World Airlines, Inc. for an Order Authorizing Discussions," CAB Docket 22908 (Dec. 21, 1970); also see "Joint Statement of American Airlines." Essentially, the argument is that markets conform to the S-shaped, nonproportional market-share versus the seat-share relationship described in Chapter 4. This, arguably, leads to a loss-producing equilibrium (see appendix to Chapter 4) unless an acceleration in rising fares postpones such losses.

71. If they did, then surely alternatives to multilateral capacity control must be considered (for example, CAB statutory control over schedules). For evidence contradicting the carriers' claim, see Joseph V. Yance, "Nonprice Competition in Jet Aircraft Capacity," *Journal of Industrial Economics,* Vol. 21 (November 1972), pp. 55–71.

rium might occur must be very small.[72] Finally, we point out that what one might interpret as loss-producing behavior is really a case of predatory service competition.[73] The rationale for the aggressive firm is the hope of driving out the competition and then offsetting the short-term losses with long-term excess profits. The reason why this opportunity might afford hope of success is that the Board can be relied upon to restrain reentry into the market.

On a different aspect of the agreements, as might have been predicted, and as discussed by Eads,[74] despite carte blanche to discuss and negotiate any relevant proposal, the carriers found it difficult to resolve their differences and reach an agreement. For example, out of the fifteen city-pairs originally proposed, agreement was reached on only four. Also, carriers not a party to the arrangement have objected to what they detect as an abuse of the agreement: member carriers' using freed capacity to compete in other competitive markets.[75]

Placing the matter in perspective, it should be noted that the Board approved the initial transcontinental capacity agreement reluctantly.[76] In limiting the terms of the agreement to only one year, the Board indicated its presumption that in future months the industry's financial picture would be rectified and that in the future such agreements would be inappropriate.

72. See Joseph V. Yance, "The Possibility of Loss-Producing Equilibria in Air Carrier Markets" (1971; processed). Also, some preliminary research undertaken by the authors indicates the same conclusion: namely, that the set of loss-eligible markets is very small. In any event, the long-run implication of such a set of conditions is the exit from each market of all but one or a few carriers, which, in turn, would earn profits.

73. See James L. Hamilton and Michael K. Kawahara, "Predatory Nonprice Competition: The Case of Hawaii Interisland Air Transport," *Antitrust Law and Economics Review,* forthcoming. Another alleged case of predatory service competition is when American Airlines merged with Trans Caribbean Airways in 1971 and then began pouring capacity into the New York–San Juan market. CAB Order 72-1-86 (Jan. 25, 1972).

74. George C. Eads, "Competition in the Domestic Airline Industry: Too Much or Too Little?" in Almarin Phillips (ed.), *Competition and Regulation* (Brookings Institution, 1974).

75. See CAB Order 72-4-63 (April 13, 1972) describing objections raised by Braniff, Eastern, and Northwest, and Board dismissal of their complaints.

76. Said the Board's order: "We regretfully have concluded in view of the evidence of continuing low load factors in the major markets in question that [economic forces] are acting too slowly in the immediate circumstances. In our judgment, a limited departure from our normal policy of leaving scheduling and capacity to the free play of competitive forces is justified at this time." CAB Order 71-8-91 (Aug. 19, 1971), p. 5. (Also see pp. 3–10, especially p. 3.)

However, succeeding Board orders pertaining to capacity limitation agreements have backed away from this stance, culminating in a recent Board decision to "put all parties on notice that the Board has tentatively concluded that capacity limitation agreements may in many circumstances be in the public interest and that the Board is prepared to consider requests for authority to discuss capacity reduction agreements in specific markets and to judge resulting agreements on their merits."[77] The Board also expressed the view that "the concerns of the Board earlier expressed about capacity limitation agreements may have been misplaced."[78] This would appear to signal the institutionalization of capacity limitation agreements, perhaps on a grand scale. If so, then this represents one of the most anticompetitive steps ever taken by the Board.

Fuel Reduction and Rescheduling Agreements

During the height of public concern over the "energy crisis," Congress amended the Economic Stabilization Act of 1970 to give the President or his delegate the power to allocate petroleum products.[79] In the face of anticipated petroleum shortages, the Energy Policy Office adopted a mandatory fuel allocation program in October 1973 which in essence limited U.S. air carriers to levels of aviation fuel consumed in 1972. Overall, this represented a reduction in fuel consumption in the neighborhood of 10 percent from the anticipated 1973 amount.

The Board responded to this action unilaterally by granting antitrust immunity and encouraging carriers to meet and "rationalize" their forced schedule cutbacks. Such meetings were to be held in Washington, D.C., and would be open to the public.[80] Pursuant to this invitation, American, TWA, and United reached agreements to curtail capacity in twenty markets, and their plan was approved expeditiously by the Board.[81] The Board also designated Pan American to orchestrate schedule reduction agreements for international carriers a few days later.[82] Finally, in an effort to encourage more agreements, the Board authorized the carriers to bypass formal,

77. CAB Order 73-4-98 (April 24, 1973), p. 1.
78. Ibid., p. 2.
79. Public Law 93-28 (April 30, 1973).
80. CAB Order 73-10-50 (Oct. 12, 1973).
81. CAB Order 73-10-110 (Oct. 31, 1973).
82. CAB Order 73-11-34 (Nov. 8, 1973).

publicly monitored session requirements and communicate privately by telephone and telegraph.[83]

From an economic efficiency standpoint, all this is highly questionable. First, even with the reduced fuel availability, profit incentives would cause carriers to provide the limited service wherever it was most desired. In short, schedule reduction agreements are not necessary to achieve this end. Second, for any given level of fuel utilization, there exists a plethora of scheduling patterns which will increase industry profits, at the expense of public convenience, over those under noncoordinated scheduling. Thus, the incentive for carriers to agree on schedule control is the opportunity for earning excess profits. Finally, in view of the ever-present temptation for carriers to orchestrate mutually beneficial reductions in other means of nonprice competition, increases in price, or both, it would appear that the Board's granting of antitrust immunity for carriers to discuss their problems informally over the telephone sets a dangerous precedent.

Congestion Agreements

As mentioned earlier, in 1968 airline congestion reached "crisis" proportions with aircraft stacked over major airports typically for an hour or more. The difficulty was triggered when air traffic controllers refused to exceed established standards for safe separation between aircraft and thus slowed down the rate of airport operations. Amid the controversy and charges of unsafe procedures, the Federal Aviation Administration announced that it was applying quotas to all airports, that operations simply would not exceed the predetermined maximum safe rates. Meanwhile, the Board authorized carriers to discuss how they might "rationalize" their flights into the congested airports, and on December 3, 1968, it approved three agreements whereby carriers would self-regulate through scheduling committees at five airports: LaGuardia, Kennedy, Newark, Washington National, and O'Hare.[84]

The economic consequences of congestion and nonmarket allocations of scarce airport and airway space were discussed briefly in the previous chapter. Our particular focus here is on the effects of the congestion agreements. One would expect, from economic theory, airlines to allocate their landing and takeoff slots among those flights offering the most profit potential. In a study of quota allocation at Washington National Airport,

---

83. CAB Order 73-11-50 (Nov. 13, 1973).

84. See CAB, *Handbook of Airline Statistics, 1971*, p. 493. Subsequently Newark was dropped from the agreement, as quotas there proved unnecessary.

Joseph V. Yance reports that "airlines have generally increased flight frequency from [Washington National] in high-profit markets and reduced it in low-profit markets."[85] Generally, this represents a more efficient allocation of resources, and also a transfer of excess profits (rents) to the air carriers. Accordingly, it should come as no surprise that the airlines adamantly oppose market solutions to airport and airway congestion, preferring instead CAB-sanctioned nonprice allocations.

Mutual Aid Pact

As with most cases of industry-wide bargaining, the labor unions in commercial aviation have attempted to whipsaw carriers in hopes of obtaining more favorable settlements. In reaction to that technique, involving a strike on Capital Airlines in 1958, six carriers (American, Capital, Eastern, Pan American, TWA, and United) entered into an agreement whereby member airlines which were struck would receive financial aid from member competitors, with transfers computed on the basis of a complex formula related to the windfall revenues of the carriers that were not struck.[86] The Board approved this agreement as not being adverse to the public interest. Four additional trunk carriers joined in 1960.[87] In 1962 the pact was renewed, with a few modifications.[88] In October 1969 the carriers requested additional modifications, and in December 1970 they petitioned to allow the inclusion of the local service carriers.[89] In a March 1972 decision, the administrative law judge recommended that the proposal extending the pact be approved but generally without modification. The Board, however, reversed the administrative law judge's decision, approving the agreement substantially as proposed.[90]

85. Joseph V. Yance, "Airline Demand for Use of an Airport and Airport Rents," *Transportation Research*, Vol. 5 (1971), p. 267.

86. This discussion of the background of the airlines' mutual aid pact is based on "Initial Decision of Arthur S. Present, Hearing Examiner," CAB Docket 9977, "Airlines Mutual Aid Pact" (March 27, 1972), pp. 4–11.

87. National, one of those that joined in 1960, withdrew at the end of 1961. Also that same year Capital effectively withdrew, merging into United. During the 1957–61 period, there were fifteen strikes covered by the agreement, with a total of $16,160,000 in revenue sharing.

88. Specifically, the struck carrier was always to receive a minimum of 25 percent of its normal operating revenues.

89. Between 1962 and 1969 there were eleven strikes covered by the agreement, involving $87,740,000 in revenue sharing. Also, it is interesting to note that Delta has never been a member of the pact, is not unionized, except for its dispatchers and its pilots, and has not been struck.

90. CAB Order 73-2-110 (Feb. 27, 1973).

The consequences of the mutual aid pact on economic efficiency cannot be assessed a priori. While the agreements doubtlessly enhance the carriers' position in collective bargaining, this must be set off against the power and unusual leverage possessed by the unions. In this industry, for example, there are many labor strata represented by separate unions. Moreover, the work of many, perhaps all, is absolutely essential for the operation of the firm, even in the very short run. While this is clearly true for pilots, it is also the case for flight attendants and other personnel because of Federal Aviation Administration regulations. Although the unilateral power of various labor groups within the same industry is not unusual, in the airlines it does not derive simply from each union's respect of the other's pickets.

The mutual aid pact, together with union leverage and the shelter of regulation, suggests that labor negotiations are likely to be resolved to the mutual advantage of the carriers *and* the unions to the detriment of the general public.[91] The public reaction to suspension of service because of a strike, lockout, or both is vastly greater than the ill-perceived ultimate effect of its resolution on costs. Moreover, since in the last two decades the industry has enjoyed above-average increases in productivity, the effect on unit costs is further masked from view.

It is difficult to assess wage levels in the airline industry by comparison with those in other industries. However, a CAB study of wages and productivity indicates that the wages of airline employees have increased at rates approximately 50 percent higher than the average for all nonfarm industries.[92] While the increasing productivity derived from the introduction of jet aircraft caused unit labor costs in the industry to fall over the period 1958 to 1967, they have risen sharply since then.

The Air Transport Association

The Air Transport Association of America (ATA) is the principal trade association in commercial aviation, to which belong all the domestic trunks and local service carriers, Pan American, the two Hawaiian carriers, three Alaskan carriers, the Flying Tiger Line (all-cargo), two helicopter airlines,

91. See H. T. K. Paxson and S. R. L. Brown, U.S. Civil Aeronautics Board, "Productivity and Employment Costs in System Operations of the Trunk Airlines and Pan American, From 1957 Through 1970" (CAB, July 1971; processed).

92. While one would expect above-average increases in productivity to be reflected in somewhat greater than average increases in wages in an expanding industry, some of these productivity gains would normally be reflected in lower unit costs and prices. (See Paxson and Brown, "Productivity and Employment Costs.")

and two Canadian carriers (as associated members).[93] The organization performs many functions for its constituents, the main ones being lobbying for legislation favorable to the airlines, educating the public about the advantages of air travel, serving as a watchdog to inform member carriers of governmental policy developments which may affect their operations, acting as a public spokesman for the industry on aviation policy issues, and serving as a neutral forum where carriers may work out formal agreements, usually under Board supervision.[94]

Because the association provides such an obvious opportunity for extra-legal collusion, the Board recently has been careful to monitor its activities. After approving the ATA's Articles of Association in 1940, the Board left the ATA pretty much to itself until a general investigation of the association's activities was ordered in 1959.[95] This resulted in the ATA's offering to modify its rules and procedures somewhat, in hopes of getting the Board to terminate the investigation.[96] The Board disapproved this offer because it objected to two provisions, one of which is of concern here.[97]

In essence, the ATA maintained the right to provide legal services to member carriers, and thus invoke professional privilege to bar the CAB from inspecting ATA's files. The Board found this provision adverse to the public interest. The ATA then filed a motion of reconsideration, to which the Board partially acceded. However, the CAB did not back away from the collusion issue, stating that "the potentiality of a central legal bureau, unrelated to ATA's own legitimate activities and operating behind a cloak of asserted attorney-client privilege, as a source of collusive activities violative of the principles of the antitrust laws and of the public interest generally, seems to us to outweigh completely any conceivable benefit to be derived."[98] The Board did allow the ATA to keep a tiny fraction of its correspondence with member carriers confidential, provided that periodic

93. Air Transport Association of America, *1970 Air Transport Facts and Figures* (Washington: ATA, 1970), p. 48.

94. A summary and evaluation of the ATA's activities may be found in Emmette S. Redford, *The Regulatory Process: With Illustrations from Commercial Aviation* (University of Texas Press, 1969), Chap. 6, "The Air Transport Association."

95. CAB Order E-13597 (March 10, 1959).

96. Air Transport Association of America, "Motion to Terminate Inspection and Review Pursuant to Offer of Settlement by Air Transport Association" (July 16, 1962). Reproduced in *Civil Aeronautics Board Reports,* Vol. 39 (September 1963–February 1964), p. 888. The settlement offer was the result of negotiations between the ATA and the CAB staff.

97. CAB Order E-19260 (Jan. 31, 1963).

98. *Civil Aeronautics Board Reports* (September 1963–February 1964), p. 884.

reports were made on the general subjects of discussion; all else would be open for Board inspection. Thus, in theory at least, the ATA is barred from facilitating extra-legal collusion.

Travel Agents' Commissions[99]

A semi-independent arm of the ATA is the Air Traffic Conference of America (ATCA). One of the main functions of this group is to accommodate carrier agreements regarding the commissions paid travel agents. During fiscal year 1968, travel agents accounted for the sale of approximately one-third of all air transport sales.[100] As with other forms of non-price competition, the carriers have an incentive to self-regulate, to impose limits. The CAB heartily obliges. In a decision rendered at the end of 1970, the Board set rates for point-to-point sales at 7 percent of the ticket price.[101] This applies to all carriers, with no deviations in rates allowed.

In justifying its decision, the Board pointed to what it believed to be a danger of "destructive competition" if such commissions were not regulated:

We continue to view an "open" commission structure as creating a climate conducive to the maintenance of destructively competitive practices with limited, if any, benefits. . . .

We reach these conclusions out of an informed conviction that without a uniform commission structure there will exist the irresistible temptation . . . to bid up commission rates to the highest level the market will bear.[102]

Moreover, the Board saw in an open rate climate an additional danger: the travel agent would not serve his client, the traveler, but would route him on the airline offering the highest commission.

Dealing with the second objection, the danger imposed by competition flows out of the institution of having the producer of the service, the airline, pay the agent rather than the purchaser. Actually, the Board recognized this problem and gave approval for travel agents to bill customers for services rendered beyond the simple sale of the airline ticket.[103] The destructive

---

99. On this also see Linda Kleiger, "Maximization of Industry Profits: The Case of United States Air Transportation" (Ph.D. dissertation, University of California, Los Angeles, 1967).

100. See CAB Order 70-12-165 (Dec. 31, 1970), p. 6.

101. Ibid., p. 17.

102. Ibid., p. 9.

103. Ibid., p. 33. Of course one would expect repeat customers to be able to judge for themselves whether they are being well served by a specific travel agent.

competition point is likewise fallacious. A counter-example demonstrates. Generically, travel agents' commissions and advertising expenditures are the same: both are nonprice means of attracting passengers. Yet, one does not observe destructive competition in airline advertising, and there is no reason to believe that travel agents' commissions are any less characteristic of diminishing returns.

To the Board's credit, it has ordered an investigation of the ATCA, especially its bylaws relating to unanimous approval by member carriers of all agreements. This rule is alleged to further restrain the level of commissions paid.[104] Also, in the order approving the latest ATCA agreement, the Board rejected a proposal to limit entry among travel agents selling airline services.[105] However, it should be obvious that the Board plays a necessary cooperative role in the industry's collusion over rates paid to travel agents.

Extra-Legal Collusion

Extra-legal collusion has not played an obvious role in the airlines. To the best of the authors' knowledge, with one minor exception, the airlines have never been prosecuted for a violation of the antitrust laws.[106] An agreement in restraint of trade can be prosecuted unless it has been immunized by the Board under section 412 of the Federal Aviation Act, but extra-legal agreements are very difficult to uncover, much less to prove.

On the other hand, there are many instances of what *appears* to be collusive behavior by air carriers.[107] A typical scenario for an industry-wide

---

Also, the same problem arises when an individual calls an airline for reservations: the carrier called has an incentive to route the passenger over his flights, not necessarily at the passenger's convenience.

104. See CAB Order 71-6-127 (June 24, 1971).

105. See CAB Order 70-12-165, p. 36.

106. In 1963 the Supreme Court remanded to the CAB a determination of whether Pan American, in setting up Panagra, Inc., in the 1920s, had acted in the public interest. This case, presented by the Justice Department on behalf of the Board, was decided on section 2 of the Sherman Act. See 371 U.S. 296 (1963); 193 F. Supp. 18.

107. For example, until recently American Airlines was considered to be the industry price leader. For a discussion of price leadership and the tradition of carrier unanimity on fare changes, see Paul W. Cherington, *Airline Price Policy: A Study of Domestic Airline Passenger Fares* (Harvard University, Graduate School of Business Administration, 1958), pp. 410–14. In the Domestic Passenger Fare Investigation, however, American proposed an unconventional fare scheme, rejected by the other carriers. For a discussion, see the next chapter.

fare increase is that following a downturn in industry profits, airline presidents will begin issuing public statements to the effect that the industry needs additional revenue to survive. The ATA will decry the Board's "undue inflexibility" over rates and will point to the industry's historical gap between actual return on investment and that termed reasonable by the Board. More publicity will surround carrier financial needs, with various proposals being discussed in the trade press and at professional meetings. Then, some carrier, usually American, will propose a specific fare increase to the Board. Almost immediately, other carriers will follow suit, matching the original proposal in all of its details.[108]

Aside from what appears to be implicit collusion over fares, there is evidence in some markets which gives the appearance of carrier collusion over service quality. For example, Christopher Barnekov has compiled indexes of market competitiveness which incorporate both the average yield (in relation to a cohort city-pair) and service quality (measured by the inverse of load factor). His results are consistent with expectation: on average, the greater the number of carriers in a market, the more competitive it is. Also, interestingly enough, the results show that when comparisons are made among city-pair markets having the same number of competitors, some are very close to the competitive norm, whereas others are much further away (toward monopoly price and output). This leads Barnekov to suggest that "on certain of the routes the carriers may have been able to reach some sort of (tacit or explicit) agreement not to compete."[109]

It should be recalled that even in purely competitive theory firms act in concert. The difference is that purely competitive firms presume that individually they have no control over prices, output, or quality. The real question is whether air carriers collude outside CAB sanction and have an impact on market equilibrium. As for the first part of that question, the evidence is suggestive of collusion, but this is difficult if not impossible to prove. As for the second, the carriers' mediocre profit showing during the last decade raises great doubts about the payoffs to whatever extra-legal collusive activities may have taken place. Probably, if and where extra-legal collusion has had an impact it has been in terms of decreased technical efficiency and perversions in the price-quality options.

108. The Board does not always respond favorably, and when it does it often responds very slowly.
109. Christopher Barnekov, Memorandum to Lee W. Huff of the U.S. Department of Transportation (April 6, 1972).

Effects of Regulation on Airline Costs

CAB regulation can affect the costs of air service in several ways. First, constraint of entry into city-pair markets protects inefficient carriers at the expense of more aggressive ones; thus, costs are higher than they would be otherwise. Second, the restraint on entry of new firms into the industry has perhaps precluded service by operators which would have been more efficient than some existing carriers. Third, regulation may have led to labor costs which are higher than under a regime of free competition. Finally, the Board's policy of discouraging price competition has resulted in excessive service competition, driving up average cost still further. In this section we shall discuss some of the available evidence shedding light on these cost effects.

Relative Carrier Costs

In a study prepared by one of the authors for the U.S. Department of Transportation, an attempt was made to estimate relative carrier efficiency.[110] With the adaptation of a methodology described by Robert J. Gordon,[111] comparisons were made between actual costs per available ton-mile (ATM) and such costs as derived from a cost function estimated by applying regression analysis to trunk carrier data pooled over the period 1962–70. (See the appendix to this chapter.)

It may be recalled from the discussion of scale economies in Chapter 2 that carrier costs may be explained by several factors, primary of which is average stage length. Since the Board determines which routes each carrier may serve, stage length is largely beyond carrier management control. Also, to a great extent the size of operations and route density are independently determined. Finally, since the carriers face a fairly homogeneous resource market (aircraft, labor, and so forth), these costs too are largely beyond management's control. If it were possible to adjust for these factors, then we would have an index for comparing carrier costs on a standardized basis, the presumption being that after such adjustments are made, any

110. See "Testimony of James C. Miller III," CAB Docket 21866-7, Exhibit DOT-T-1 (Aug. 25, 1970).

111. Robert J. Gordon, "Airline Costs and Managerial Efficiency," in *Transportation Economics,* A Conference of the Universities–National Bureau Committee for Economic Research (Columbia University Press for the National Bureau of Economic Research, 1965), pp. 61–94.

divergence between actual cost and estimated or standardized cost can be attributed to carrier efficiency or inefficiency.[112]

Such a comparison is shown in Table 7-5. The method employed was to take the regression equation described in the appendix to this chapter and then calculate from the relationship what each carrier's cost would have been (given its available ton-miles, average stage length, and market density) had it conformed to the level of cost estimated by the equation to be a feasible opportunity. This estimated cost level was then compared with the carrier's actual cost level to form an inefficiency index (calculated by dividing actual cost by estimated cost and multiplying by 100). Thus, a number greater than 100 in the table indicates that the carrier during that year had costs greater than the estimated level. Similarly, a number under 100, such as 98, indicates that the carrier during that year had only 98 percent of the estimated cost. Thus, in essence, the indexes reflect the technical efficiency of the carrier during that year *relative* to the technical efficiency of all trunk carriers.

Our theory of the effects of regulation would imply that carriers protected from competition would be inefficient relative to those facing more severe competitive tests. However, a comparison of Tables 7-3 and 7-5 fails to reveal any strong relationship. Take, for example, the indexes and competitive percentages for 1970 (see Table 7-5). The average trunk-line competitive percentage for 1970 is 76.5. Among those carriers having a higher than average competitive percentage two had inefficiency indexes greater than 100, and three had indexes lower than 100.

Perhaps several factors are at play here. First, as discussed in the appendix, the results shown in Table 7-5 must be considered as no more than a first-cut attempt to quantify relative carrier costs. More sophisticated techniques may reveal considerable error in the rankings shown in the table. Second, everything else equal, less competitive markets have higher load factors. Since the regression equation used cost per available ton-mile (vis-à-vis revenue ton-mile), one would anticipate that average costs for such markets would be higher since they would include higher traffic expenses per ATM. Moreover, as was pointed out by Robert S. Villanueva, everything else equal, expenses per passenger are higher in competitive

---

112. Other variables that may affect average costs yet are beyond the control of the individual carrier include the effects of weather, a preponderance of high-cost markets in a carrier's route structure, and constraints on aircraft routing (such as excess circuity).

Table 7-5. Actual Unit Cost per Available Ton-Mile as Percent of Standard Unit Cost, 1962–70, and Percent of Revenue Passenger-Miles in Competitive Markets, 1970, by Domestic Trunk Air Carriers

Carrier	1962	1963	1964	1965	1966	1967	1968	1969	1970	Percent of revenue passenger-miles in competitive markets, 1970
American	115	113	112	113	102	99	100	98	95	83.0
Eastern	93	92	96	103	113	107	113	108	104	76.6
Trans World	115	111	113	112	114	113	111	112	109	91.1
United	103	106	101	101	107	103	103	99	97	67.5
Braniff	93	96	99	107	106	109	113	112	106	66.0
Continental	84	88	90	75	70	76	87	89	90	79.4
Delta	105	105	102	100	100	101	100	93	84	67.9
National	88	89	89	86	86	91	88	89	99	89.1
Northeast	115	127	118	119	116	120	100	119	116	88.9
Northwest	97	86	86	80	81	77	78	77	94	63.5
Western	95	89	96	101	102	a	108	108	113	73.4

Sources: Appendix to Chapter 7 and Table 7-3.
a. Not computed because of Western's merger with Pacific Northern in 1967.

markets because of nonprice competition in dimensions other than scheduling.[113]

In summary, the information contained in Table 7-5 must be interpreted with a great deal of caution. The method employed, however, does represent a significant advance over typical industry efficiency discussions which merely compare cost per ATM, unadjusted for important route and service characteristics. As for the hypothesis that protected carriers have higher costs, the evidence neither confirms nor rejects it. Perhaps in the future the Board's staff and other researchers will give this issue more attention and will be able to apply more sophisticated tests.

Regulated and Nonregulated Carrier Costs

For many years economists have argued that regulation results in great technical inefficiency in commercial air transport and that fares would be much lower under less regulation. Two studies referred to earlier provide estimates of this differential between fare and cost—the studies by Jordan and Keeler.[114]

Jordan's method compares the formerly lightly regulated California intrastate carriers and the domestic trunks.[115] It should be stressed that in the major California intrastate markets the intrastate carriers offer service comparable with that of the interstate trunks. They fly the same types of aircraft, they offer substantially the same on-board services, and they serve the same airports. Yet a comparison between the coach fares actually available in the major California intrastate markets during 1965 and fares that would have existed had CAB regulation applied to those markets shows that coach fares for similar interstate markets would have been between 32 and 47 percent lower than the CAB-regulated fares then in effect.[116]

113. "Rebuttal Testimony of Robert S. Villanueva," CAB Docket 21866-7, Exhibit TWA R-T-A (Sept. 22, 1970).

114. Jordan, *Airline Regulation in America*; and Theodore E. Keeler, "Airline Regulation and Market Performance," *Bell Journal of Economics and Management Science*, Vol. 3 (Autumn 1972), pp. 399–424.

115. Until 1965 the California Public Utilities Commission (CPUC) regulated intrastate carrier rates but not entry. Moreover, rate regulation was in the form of maximum rates, not minimums. Since 1965 the CPUC has granted route protection to established intrastate carriers.

116. Jordan, *Airline Regulation in America*, p. 111. (Also see Table 4-1 above.) Jordan also compared regulated and unregulated carriers in terms of real resource utilization (Chap. 11).

Theodore Keeler adopted a different approach, first estimating a synthetic cost function for airline service and then asserting that under deregulated conditions fares would be equal to average costs. A comparison between these estimated deregulated fares and actual trunkline fares for 1968 yields a markup for regulated fares over unregulated fares of between 20 percent for short-haul markets and 95 percent for long-haul markets.

For two important reasons the results of Jordan and Keeler overestimate what would appear to be the technical inefficiency of regulated carriers. First, the unregulated-carrier load factors are higher than in regulated markets.[117] In other words, if the unregulated fares were computed on a regulated-market load factor basis, the cost difference would be much smaller. Second, the fare comparisons do not adjust for the fact that average yield for trunk carriers is considerably less than the standard fare because of the widespread use of discount fares. Thus, the average fare for regulated carriers is lower than that used for comparison. Third, the Keeler cost estimates are based on the exclusive use of the latest, most productive aircraft. While a competitive market would bring about the adoption of the most productive technology, in an industry where productivity increases through changing technology are predictable, the opportunity cost of using capital of any vintage would reflect the anticipated obsolescence.

In summary, these two studies, while certainly implying a substantial technical efficiency difference between regulated and unregulated carriers, do not necessarily prove the point.

This does not exempt the regulated carriers from criticism, however.[118] As Jordan realized, something of value is purchased for the higher interstate fare—a higher service quality.[119] The relevant question is whether the extra quality is worth the extra cost. Applying the characteristics of the California intrastate markets to the relationships developed in our optimal load factor model outlined in Chapter 6, it appears that the unregulated California markets come much closer to matching service quality and price

117. In 1964 and 1965, California intrastate load factors averaged 74.9 percent and 63.3 percent respectively (Jordan, *Airline Regulation in America*, p. 202). Keeler assumed a 60 percent load factor in his cost estimations. Both authors (especially Keeler) refer to low load factors as indicative of management inefficiency (Jordan, ibid., pp. 200–08; and Keeler, "Airline Regulation," pp. 414–19). This contrasts quite markedly with our theory which makes equilibrium load factors a function of exogenously determined fares.

118. Recall too the question of inflated labor costs due to regulation discussed in connection with the mutual aid pact.

119. Jordan, *Airline Regulation in America*, p. 227.

with passenger preferences. The reason is that in a deregulated market carriers have the option of competing on the basis of price as well as service. Thus, it would appear that the major cost of regulation is a non-optimal price-quality mix. Technical inefficiency is important, too, although less measurable, and both costs could be reduced by allowing more freedom of entry and encouraging price competition.[120]

Appendix: Airline Cost Model for Relative Efficiency Comparisons

In this model we hypothesized that three variables—available ton-miles ATM, average stage length LEN, and market density DEN (available ton-miles per route-mile operated)—are important in explaining average cost (operating expense per available ton-mile). Moreover, we assumed that in each case the relation (if one existed) would be curvilinear, so the log forms of these three independent variables were used in estimating the effects on average cost.

Regressions were performed on airline data by carrier and by year, 1962–70.[121] This technique of "pooling" cross-section and time series data has limitations.[122] For example, if the data (with transformations) are heteroscedastic, then ordinary least squares will underestimate the standard errors. On the other hand, the lack of change in route-miles operated from year to year gives rise to multicollinearity problems between ATM and

---

120. Inferences about the effects of regulation might also be drawn from two foreign experiences. In one study, David G. Davies contrasts Australia's two airlines—one publicly owned, the other private: "The Efficiency of Public Versus Private Firms: The Case of Australia's Two Airlines," *Journal of Law and Economics,* Vol. 14 (April 1971), pp. 149–65. Davies finds that uniformly the private airline is more efficient than its public cohort. In a second study, Michael H. Cooper and Alan Maynard ("The Effect of Regulated Competition on Scheduled Air Fares," *Journal of Transport Economics and Policy,* Vol. 6 [May 1972], pp. 167–75) found that scheduled air fares in the United Kingdom are maintained at excessive levels, but that "scheduled operators respond to charter competition by lowering fares." (Ibid., p. 174.)

121. The data are taken from CAB, *Handbook of Airline Statistics, 1971,* Pts. 3, 4.

122. See Pietro Balestra and Marc Nerlove, "Pooling Cross Section and Time Series Data in the Estimation of a Dynamic Model: The Demand for Natural Gas," *Econometrica,* Vol. 34 (July 1966), pp. 585–612.

DEN; this leads to an overestimation of coefficient variance. Also, one presumes that the nature of the cost function does not change over time. This, of course, is a stringent assumption. Even so, data pooling was used because outliers have less effect the greater the number of observations and because with only eleven trunk carriers one is highly constrained by degrees of freedom.

Regressions were performed with three different dependent variables: (a) total operating expense per available ton-mile (*TOE*/*ATM*), (b) direct operating expense (sum of flying operations, direct maintenance, and flight equipment depreciation) per available ton-mile (*DOE*/*ATM*), and (c) indirect operating expense (total operating expense minus direct operating expense) per available ton-mile (*IOE*/*ATM*).[123] In addition to the *ATM*, *LEN*, and *DEN* variables, eight zero-one "dummy" variables were used in an attempt to separate out the effects of year-to-year changes in costs due either to improved technology (assumed to be neutral), which would decrease cost, or inflation (again neutral), which would raise cost.

Results of the regressions are shown in Table 7-6. The *F*-statistic for each equation is significant at the 0.01 level, meaning generally that a definite relationship exists between average cost and the independent variables taken together (though not necessarily individually). The highest coefficient of determination (corrected *R*-square) occurs in estimating *DOE*/*ATM* (regression 2), suggesting that 69 percent of the observed variations in this average cost category can be attributed to the eleven independent variables. The lowest coefficient of determination occurs when estimating *IOE*/*ATM*, and here the suggestion is that only 19 percent of the observed variations in this average cost category may be attributed to the independent variables.

The coefficients of the dummy variables (1963 . . . 1970) show, ceteris paribus, a falling level of (average) cost over the time period under review. However, the *t*-ratios of these dummy variables are not very high, suggesting that for some years their effect is not significantly different from zero. On the other hand, the *t*-ratios of the *LEN* variable are all significant (even at a 0.001 level), and, as expected, the coefficient signs are all negative. Finally, the signs of the *DEN* coefficients are all positive, meaning that given stage length and given total *ATM*s, an increase in market density

---

123. In computations, *ATM* was divided by 1,000; *LEN* was multiplied by 1,000; and *DEN* was multiplied by 10. The regression equations shown in Table 7-6 reflect these adjustments.

Table 7-6. Regression Results for Average Direct and Indirect Operating Costs, Domestic Trunk Air Carriers

Variable and regression statistic	Operating expense per available ton-mile[a]		
	Total, TOE/ATM (regression 1)	Direct, DOE/ATM (regression 2)	Indirect, IOE/ATM (regression 3)
Variable			
Intercept	84.6	42.8	41.8
Dummy			
1963	−1.28	−0.76	−0.52
	(−1.04)	(−1.66)	(−0.58)
1964	−2.74	−1.80	−0.94
	(−2.21)	(−3.87)	(−1.05)
1965	−3.42	−2.42	−1.00
	(−2.71)	(−5.13)	(−1.10)
1966	−3.11	−2.51	−0.60
	(−2.43)	(−5.23)	(−0.65)
1967	−3.86	−2.70	−1.16
	(−2.85)	(−5.31)	(−1.19)
1968	−4.52	−3.11	−1.41
	(−3.36)	(−6.17)	(−1.45)
1969	−3.76	−2.62	−1.15
	(−2.79)	(−5.19)	(−1.18)
1970	−0.97	−1.26	0.28
	(−0.70)	(−2.43)	(0.28)
Available ton-miles (log)	−0.36	−0.51	0.16
	(−0.39)	(−1.50)	(0.24)
Average stage length (log)	−12.16	−5.94	−6.22
	(−6.67)	(−8.69)	(−4.71)
Market density (log)	3.18	1.82	1.35
	(2.12)	(3.24)	(1.25)
Regression statistic			
Corrected R^2	0.46	0.69	0.19
F-statistic	8.5	21.0	3.1
Standard error of estimate	2.88	1.08	2.08
Degrees of freedom	86	86	86

Source: Basic data, covering 1962–70, are from CAB, *Handbook of Airline Statistics, 1971*, Pts. 3 and 4.
a. The numbers in parentheses are *t*-ratios.

(scheduling the same *ATM*s but reducing route-miles operated and serving more intensively those remaining) results in an increase in average cost.[124]

Regression 1 was used to derive "firm effects" for the carriers for each year, 1962–70, and the results can be found in Table 7-5. The residuals

124. Given the opposite effects of *ATM* and *DEN*, it is extremely important to postulate just how output is to expand before making any judgment as to returns to

were thus presumed to represent relative inefficiency (in positive cases) or relative efficiency (in negative cases). However, given the limitations of the pooling technique, given the relatively high level of unexplained variation (for instance, 54 percent for TOE/ATM), and given other frailties of the model (for instance, the noninclusion of service quality characteristics), these results should be viewed with considerable reservation. In particular, one should be wary of comparing the efficiency of any two particular carriers, especially in cases where their markets and operating characteristics are grossly dissimilar.

---

scale. To illustrate with an example taken from an earlier regression including only 1962–68 data, suppose that in 1968 a typical trunk line (as represented by the mean values) had increased ATMs 10 percent proportionately over the same routes. Thus, average stage length would have remained unchanged, but market density would have been increased 10 percent because of the 10 percent increase in ATMs. The result (from the equation) would have been an increase in TOE/ATM from 20.8 cents per ATM to 21.0 cents, an increase of 1 percent. On the other hand, if ATMs had been increased by expanding to new routes (LEN and DEN remaining unchanged), then TOE/ATM (according to the equation) would have fallen by \$0.00063, a reduction of approximately one-third of 1 percent. See "Testimony of James C. Miller III," CAB Docket 21866-7, Exhibit DOT-T-1 (Aug. 25, 1970), pp. 25, 26.

CHAPTER EIGHT

Theory Confronts Policy: The Domestic Passenger Fare Investigation

THE POLICY of a regulatory agency is primarily the outcome of the dynamic process of interpreting the governing statutes as they apply in specific situations. It reflects (a) powers and responsibilities bestowed on the agency by statutes, (b) policy directives explicit or implicit in the statutes, and (c) the pattern of regulation that is practiced. A regulator's policy is really delineated by its practices, which, of course, must be consistent with statutory authority and justifiable in terms of its policy directives.

Just as in civil and criminal law, the importance of decisions in individual regulatory cases in molding policy should not be underestimated. Since the Board is loath to have its decisions overturned in the courts, it tends to render individual judgments consistent with earlier ones which were successful in meeting court tests. Occasionally, however, the Board will institute an investigation of a particularly troublesome issue and will call into question prior precedent. The Board feels confident in taking this initiative since a precedent-breaking decision is unlikely to be overturned if it is reached upon a full and impartial hearing of the evidence and is conducted in accord with the governing statutes.[1]

The CAB's most important challenge to prior precedent is the Domestic Passenger Fare Investigation (DPFI) initiated in 1970.[2] In it, Board policy in nearly every area of fare regulation was open to reassessment. For several reasons this case is worth summarizing and bringing to the atten-

1. The Board may be relatively confident of successfully defending precedent-breaking decisions whether the rationale for change be an admission of error in the former decisions, or that the former decisions no longer apply because conditions have changed.
2. CAB Docket 21866, instituted by CAB Order 70-1-147 (Jan. 29, 1970).

tion of regulatory economists and practitioners. First, it indicates a new direction for CAB fare policy. Second, it shows how the direction of CAB policy can be changed and on what grounds change can be justified. Third, it provides a case study of how economic analysis, forcefully advocated by another government agency (in this instance, the U.S. Department of Transportation), may have had an impact on a regulatory agency. Finally, the model of industry behavior discussed in the case and ultimately adopted by the Board should have broad application to other quasi-competitive industries under economic regulation.

A matter of perspective should be noted at the outset. The authors participated in the DPFI as expert witnesses for the U.S. Department of Transportation (DOT), and in that capacity presented materials and advocated positions consistent with maximizing economic efficiency, given the regulatory framework and given the scope of the proceeding.[3] Our presentation in that case is emphasized in the discussion to follow.[4] Second, although we were associated with the winning side on most major issues, we cannot assess whether, in general, our economics won out because it was better, or because of luck, underlying forces, political influence of the participants, or greater persuasive powers. However, because of this relative success, we may tend to overstate what we have perceived as a new, relatively enlightened policy direction. It must be kept in mind that just as a plaintiff can and usually will sue on all grounds he thinks relevant,[5] the Board will attempt to justify its decisions with a multitude of reasons.[6] Consequently, each of the decisions rendered in this case expresses numerous justifications in addition to those we cite. As they pertain to economic analysis, however, they are generally consistent with essential points sum-

3. The authors do not necessarily endorse all the presentations made by the department in that proceeding, nor, of course, should the authors' writings necessarily be interpreted as representing departmental policy.

4. For a summary of the positions of the various parties in the case, see James C. Miller III, "The Domestic Passenger Fare Investigation and the Future of CAB Regulation" (paper delivered at a seminar on Problems of Regulation and Public Utilities, Dartmouth College, 1971; processed).

5. For example, an airline may petition the Board to suspend or find unlawful a competitor's fare reduction under sections 404(b) (Discrimination), 411 ([Unfair] Methods of Competition), and 1002(d) (reasonableness, and so forth) of the Federal Aviation Act.

6. In other words, the Board will give reasons A, B, and C for a decision, even though each may appear to be separately sufficient. The reason is that should the decision be challenged in court it is hoped that at least one of the justifications will hold up.

marized. In any event, we do not mean to imply that the Board's decisions in this case can serve either to confirm or to question the validity of our economic analysis.

A related issue is the permanency of this new policy direction. Since Board decisions are rendered in closed sessions, the public does not necessarily learn the real reasons for the positions chosen. Since professional staff members draft the decisions and since their job is to write a tight opinion that will stand up in court, the underlying rationale may never show through. In short, it is hazardous to impute to Board members the same decision calculus expressed in the formal decision. Thus, while it might appear that the Board has moved toward a policy consistent with economic efficiency, this change may have been simply expedient. If so, then if certain conditions change, Board policy may too. In fact, as we shall describe later, one already may observe the Board's retreat from the DPFI findings.

Nature of the DPFI

The Domestic Passenger Fare Investigation is the Board's second general, in-depth investigation of airline pricing policies. The first was held over the period 1956–60, and became known as the General Passenger Fare Investigation (GPFI).[7] It was brought on principally by congressional pressure to see that the Board correctly discharged its rate-making responsibilities, by carrier filings for fare increases during the 1951–56 period, and by the Board's need to determine what kind of fare increase, if any, might be warranted and what standards should be adopted to judge future fare filings.

Although considerable resources were devoted to the GPFI, the results were disappointing because little was decided. In brief, the final conclusions were (a) the reasonable rate of return on investment in commercial aviation is 10.5 percent,[8] and (b) the overall fare level should reflect the costs the

7. For a thorough review of the GPFI, see Emmette S. Redford, "The General Passenger Fare Investigation," in Edwin A. Bock (ed.), *Government Regulation of Business: A Casebook* (Prentice-Hall, 1965). The Board's final decision in the case was issued on November 25, 1960, and is contained in Order E-16068 (Nov. 25, 1960).

8. After taxes, but before interest payment on debt. The investment base was taken to be equity plus long-term debt. An operating ratio approach to reasonable return was explicitly rejected.

carriers actually incur in providing service.[9] These limited findings subsequently circumscribed CAB fare policy throughout the 1960s.

What brought on the DPFI was almost surely the Moss Case of 1970.[10] When the airlines' profits began falling in 1969, the Board, concerned about the carriers' plight, began holding ex parte informal meetings to work out alternative solutions. A group of congressmen, headed by John E. Moss, Democrat from California, complained of these actions and requested at minimum permission to attend. This petition was rejected. Subsequently, the carriers filed new fare increases. Although the Board rejected this proposal, it in turn indicated a fare formula based on mileage that would be acceptable. The carriers then filed the formula suggested by the Board.

The Moss petitioners carried this action to court, arguing that in its haste to be responsive to the carriers, the Board had ignored certain statutory requirements. Partly in an effort to relieve public pressure and partly, perhaps, to affect the outcome of the court's decision, the Board announced the DPFI on January 29, 1970, citing as reason "an exploration of the issues raised by the [Moss Group]."[11]

In its written opinion, the court scolded the Board for its "blatant attempt to subvert the [Federal Aviation Act]" and for an "intimation . . . that its responsibilities to the carriers are more important than its responsibilities to the public."[12] The court further declared the fares that had been approved by the Board unlawful because of procedure and remanded the case to the Board for further proceedings. The Board then merged certain of the court-raised issues into the DPFI, and announced a separate investigation to determine the lawfulness of the fares then in effect.[13]

The order defining the scope of the DPFI set forth nine separate

9. An attempt by the Board's Bureau of Air Operations to incorporate load factor standards was contemplated but rejected.

10. *John E. Moss et al.* v. *Civil Aeronautics Board.* For a summary of this case, see Judge J. Skelly Wright's opinion in the unanimous decision rendered in the U.S. Court of Appeals for the District of Columbia Circuit, No. 23,627, decided July 9, 1970, reprinted in the *Congressional Record,* Vol. 116, Pt. 17, 91 Cong. 2 sess. (1970), pp. 23575–79.

Certain issues in the DPFI would have been reviewed anyway. For example, the Board was under court order to reassess the lawfulness of youth discount fares, and an investigation of joint fares had already been instituted.

11. CAB Order 70-1-147, p. 2.

12. *Congressional Record,* Vol. 116, Pt. 17, p. 23577.

13. CAB Docket 23140. The Board has since determined that the fares charged during this period were not, in fact, unjust and unreasonable. See CAB Order 73-7-39 (July 13, 1973). However, this case is now in the court of appeals.

phases:[14] (1) Aircraft Depreciation, (2) Leased Aircraft, (3) Deferred Federal Income Taxes, (4) Joint Fares, (5) Discount Fares, (6) Load Factor and Seating Configuration,[15] (7) Fare Level, (8) Rate of Return, and (9) Fare Structure. The first three phases would be handled by rule-making proceedings, with the remaining six scheduled for public hearing.[16]

Cases involving airline fares are, by convention, broken down into issues involving fare level, or average yield, and fare structure, or the relationship one fare has to another. The fare level issues in the DPFI are contained primarily in phases 1, 2, 3, 6, 7, and 8. Fare structure issues are the principal subjects of phases 4, 5, and 9.

Fare Level Issues[17]

Essentially the Board's responsibility in the fare level phases of the DPFI was to decide between two opposing regulatory philosophies. The traditional industry view held that the Board's function is to determine the actual, or reasonable, costs of performing service and then to regulate fares to cover these costs. This meant, in essence, observing whether the carriers' rate of return was excessive or insufficient, and then, based in part on predicted costs and revenues, regulating fare levels (taking into account demand price elasticity) in such a way as to match total revenues with total costs, including a reasonable return on investment.[18] The proponents of this position based their case primarily on section 1002(e)(5) of the Federal Aviation Act, which states that the Board must take into consideration "the need of each air carrier for revenue sufficient to enable such air carrier, under honest, economical, and efficient management, to provide adequate and efficient air carrier service." Oversimplifying a bit, the carriers argued that unless the Board could prove dishonesty or gross inefficiency, it had

14. CAB Order 70-2-121 (Feb. 26, 1970), p. 2.

15. By Order 70-11-91 (Nov. 19, 1970) the Board separated phase 6 into phase 6A, Seating Configuration, and phase 6B, Load Factor.

16. Rule-making proceedings involve only exchange of written communication. Public hearings involve cross-examination of witnesses before an administrative law judge (formerly "hearing examiner"), and usually, though not always, oral argument before the full Board (see the appendix at the end of the book).

17. In this overview we shall skip phases 1, 2, and 3. For a summary of the decisions in these phases see Miller, "Domestic Passenger Fare Investigation."

18. The Board's existing policy toward fare level regulation may also be characterized as attempting to match revenues with predicted costs, including a reasonable return on investment (see Order E-16068). Although the Board retained the right to disallow certain costs from inclusion in the rate base, it never went so far as attempting to regulate the level of output and the overall quality of service.

to accept carrier costs as being justified and therefore had no choice but to adjust revenues to cover the costs of whatever levels and qualities of output the carriers anticipated providing.

The alternative view held that the Board need not accept carrier costs as sole evidence of a reasonable fare level. Its advocates took several different perspectives. Some simply argued that "the public should not be made to pay for excess capacity," as evidenced by aircraft flying on average less than half-filled. Some suggested that carriers be penalized for flying excess schedules by not counting in their rate base the costs of flights averaging less than some minimum load factor. The Department of Transportation argued that load factor and service quality are, in fact, endogenous to the market equilibrium—that once price is determined, nonprice competition (primarily in the form of schedule frequency) results in a (zero excess-profit) market equilibrium quality of service. Moreover, the department implied that the Board's preoccupation with determining and aggregating the carriers' costs and with adjusting fares so that revenues will match these estimated costs not only constitutes a naive and basically incorrect interpretation of airline industry competitive dynamics but overshadows the trade-off between price and quality which should be of crucial concern. In short, the department argued that the appropriate fare level depends on an estimate of the optimal feasible combination of fare and quality.

In the end, the Board accepted an endogenous quality-of-service model consistent with the analysis presented in this book. Recall from Chapter 4 the model of nonprice competition in the industry, particularly the trade-off between fare level and equilibrium load factor (Figure 4-2). Compare this with the Board's phase 6 opinion:

We find, as DOT has stated, that the higher the fare level in relation to cost, the more capacity carriers will offer and the lower load factors will be; and, conversely, the lower the fare level, the less capacity carriers will operate and the higher load factors will be.[19]

In any given market, the carrier with the greatest number of schedules will normally carry the largest number of passengers. Thus, the desire to maximize market participation creates powerful incentives to add capacity. The countervailing incentive is supplied only by the imperative of economics: Schedules cannot be added indefinitely if the load factors achieved are insufficient, at the prevailing fare levels, to permit the carriers to cover costs and return a profit.[20]

This decision, which reversed the recommended opinion of the administrative law judge, clearly breaks with tradition.

19. CAB Order 71-4-54 (April 9, 1971), p. 23.
20. Ibid., p. 5.

Of course, a load factor standard must presume something about aircraft seating density. The Board's preliminary decision on this issue did not employ the model of nonprice competition and basically was inconsistent with the decisions rendered in other phases. Rather then basing fares on a standard load factor which, in turn, assumes some representative seating density, the Board announced that if carriers wished to configure their aircraft at lower than standard seating densities, they would have to collect minimum surcharges.[21] In its final order on the seating question, however, the Board changed its mind. It reverted to the model of nonprice competition, saying that it would base fares on standard seating densities and would not require surcharges.[22] Interestingly, the Board also stated that it would be receptive to proposals for fare reductions by carriers which chose to remove their coach lounges and utilize the higher-density standard seating.[23] Under this provision TWA was successful in reducing its one-way coach fare between New York and Los Angeles by $10 for aircraft not having coach lounges.[24]

In its decision on rate of return, the Board similarly accepted the model of nonprice competition outlined earlier and took due notice of the potential destabilizing effects of a policy of attempting to regulate rate of return through changes in fares. As explained in Chapter 4, if the Board attempts to regulate carrier rate of return at some level other than the weighted average of carriers' required internal rate of return, then such attempts will be frustrated by variations in equilibrium load factor and other service quality dimensions. Thus, much less important than the rate of return actually deemed reasonable (the Board settled on 12 percent[25]) is the man-

21. CAB Order 71-4-48 (April 8, 1971).

22. CAB Order 72-5-101 (May 26, 1972).

23. The petitioning carrier also had to prove that as a result of utilizing the higher-density configuration it was sustaining a significant adverse competitive impact from carriers which had retained their lounges and charged the established fare.

24. See CAB Order 73-1-69 (Jan. 23, 1973). Also see CAB Order 73-6-102 (June 26, 1973) clarifying the Board's position on such fare differentials. It might be noted that Continental Air Lines has taken this case to court, arguing that it should be allowed to match the $10 fare reduction and at the same time retain its coach lounges.

25. See CAB Order 71-4-58 (April 9, 1971). The figure of 12 percent appears to overestimate the carrier's actual cost of capital inasmuch as in making this assessment the Board utilized an optimal debt/equity ratio of 45/55 rather than the actual ratio of 60/40. Based on estimated costs of debt (6.20 percent) and equity (16.75 percent), using the actual debt/equity ratio would imply a reasonable return of only 10.42 percent.

ner in which the rate is to be regulated.[26] The Board realized the futility of attempting to regulate rate of return precisely and, in essence, decided to use the calculated reasonable rate only as an aid in imputing a normal profit "cost" to be covered by a reasonable fare level. To quote the Board,

The rates of return specified herein will be used as standards for measuring the reasonableness of the general domestic passenger-fare level. They are not in any sense to be regarded as guarantees that any individual carrier will earn the standard return in any given year or period of years, or that the industry as a whole will achieve the specified rates in particular periods.[27]

Furthermore, in its fare level decision, the Board said:

The fact that earnings in a particular year are either above or below the standard rate of return would not be an occasion for fare adjustments unless the fares were significantly out of line with those required to produce reasonable earnings at a standard load factor. The Board believes that a firm adherence to this policy will enable the industry, during representative periods, to cover its cost of capital and provide investors with reasonable compensation for the risks taken and permit the carriers to attract needed additional capital.[28]

As for the "ratchet" effect (Figure 4-2), the Board stated in its load factor decision:

Increasing the fare level for the purpose of achieving profitable operations at the lower load factor lowers the break-even load factor and thus encourages the addition of more capacity, leading again to lower profits and demands for further fare increases. It is obvious that the actual capacity scheduled by the carriers is not the proper basis for determining reasonable future fares and that it is the duty of the Board to establish reasonable load-factor standards in order to discourage the uneconomic cycle of excess capacity and higher fares.[29]

While it is clear that in the fare level issues the Board implicitly accepted the model of nonprice competition, in selecting the specific load factor standard it neither endorsed the model presented in Chapter 6, nor did it approach the question of the optimal combination of price and quality in a sophisticated way. In fact, the decisions contain little justification for the standard chosen: "For any fare-level adjustment that may be necessary at the conclusion of the *Fare Structure* phase, we intend to apply an overall trunk load-factor standard of 54 percent."[30]

26. Another reason we considered the actual rate chosen relatively unimportant is that since the airlines' ratio of yearly revenue to total investment exceeds unity, a given percentage change in the estimated reasonable rate of return would mean a smaller percentage change in the cost-recovery level of fares.

27. CAB Order 71-4-58, p. 3.

28. CAB Orders 71-4-59 and 71-4-60 (April 9, 1971), pp. 73, 74.

29. CAB Order 71-4-54, p. 21.

30. CAB Orders 71-4-59 and 71-4-60, p. 50.

The Board selected this particular standard primarily on the basis of calculations provided by its Bureau of Economics. In those, monopoly routes were presumed to attain load factors of 62 percent, and then an additional aircraft of average capacity for that route was added for each additional carrier in competitive markets.[31] Under these limiting assumptions, the average industry load factor was 54 percent. The 62 percent figure was argued to be feasible, having been attained during a number of preceding years, and yet not so high as to turn away too much traffic in monopoly markets. The resulting average of 54 percent was argued to be feasible and yet striking a balance between attainable economies of aircraft utilization and the availability of service.

Fare Structure Issues

As discussed in Chapter 5, efficient resource allocation requires not only that average fares be equal to marginal and average costs including a normal profit, but also that fares in individual markets approximate as closely as possible their respective marginal and average costs. In the order instituting the investigation, the Board appeared to endorse such a policy of efficient pricing in saying,

A fare structure that provides a closer relationship between the fares and the costs of service relating to various markets would also produce more equitable results among the carriers in terms of the ability of individual carriers to achieve a fair return on investment. Further, fares based upon reasonable costs and load factors would benefit the communities served by the carriers by discouraging uneconomic scheduling in some markets and encouraging a better balance of service on all the carriers' routes. The establishment of fares on an economic basis would also provide assistance in future determinations of the need for and adequacy of air service to various communities.[32]

Although it would be inaccurate to claim that the Board overwhelmingly endorsed efficient pricing for determining fare structure, on most of the major issues thus far decided it at least moved in this direction, sometimes breaking precedent with the past.

In the joint-fares phase of the DPFI, the major questions were: (a) what discount for through service should be allowed or required, and (b) in the event there is a discount, what constitutes a reasonable division among

31. No adjustment was made for the traffic-generating effect of additional flights and lower load factors (that is, decreased schedule delay).
32. CAB Order 70-1-147, p. 5.

carriers of the revenue collected from the traveler?[33] In its decision, the Board concluded that on average the carriers save $4 per interline connection. This saving accrues mainly from single ticketing and through-routing of baggage. Accordingly, the Board ordered carriers to provide a minimum $4 discount for each intercarrier connection. The Board also allowed larger discounts for "competitive" interline fares. (These are instances where two carriers, not certificated for direct service between two points, may match the direct-service fare of a third carrier.)

On the question of dividing joint-fare revenue among the participating carriers, the Board chose in principle to price according to the relative costs of providing the service:

It is an elementary principle of regulation that revenues be geared as closely as possible to the costs of service. With costs as the touchstone of regulation, efficiency is promoted, and inefficient misallocations of resources are discouraged; and as long as rewards are commensurate with reasonably attainable costs, sound economic conditions will be fostered.

Since the carriers' inputs of services in interline carriage are represented by the cost of service, a division formula which rewards each carrier in proportion to the cost of the services it provides . . . must be deemed to be a just, reasonable and equitable basis for divisions.[34]

In applying this principle, the Board adopted a line-haul cost formula developed by its Bureau of Economics as the standard for revenue division. Although certainly constituting a rough-and-ready approach, the essence of the joint-fare decision can be viewed as a proxy for efficient pricing.

The discount-fare question was an extremely sensitive one for the Board inasmuch as special favors had been given to young people, among others, and to withdraw this privilege would give the public appearance of being antiyouth. Furthermore, the Board would be reversing its previous endorsement of discounts, and this would require explicit justification. In spite of these difficulties, the Board did conclude such discounts to be unlawful. Reflecting the DOT arguments, the Board found in essence that discounts are instances of third degree price discrimination, that therefore they have

33. Joint fares are rates charged to passengers traveling over the lines of two or more carriers with a single ticket. An example would be a passenger flying from Los Angeles to Charlottesville, Virginia, via Washington, D.C. He might fly from Los Angeles to Washington on TWA, then transfer to Piedmont for the Washington–Charlottesville portion of the journey. At Los Angeles, he would buy a single ticket which might or might not include a "discount" on the sum of the normal Los Angeles–Washington and Washington–Charlottesville tariffs.

34. CAB Order 72-4-42 (April 10, 1972), p. 31.

significant allocative efficiency costs, and that the abolition of discount fares would bring a downward adjustment in the level of normal fares.

Portions of the discount fare decision are worth quoting:

Assuming that average seat-mile costs remain constant, the industry's break-even load factor levels will necessarily increase as average fares are reduced and will decrease if average fares increase.

The introduction of discount fares reduces the average fare, thus increasing the breakeven load factor. As the Department of Transportation has shown, if the discount fares have the effect of bringing the breakeven load factor above the actual load factor, then the carrier has two choices: either it must adjust its schedules in order to raise the actual load factor to breakeven or the fare level must be raised in order to lower the breakeven load factor. In either event, the normal-fare passenger is burdened. In the first instance, his fare remains the same but there will be fewer seats available to the normal-fare-paying passenger, and there will thus be a decline in the quality and adequacy of the services provided to the normal-fare payer, unaccompanied by any reduction in his fare. On the other hand, if the carrier increases its fares to cover the declining average yield, then the normal-fare payer is burdened by having to bear a fare increase in order to cover the short-fall created by the discount fares.[35]

The Board went on to say that promotional fares of a short-run duration (essentially those of a loss-leader, information-generating variety) would be permitted so long as they served their purpose and did not remain in effect for an extended period.[36]

To implement its findings, the Board declared that within an 18-month period all youth, family, and Discover America discount fares would have to be eliminated. Moreover, it recognized that it would be necessary to revise downward the level of normal fares and announced its intention to institute another proceeding which would determine the required readjustment.[37]

---

35. CAB Order 72-12-18 (Dec. 5, 1972), pp. 45, 46.

36. It is worth noting that in the discount-fare phase the Board drew tentative conclusions regarding scale economies of particular relevance to the question of airline mergers: "The effect of scale on the economics of airline operations was considered by the Department of Transportation. That party submitted evidence in support of the proposition that the airline industry is one of constant returns to scale. . . . No party has seriously challenged the DOT evidence, and without necessarily adopting its methodology and conclusions in all of its details, the Board finds that the general conclusions reached are sound." (Ibid., p. 48.)

37. Immediately after the Board's decision on discount fares a number of bills were introduced in Congress which would either grant the Board explicit authorization to approve discounts for youth, the elderly, and so on, or actually force the

The remaining fare structure issues were drawn into focus in the fare structure phase of the investigation. The most important issue concerned the appropriate fare taper. As indicated before, there is evidence that carriers are breaking even at various lengths of haul, given the present fare structure;[38] moreover, a change in fare structure within reasonable limits would, over time, result again in equilibrium for the various distances with zero excess profits. Given that in the short run costs are not very variable and that short-run demand is fairly inelastic, generally it would be to the advantage of a carrier to have its fares raised or for the fare structure to be altered so that fares rise for his weighted-average stage length. Such a fare increase would thus bring about excess profits until nonprice competition eliminated them.

As a whole, the carriers accepted as an article of faith that some fare formula based on mileage would be adopted in the proceeding.[39] Eight different fare formulas were advanced, with the remaining parties indicating a preference for one of these eight. Consistent with the point raised above, it is interesting to note that TWA, which has the longest average length of haul, proposed to reduce fare taper and raise fares noticeably in long-haul markets. Braniff, which has the shortest stage length, proposed to increase short-haul fares and decrease long-haul fares.

In its final decision in this phase, the Board concluded that "the statutory scheme is best served in the long run by a fare structure which conforms as closely as possible to costs—rather than one which merely uses costs as a point of departure for value-of-service adjustments."[40] Accordingly, the Board moved in the direction of increasing the fare taper, raising short-haul fares some 9 percent at 300 miles and lowering long-haul fares some 6 percent at 2,200 miles. Moreover, the Board announced its intention of making future adjustments in fare taper to conform fully with the taper of cost. According to the Board's figures this would mean a further increase

---

Board to have such fares reinstituted. To date, no formal action has been taken on such bills.

38. With the cost taper (for constant load factor) exceeding the fare taper, one would predict generally declining load factors with increasing distance. Such is the case—see Chapter 4, equations (1) and (2), and Figure 6-4.

39. Essentially a fixed charge plus a constant (or variable) rate per mile (see Figures 6-3 and 8-1).

40. CAB Order 74-3-82 (March 18, 1974), p. 68.

in short-haul fares on the order of 6 percent (at 300 miles) and a reduction in long-haul fares by some 3 percent (at 2,200 miles).[41]

Importantly, one reason the Board gave for basing the fare taper on the cost taper is that in its opinion cross-subsidy by length of haul is no longer in the public interest. Aside from the question of efficient resource allocation, the Board concluded that as a general proposition attempts to cross-subsidize prove fruitless inasmuch as the excess profits from long-haul service tend to be eliminated through excessive service and that in short-haul markets carriers simply curtail service in order to drive up actual load factors as a means of covering costs.[42]

Additional issues in this phase of the investigation were brought into focus. For example, should the fare taper incorporate the load factor standards which the Department of Transportation recommended as consistent with its estimated optimal level and structure of fares (Chapter 6)? Also, as DOT recommended, should peak-load pricing be encouraged to a greater degree? Should airports be encouraged to ration off landing slots and gates through the price mechanism? What are the appropriate relationships among fares for first class, coach, and economy services?

As for the question of load factor standards, the Board stated:

DOT argues that load factors should increase with distance, on the theory that as distance increases, the benefit to the passenger of having a lower fare at a higher load factor tends to outweigh his "time" cost of having a smaller number of flights to choose from (and thus having to wait longer for a flight), while at shorter lengths of haul a choice among more frequent flights would justify a higher-fare, low-load-factor service.

... DOT's analysis which ... attempts to define a reasonable trade-off between fares and quality of service from the *passenger's* viewpoint, has considerable theoretical merit. However, its application depends on a determination of the value passengers place on their time, and the record is not sufficient to support any findings on this crucial element of DOT's analysis. On the other hand, basing load-factor standards for structure purposes exclusively on historical patterns is an untenable alternative, because the historical patterns are necessarily influenced by the then-existing fare structure.[43]

For purposes of the proceeding the Board accepted the load factor standards suggested by its Bureau of Economics, "not as perfection, but as the

41. Ibid., p. 76.
42. Ibid., especially pp. 66–72.
43. Ibid., pp. 41, 42.

best approximation."[44] In effect, the Board left open the issue of optimal load factor standards by the expedient of finding the record "not sufficient."

On other issues, the Board found the record insufficient to make a determination of the reasonable off-peak fare to be charged for night-coach service and ordered a new investigation to answer this specific question.[45] Other peak–off-peak fares were considered but rejected.[46] The Board did, however, adjust the differential between first class and coach fares to reflect more fully the difference in cost: by July 1, 1976, first class fares must range from 150 to 163 percent of coach fares (depending on distance), up from the present, uniform 130 percent.[47] Finally, the Board concluded that the discount for economy service (primarily coach service without meal) must be no greater than $4.[48]

Measures to Increase Price Competition

One theme of this book is that the Board essentially sets price, albeit with help from the carriers, and then the carriers compete on quality of service, taking price as a parameter. The result is that the level and structure of price-quality options are not optimal—as best we can determine. Furthermore, in competitive markets there is little quality differentiation and practically no variation in combinations of price and quality, except for the difference between first class and coach service. If there were price competition, then market tests would lead to a more efficient level and structure of price and quality and also to more price-quality differentiation.

In the fare structure phase of the DPFI, proposals were advanced to promote price competition. Essentially, the idea was that the Board should establish a "zone of reasonableness" within which carrier fare filings would be per se or else prima facie reasonable.[49] This zone of fare flexibility would not be without the usual restraints on discrimination, preference, and

44. Ibid., p. 43.
45. Ibid., p. 146.
46. Ibid., p. 147.
47. Ibid., pp. 123–28.
48. Ibid., pp. 129–35.
49. Section 1002(d) of the Federal Aviation Act gives the Board the power to "determine and prescribe the lawful rate, fare, or charge (or the maximum or minimum, or *the maximum and minimum thereof*)" (emphasis added).

Figure 8-1. Zone of Reasonableness Proposal to Increase Price Competition among Air Carriers[a]

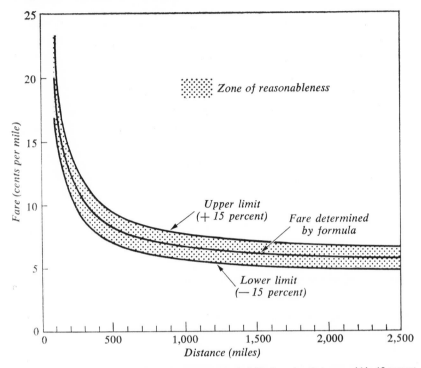

a. Under the proposal, changes in air fares initiated by individual carriers that were within 15 percent plus or minus of a predetermined fare formula would be considered reasonable and allowed to stand

prejudice; however, under the proposal, carriers could initiate limited fare changes without fear that they would be suspended and put down for investigation on grounds that the new fares were unreasonably high or unreasonably low.[50]

The zone of reasonableness concept advanced in the case is summarized in Figure 8-1. Starting with a fare-mileage formula, carriers would be allowed to establish and change specific fares anywhere within this zone. Fares could also be proposed outside the zone, but they would not be assumed reasonable and would have to go through the same procedure as at present.

This proposal for pricing flexibility had its most ardent advocates in two

50. A further restraint, of course, would be section 411 ([Unfair] Methods of Competition) of the Federal Aviation Act.

government agencies, the Departments of Transportation and Justice. Representatives of these two departments saw the proposal primarily as a means of encouraging carriers to compete on price as an alternative to competing on service quality. They also took the more extreme position on the zone, such that rates within the boundaries would be per se reasonable. Under their proposal, rates would be allowed to vary 15 percent, plus or minus, from a predetermined fare formula, thus yielding an established zone 30 percent wide.[51]

Other parties to the investigation also advocated some fare flexibility, but they suggested a zone in which fares would be only prima facie reasonable—that is, presumed reasonable unless proved otherwise. The outstanding proponent of this scheme was American Airlines, traditionally the industry's pricing leader, which, in proposing a 15 percent variation plus and minus, stated that in regulating fares "the Board should . . . attempt to achieve two goals. First, it should give the carriers a real opportunity to develop prices which reflect differences in costs and marketing considerations among different markets. Second, it should give the public the benefit of meaningful price competition."[52] The other parties advocating pricing flexibility were more conservative. Continental, Delta, four local service carriers, and the Board's Bureau of Economics all advocated a zone of 10 percent, that is, a variation of 5 percent, plus or minus, from the predetermined fare.[53] Rather than emphasizing price competition, however, their arguments were predicated primarily on the need for limited carrier management discretion in establishing rates.

Of the remaining major parties, only Allegheny and Ozark endorsed the concept of fare flexibility. The rest either ignored it or opposed it outright. Strongest among those in opposition were Eastern, TWA, and United. For example, Eastern argued that "the wide disparity among carriers as to . . . inherent strength . . . requires that fares be controlled and maintained at a level which will permit adequate returns to the 'need' carriers and protect them from the adverse effect of fare competition with carriers

51. Obviously this was a means of partially deregulating the airlines. In commenting on the earlier version of the material contained in this chapter, Richard Caves remarked, "Denied the option to deport the CAB wholesale, Miller and [Douglas] have chosen instead to offer it a lifetime supply of sleeping pills." (Richard E. Caves, discussion of Miller paper at Dartmouth seminar.)

52. See Brief of American Airlines, Inc. to the Civil Aeronautics Board, CAB Docket 21866-9 (May 22, 1972), p. 16.

53. Congressman Moss and his colleagues advocated a zone of minus 15 percent.

Table 8-1. Comparison of Policies Adopted by the Civil Aeronautics Board as a Result of the General Passenger Fare Investigation, 1960, and the Domestic Passenger Fare Investigation, Concluded in 1974, and Interim Policies

Phase of DPFI and policy issue	Policy adopted after GPFI	Interim policy	Policy after DPFI
1. Aircraft depreciation	Straight-line write-off	...	Affirmed
2. Leased aircraft	...	Not included in rate base	Affirmed
3. Deferred federal income taxes	Included as current expense	...	Affirmed
4. Joint fares	...	a. Rate based on sum of local rates minus cost saving	a. Affirmed
		b. Revenue division based on local rates	b. Revenue division based on relative carrier costs
5. Discount fares	...	Discriminatory discounts encouraged	Discriminatory discounts disallowed
6A. Seating configuration (standards)	...	...	Standards adopted, regulation implicit
6B. Load factor (standards)	Rejected	...	Standards adopted, regulation implicit; no analysis of price versus quality

7. Fare level	Unable to determine reasonable fares from record	Fares based on actual costs, reflecting carrier revenue need	Fares based on average cost of providing reasonable quality of service
8. Rate of return	a. 10.5 percent overall return, based on cost of capital and actual debt–equity ratio b. Implication of guaranteed return	...	a. 12 percent overall return, based on cost of capital and optimal debt–equity ratio b. Guarantee explicitly rejected; actual return left to market forces; no ratchet effect
9. Fare structure	...	Gradual increase in fare taper; promulgation of industry-wide fare formula; no zone of reasonableness fare flexibility	Adoption of cost taper as standard for fares; zone of reasonableness fare flexibility rejected

Sources: CAB Orders E-16068, 70-1-147, 72-4-42, 72-12-18, 71-4-54, 71-4-58, 71-4-59, 71-4-60, 71-4-48, 72-5-101, 74-3-82, and others. The date of each order is given in the note in Chapter 8 in which the order first appears.

who are stronger."[54] In essence, those opposed to pricing flexibility voiced fears of "destructive competition" and raised the specter of open "rate wars."

The administrative law judge's recommended decision in the fare structure phase forcefully argued against allowing fare flexibility, saying that by doing so the Board would abdicate its fare-regulating responsibilities. The Board agreed, despite a preliminary indication that it might find some degree of fare flexibility acceptable.[55] To quote the Board:

In general, the [zone of reasonableness] proposals rest on an erroneous understanding of the Board's past practices with respect to fare policy, and on unrealistic assumptions as to how the industry would respond to a policy of partial deregulation of fares. In our opinion, adoption of any of these proposals would be tantamount to abdicating our statutory responsibility to protect the public interest in reasonable fares. Moreover, we believe that the proposals would inevitably lead to an irrational and inequitable fare structure and to an unwarranted escalation of the fare level.

... for over thirty years the carriers have been free to file tariffs proposing changes in their normal fares, either upward or downward, subject to the Board's power to suspend and investigate. The history of carrier-initiated fares under this regime inspires little confidence in the likely end-results of the zone proposals. For, aside from the patchwork fare structure which evolved, the fact is that, for all practical purposes, the only proposals to adjust normal fares during this entire period involved increases. Price competition in normal fares has been virtually nonexistent.[56]

Thus, in the Board's opinion, based on historical evidence, pricing freedom would not result in fare competition, but merely uniform fare increases up to the limit of the zone. The point missed in this opinion is that significant costs are associated with competing on the basis of price

54. See Brief of Eastern Air Lines, Inc. to the Civil Aeronautics Board, CAB Docket 21866-9 (May 22, 1972), p. 42.

55. In its fare level decision, the Board agreed with American that in certain short-haul markets it might be expedient to retain the existing fare instead of raising it the authorized 9 percent. (CAB Orders 71-4-59 and 71-4-60, pp. 78–80.) In effect, however, this decision really authorized the carriers to select either the old fare or to take the full 9 percent increase. The zone was narrow (only 9 percent, or 4.5 percent, plus and minus) and was limited to the extremes. Since a significant fare increase had been wholly anticipated and capitalized, the carriers immediately raised nearly all such rates the authorized amount.

A zone that is too narrow not only limits the degree of price competition but also facilitates price collusion. Thus, to have the desired effect, the Board must allow for a broad range for price action; the authors expressed the opinion that 15 percent plus and minus represents a minimal standard.

56. CAB Order 74-3-82, pp. 115, 116.

under the present regime. To accomplish a fare reduction a carrier must announce the change 30 days in advance. Then, it must face the prospect that competing carriers will object to the fare reduction and have it suspended, rejected, or both on grounds that it is unreasonable, unjust, or predatory. Given these impediments, it is little wonder that price reductions have been scarce. In short, the Board's rationale is weak, and it is regrettable that the regulator has passed up an excellent opportunity to enhance the performance of the industry by allowing a modicum of true competition.

Summary of DPFI Policy Changes

Table 8-1 summarizes the findings of the DPFI in comparison with the outcome of the General Passenger Fare Investigation in 1960. Since questions about fare structure were explicitly set outside the scope of the GPFI (and thus no opinions were rendered at that time on such issues as joint fares, discount fares, and fare taper), comparisons on these issues of structure are based on policies developed subsequent to the GPFI.

As indicated in the table, on a number of important issues (phases 5, 6, 7, and 8) the Board clearly broke with tradition. Generally, these changes may be attributed to two underlying policy emphases which evolved from the investigation. First, there has been an acceptance by the Board of the model of nonprice competition outlined in this book. Second, greater emphasis has been placed on costs as the standard for individual fares; accordingly, there is less emphasis on "value of service" and other subjective criteria. However, the Board rejected the notion of fare flexibility and is not likely to encourage price competition among the carriers. Moreover, the DPFI dealt only with fare issues, not with questions of entry and exit. Arguably, a general investigation of entry policy would result in more liberal standards. Thus, while the policy actions taken in the DPFI are encouraging, many additional policy changes appear warranted on grounds of economic efficiency.

CHAPTER NINE

Summary, Conclusions, and Policy Recommendations

THIS STUDY has presented a model of domestic trunk-line behavior under economic regulation wherein carriers take price as set by the Civil Aeronautics Board and compete in quality dimensions, primarily the frequency of scheduling. Because of diminishing returns from efforts to attract new passengers through adding capacity, the profit-maximizing carrier will limit such activity, depending on price, the elasticity of demand, and other factors. Moreover, in markets where there are several carriers (or where a carrier anticipates that its competitors will retain frequency at given levels or where frequency competition is expected to have a disproportionate impact on market share), excess profits will tend to be eliminated because of the inverse relation between average cost and capacity utilization. The empirical evidence appears to comport with this model, at least more so than with competing views of the industry.

An important conclusion which can be drawn from this analysis is that the nature of the market equilibrium depends upon the regulator's choice of a price. In other words, there is a broad range of alternative combinations of price and quality which are consistent with a market equilibrium having zero excess profits. Essentially, then, the airlines should be relatively indifferent to price, at least within the feasible range.[1] On the other hand, the traveler is not indifferent, since his full cost of transport is a function of

---

1. This, obviously, is an oversimplification. Consistent with numerous "satisficing" models of economic behavior (William J. Baumol, Oliver E. Williamson, Harvey Averch and Leland L. Johnson, and others), the airlines seem interested in overall size and rate of growth as well as profits. See the discussion of CAB regulatory objectives later in this chapter; also see Fritz Machlup, "Theories of the Firm: Marginalist, Behavioral, Managerial," *American Economic Review,* Vol. 57 (March 1967), pp. 1–33; and William J. Baumol and Alvin K. Klevorick, "Input Choices and Rate-of-Return Regulation: An Overview of the Discussion," *Bell Journal of Economics and Management Science,* Vol. 1 (Autumn 1970), pp. 162–90.

both the ticket price and the imputed cost of time spent in transit. There is a direct relationship between price and quality, or, more specifically, an inverse relationship between price and expected delay. At a high price, market equilibrium will be characterized by high schedule frequency and low load factors; thus, frequency delay, stochastic delay, and total, or schedule, delay will be relatively small. At a low fare, the market equilibrium will be characterized by a much greater expected delay. Depending on the passenger's value of time and other factors, there is a combination of price and quality which minimizes his total trip cost. Our empirical analysis strongly suggests that the regulator's chosen level and structure of fares is inefficient, in that another set of alternatives would significantly lower passenger trip costs, yet yield normal profits to the carriers.

Since the airlines presumably have profit motives and since they are subjected to considerable nonprice competition, we would expect the industry to be characterized by a level of technical efficiency not too far removed from the optimal feasible level, given the quality of service, given the levels of input costs, and given regulator-imposed production restraints. As best we can determine, carriers do vary in their ability to achieve technical efficiency. Moreover, one may argue that Board restriction on the entry of new competing trunks has served to increase the cost of a given quality of service. Finally, even if one presumes that the existing trunk carriers are technically efficient, given their feasible opportunities, we may easily identify Board policies which serve to raise unit costs. These include restrictions on aircraft routing and service provided, costs attendant on litigating rate and route cases, and formal CAB-sanctioned carrier collusion.

It would appear to us that while undoubtedly allocative and technical efficiency costs in the airlines are significant, the greatest welfare loss comes from a nonoptimal level and structure of price-quality options. Technical inefficiency in the airlines is extremely difficult to measure since we have no truly comparable unregulated standards with which to compare the trunk carriers.[2] The allocative efficiency costs likewise are difficult to estimate, but are probably a great deal less extensive than commonly supposed because of the variability of quality and cost in response to price. However,

2. Comparison with foreign air carriers is not very relevant, since typically they face different levels of resource costs, and even adjust input mixes accordingly. See Mahlon R. Straszheim, *The International Airline Industry* (Brookings Institution, 1969), Chap. 4. The most obvious domestic comparison would be that of the intrastate California (or Texas) carriers, but here the price-quality option is grossly different than in comparable interstate markets; note too that several of the interstate carriers compete in the intrastate markets with varying degrees of success.

by making some heroic assumptions and using the model developed in Chapter 6, we can provide a crude estimate of the welfare loss due to nonoptimal price-quality level and structure.

What we shall do is to estimate the passenger's full cost of travel under the present regime and his lowest feasible cost (choosing the optimal price-quality combination), then aggregate this difference across all travelers. During 1969, the latest year for which we have requisite data, domestic trunk-line revenue totaled $6,514 million (Table A-1). Had the price-quality options been at optimal levels consistent with a $10 per hour evaluation of passenger delay time, total passenger revenue would have been approximately $6,148 million; for an optimal configuration reflecting a $5 per hour passenger evaluation of delay time, total passenger revenue would have been approximately $5,976 million.[3] In other words, during 1969 passengers paid excess fares, ranging from approximately $366 million to $538 million.

However, for this additional price, passengers purchased reductions in delay time—valued at approximately $118 million in the configuration consistent with a $10 per hour waiting time evaluation, and approximately $182 million in the $5 per hour configuration. This leaves a 1969 dead-weight welfare loss which (given the assumptions) ranges between $248 million and $356 million.

We wish to stress that this estimate is not meant to be precise and under present data limitations cannot be. The important point is that the trade-off between price and quality is an important element in defining the efficiency of an airline market. A precise estimate of the welfare loss is just not that important. The obvious concern is that ignoring the trade-off between price and quality results in a welfare loss which is, or can be, significant.

The Board's Implied Regulatory Objectives

Thus far we have considered regulatory policy to be exogenous. For purposes of appraising industry performance and describing the behavior of the airline industry subject to government regulation, this has been an

3. These estimates are based on the cost model outlined in the appendix to Chapter 2 and the delay model specified in the appendix to Chapter 6. A further assumption is that all markets are characterized by a demand density of 400 daily passengers. Data sources are CAB Docket 21866-9, Exhibits BC-2124 and BC-2200 (Nov. 20, 1970).

appropriate and relatively unimportant assumption. But in order to address the regulator and make recommendations for policy improvement, it is useful to characterize the industry's decision calculus.

On the one hand, we might develop a truly endogenous model, whereby the Board would respond to key variables in the industry's market equilibrium, and, in turn, the industry would respond to changes in regulator policy. Presumably, such a model would be stable, converging to an equilibrium after any exogenous stimulus. While such would appear to be a fruitful endeavor, we take here the simpler approach of trying to characterize the objectives of the regulator.

There are several ways to go about identifying the Board's objectives. First, we might review closely the Federal Aviation Act. As described in the appendix, the formal legislative "Declaration of Policy" gives to the Board a set of objectives that are incapable of being maximized simultaneously and that are generally subjective and ambiguous. Other sections of the act give even less information concerning regulator objectives. In short, any of a broad range of specific objectives are consistent with the act. Another alternative is to read Board decisions in individual cases and to draw from the arguments presented the ultimate objectives of the regulator. But as described briefly in the previous chapter, a major requirement of a Board opinion is that it serve to defend a position against any adversary; thus, one treads dangerously if he seeks to infer from written decisions the true objectives of the regulator. A third approach is to infer objectives from the regulator's behavior. This, admittedly, is an indirect approach, but one which is relatively free from bias and subject to empirical tests. We shall utilize this approach in the following discussion.

First, let us characterize the early history of industry regulation. Clearly, Congress implied in the Civil Aeronautics Act of 1938 the promotion and development of an infant industry. Broadly interpreted, the statute implied that the technology of the industry would be aided and advanced, and that service would be expanded to as many markets as was feasible. This meant the maintenance of service in markets where adequate schedules would not be profitable. Accordingly, two techniques were used to elicit such unprofitable services: direct subsidy of airmail service, and indirect or cross-subsidy, wherein excess profits were maintained on some routes to subsidize losses on others. It is commonplace in regulation that indirect subsidy is preferred to direct subsidy. Accordingly, the air regulator developed a policy of restraining entry into monopoly markets in order that carriers might earn profits there to offset losses in markets where exit was restricted.

Over time, however, air traffic grew at a rate many times that of gross national product, being a superior good and reflecting lower costs and improved service resulting from changes in aircraft technology. The structure of the industry also changed, with local service carriers and commuter airlines inheriting the subsidized markets. Hence, with the trunk industry's maturation, the underlying need for direct subsidy and cross-subsidy disappeared.[4] This fundamental fact completely changed the nature of efficient and effective trunk-line regulation.[5] The regulator, however, has not recognized this fundamental change. Having fulfilled its initial objective, it now finds itself successful without really knowing where to go next. Under such circumstances, clear-cut, consistent Board objectives are not easily identified.

Below, we shall consider several alternative regulatory objectives that could be or have been raised. The list is not meant to be exhaustive nor is it presumed that only one objective is overriding. However, one alternative does appear to be more descriptive than the others.

1. *Maximize economic efficiency.* This study attests to the Board's shortcomings if efficiency be the major objective. Conceivably, the Board has attempted to maximize economic efficiency, yet because of shortcomings in its analysis, especially its understanding of the welfare costs of nonoptimal price-quality level and structure, it has not succeeded. The outcome of the Domestic Passenger Fare Investigation (DPFI) does set a precedent for greater efficiency in some areas, but whether in the history of CAB regulation this will be viewed as a watershed remains to be seen.

2. *Maximize industry profits.* It is tempting to take the skeptical and fashionable view that the industry under regulation is simply a sanctioned cartel, run for the benefit of the carriers, to maximize their profits. As L. J. Kleiger has shown, the Board practices many of the necessary conditions of a profit-maximizing cartel agent.[6] For example, the regulator restricts entry, facilitates price collusion, and limits the prices paid for some resources. On the other hand, there is considerable countervailing evidence.

4. Except for minor payments to Northeast for low-density New England service during the period 1964–68, the trunk carriers have been off subsidy since 1959. U.S. Civil Aeronautics Board, "Subsidy for United States Certificated Air Carriers" (August 1972; processed), App. 7.

5. On the other hand, it raises the basic question about the necessity of any economic regulation of the industry—a question to be discussed later.

6. Linda Kleiger, "Maximization of Industry Profits: The Case of United States Air Transportation" (Ph.D. dissertation, University of California, Los Angeles, 1967).

Over the past few years the Board has granted existing firms extensive new entry into specific city-pair markets, effectively eliminating monopoly routes of any consequence. This pattern of certification has heightened nonprice competition, with obvious increases in costs and reductions in profits. Perhaps the most persuasive countervailing evidence is that industry profits over the long term have not been significantly out of line with a normal return on investment (see Table 2-5); certainly they fall short of a profit-maximizing level.

3. *Minimize "squawk."* Several economists have hypothesized that regulatory agencies choose policies which through carefully planned compromise and cajoling minimize hostility among regulatory participants.[7] A reason for this is that generally Congress and the Executive are likely to be satisfied with an agency's performance so long as they do not receive too many complaints. Moreover, one can detect in individual regulatory proceedings a tendency of both administrative law judges and the CAB to compromise whenever there is significant divergence in the positions of the major intervenors. This is especially true in instances where the presumed outcome will have distributional effects on the carriers. Since until recently there have been few forthright public interest advocates in most proceedings, the squawk-minimization objective is consistent with cartel-like behavior.[8]

4. *Maximize Board members' human capital.* Presumably, most people are concerned about future as well as present income. Because of "experience ladders," access to information, personal contacts, and so on, a person who is a member of the Board typically can maximize his future income by pursuing a career in air transportation, whether remaining as a Board member or taking a job on the outside. To some extent, Board membership may be "on the job training"; thus, one would expect a person's future income to be augmented by experience on the Board. The important question is whether the prospect of future income augmentation affects Board member decisions in regulatory cases. On the one hand, a member may prefer to remain on the Board, in which case he may be tempted to reach decisions which will maximize his chances for reappointment—that is, by

7. See, for example, Ross D. Eckert, "The Los Angeles Taxi Monopoly: An Economic Inquiry," *Southern California Law Review,* Vol. 43 (Summer 1970), pp. 407–53; and George W. Hilton, "The Basic Behavior of Regulatory Commissions," in American Economic Association, *Papers and Proceedings of the Eighty-fourth Annual Meeting* (*American Economic Review,* Vol. 62, May 1972), pp. 47–54.

8. Hilton also notes that it is consistent with objective 4 below (ibid., p. 49).

maintaining good relations both with the Executive and with Congress as well as with the industry. Or, the member may see opportunities on the outside, and thus be tempted to reach decisions consistent with maximizing his value on the outside—good relations with other Board members and CAB staff, good relations with industry leaders, and so forth.

Unfortunately, this is the kind of speculation which cannot be supported by clear-cut evidence. Some of the evidence at least appears consistent with this regulatory objective, although it is also consistent with alternatives. For example, of the thirty-one persons who had served on the Board through 1970, eleven were appointed to a second term, and five were appointed to a third term.[9] Also, a number of Board members after retirement became prominent members of the industry. This includes a number of lawyer representatives of carriers, a president of Northwest Airlines, a vice-president of Pan American, a chairman of the board of Slick Airways, and the head of the local service carrier trade association.

5. *Maximize industry size.* In our view, this appears to be the most compelling explanation of past regulatory policy. There are several dimensions in which size could be measured: total industry revenue, total industry cost, total number of flights, total number of aircraft, or total investment base. Actually, because of relatively fixed input relationships, the maximization of any one of these is tantamount to the simultaneous maximization of the others. Maximization of industry size is also consistent with simply promoting the industry.

Considerable evidence supports this hypothesis.[10] First, discount fares can be interpreted as price discrimination for the purpose of increasing total revenue. Second, attempts to price discriminate through cross-subsidy (for example, long-haul versus short-haul) have tended to increase total revenue.[11] Direct subsidy, of course, has augmented airline revenue. Finally, and perhaps most importantly and surprisingly, it would appear from our model of nonprice competition that the present level of fares maximizes total capacity and thus investment in flight equipment. From equation (30) in the appendix to Chapter 4 we have a relationship which can be inter-

9. U.S. Civil Aeronautics Board, *Handbook of Airline Statistics, 1971 Edition* (1972), p. 550.

10. See also Arthur De Vany, "Quality Competition in Regulated Industries: The Case of the Airlines" (November 1973; processed).

11. One typically hears from industry spokesmen the argument that short-haul fares cannot be raised, for to do so would drive air passengers to competing modes of travel.

preted with cost data from Chapter 2 to mean that total flights are max-imized for some value of demand price elasticity within the range -1.36 to -1.25. Most empirical estimates of price elasticity fall near or within this range, including those of the Board's staff.[12]

We reiterate that this short list of regulator objectives is not meant to be exhaustive. Nor do we presume that any one objective has been over-riding—probably Board behavior may be better described as incorporating a multitude of objectives.[13] However, except for the first, all are incon-sistent with achieving economic efficiency, which, for the purpose of this study, is considered to be the public interest objective. Accordingly, we frame proposals below which are intended to force the Board to move in the direction of greater economic efficiency.

Policy Recommendations

Our policy recommendations are of two types. First, given the existing institutional framework, there should be greater efficiency in the Board's choice of price and other regulatory parameters. Second, to the degree politically feasible, there should be movement in the direction of deregulat-ing airline service. While this study has been cast primarily in the context of increasing industry economic efficiency through enlightened regulation, we must recognize the powerful arguments for deregulation, or at least movements in that direction. Thus, we outline below our tentative ap-praisal of the efficiency of a deregulated airline market.

Although it is tempting for economists to attribute a perfectly competi-tive (efficient-market) outcome to a deregulated industry, we concede that the airline industry, if deregulated, would probably contain certain market imperfections so that further improvements in efficiency might be possi-ble. However, it would appear that a deregulated trunk-line industry would

12. In the fare level phase of the Domestic Passenger Fare Investigation, the Board's Bureau of Economics presented two studies of demand price elasticity: one, a time-series analysis, came up with a figure of -1.249; the other, a cross-section analysis, estimated price elasticity at -1.276. See CAB Orders 71-4-59 and 71-4-60 (April 9, 1971), pp. 59–61.

13. We note briefly three additional problems in identifying a regulator's objec-tive function: (a) objectives of individual Board members may change over time, (b) Board membership changes over time, and (c) Board decisions are rendered on the basis of majority rule, thus bringing into consideration a number of public-choice complications.

be more efficient than it is at present under regulation. On the one hand, the preconditions for pure competition appear to be present: insignificant scale economies, fairly elastic (firm) demand, difficulty of coordinating price and output policies, relatively free entry and exit (without a regulator).[14] Moreover, empirical evidence indicates the viability and efficiency of quasi-regulated markets in the California intrastate service, the Texas intrastate service, and the plethora of unregulated commuter-carrier interstate and intrastate services. Finally, as this study attests, the principal sources of economic inefficiency in air service may be ascribed to regulator-imposed restraints on competition.

A deregulated market, however, would probably be characterized by some inefficiencies. First, whereas extra-legal collusion is presently unimportant, the incentive for this type of activity (and presumably its extent) would be greater without the Board as agent for lawful collusion. Second, the small scale of demand relative to cost in many markets would perhaps lead to the emergence of a quasi-monopolist.[15] Third, deregulating air transportation to some extent would merely replace regulation by independent commission with "regulation" by the courts through the antitrust laws. Finally, in a deregulated environment the provision of service might occur with excessive frequency, utilizing inefficiently small aircraft.[16]

From this we conclude that, despite problems of market imperfections, a deregulated airline industry would probably be much more efficient than the existing regime.[17] In reforming regulation in the direction of deregulation, however, two things must be kept in mind. First, during a transitional phase there will be a learning experience on the part of firms as they adapt to the new environment. There may be turnovers in carrier management, as existing managers are people who perform well within the existing regulatory framework. There may also be changes in service and in ownership and identification of carriers. In short, there is something to be said

14. This is not to say that under deregulation each market would necessarily be served by a large number of firms. However, because of insignificant scale economies the possibility of entry would effectively restrain firms in the larger markets to reasonably competitive behavior.

15. That is, the emergence of a single firm which did not maximize short-run profits, but earned excess profits just short of attracting entry.

16. See George W. Douglas, "Equilibrium in a Deregulated Air Transport Market" (paper delivered at a seminar on Problems of Regulation and Public Utilities, Dartmouth College, 1972; processed).

17. The principal efficiency gains would come in densely traveled and long-haul markets.

for a transitional phasing of deregulation—over a two-year period, for example. In any event, proposals should keep in mind possible transitional difficulties. Second, it is ambiguous to speak of any particular policy change as an instance of deregulation. The problem is that of ceteris paribus. For example, to deregulate price but simultaneously to approve capacity agreements or limit entry may lead to a deterioration in economic efficiency, even though one policy change appeared to be in the direction of deregulation. Unfortunately, advocates of deregulation often find their proposals subverted by compromise agreements which tend to serve opposite ends.[18]

Reforms under Existing Legislation

Under the Federal Aviation Act the Board has considerable latitude in framing regulatory policy. We shall here describe a number of recommendations which are possible under the existing statute. First, a set of possible actions that should not be attempted.

1. *Do not attempt to regulate return on investment.* As described in Chapter 4, carriers will employ nonprice competition to a point where the anticipated return on additional investment is equal to the carriers' own internal required rate of return. Board attempts to regulate this return precisely as a predetermined reasonable rate will prove fruitless and will lead the market equilibrium away from the efficient combination (see Figure 4-2).

2. *Do not approve capacity agreements.* As described previously, the long-range effect of capacity agreements is carrier inefficiency in matching capacity with demand. Another result is excess profits in capacity-controlled markets, provided fares are not adjusted downward accordingly, which represent an allocative efficiency cost.

3. *Do not approve fuel reduction and rescheduling agreements.* Restrictions on fuel supplies to airline firms obviously limit the amount of capacity they can offer. Competition among firms in planning schedules leads generally to an efficient overall network, that is, capacity offerings responsive to passenger demand. Not only are rescheduling agreements not needed, but they lead to inefficiencies and create excess industry profits.

18. A case in point is the administration's recent effort to deregulate surface transportation. See American Enterprise Institute for Public Policy Research, *Transportation Legislation,* Legislative Analysis 22 (AEI, 1972).

4. *Do not limit entry to protect incumbent carriers.* As described in Chapter 7, entry controls insulate existing carriers from competition. If a prospective entrant appears likely to succeed in the market to the detriment of an incumbent carrier, then this may be an indication that the new carrier is more efficient. Protests from incumbent carriers are to be expected, but to give them great weight is to encourage technical inefficiency.

5. *Do not suspend or find unlawful fare decreases on grounds of protecting competitive carriers.* Understandably, whenever one carrier proposes to reduce a fare its competitors will object, preferring instead the existing fare level. Refusing to approve such an initiative protects less efficient carriers and constrains differentiation in price-quality options.

6. *Do not limit exit from service.* If a carrier wishes to suspend or abandon a market, its decision is an indication that the social value derived from the service is less than the cost of providing it. To constrain exit is inefficient. (However, the Board should be liberal in certificating a new carrier in any abandoned market.)

7. *Do not regulate commuter carriers.* Continuing the exemption for commuter carriers is a good way of testing the efficiency of trunk and local service carrier service. That is, if a commuter carrier can provide service under regulator-imposed cost disadvantages,[19] then this is a market test of the inefficiency of trunk-line and local service carrier provision.

8. *Do not further restrict (charter) operations of the supplemental carriers.* The supplemental carriers provide a vital function in competing with the scheduled carriers. Not only do they provide benchmarks of technical efficiency, but they reveal the need for lower price-quality options in scheduled service. Without the supplementals the inefficiencies of trunk service would be partially masked.

Now let us consider a series of feasible proposals of an affirmative nature.

1. *Determine and bring about the optimal level and structure of fare-quality options.* Hold a specific hearing in which the trade-off between fare level and quality is brought under close scrutiny and a determination is made concerning the optimal level and structure of fares and quality. At the same time, explore the feasibility of increasing the number of price-quality options.

2. *Hold general investigations regarding policies toward entry, exit, merg-*

19. Because of a limit on aircraft size, the commuter carrier is penalized in terms of per-seat or per-passenger capacity costs. However, the commuters do appear to pay lower prices for some resource inputs, particularly pilot services.

ers, and collusion. At present, all of these matters are treated on an ad hoc basis. An investigation which looked at these issues in the same depth as the Domestic Passenger Fare Investigation looked at fares would be appropriate and presumably would lead to the identification of more specific, efficiency-inducing policies.

3. *Encourage price competition and market tests of price-quality options.* Conclude that under section 1002(d) of the Federal Aviation Act a zone of reasonableness for fares is in the public interest. Such a zone might work either in terms of per se reasonableness (meaning lawful on grounds of reasonableness whatever the case), or prima facie reasonableness (that is, presumed to be lawful on grounds of reasonableness unless proven otherwise). This might also be coupled with a stated policy of giving less weight to questions of alleged discrimination, preference, or prejudice. The zone might also allow for broad variations in price-quality options, thereby giving market tests of the preferred combinations.[20]

4. *Reform the decision-making process.* It would enhance economic efficiency if in the adversary process more emphasis were placed on substance and less on form. Also, it would improve the quality of decisions if more economics expertise were required of administrative law judges and Board appointees. Finally, in view of the tendency of the Board to minimize squawk, public or private interest advocates with economic efficiency positions should be encouraged to present their case.[21]

While the above reforms do not exhaust the possibilities feasible under existing legislation, they include some of the more important ones, and, if adopted, would go far toward increasing the efficiency of airline markets.

Reforms Requiring Additional Legislation

Even more substantive reforms are possible with new legislation. Essentially, initial legislation setting up a regulatory agency specifies broad

20. Other options for increasing price competition and market tests of price-quality options (within existing statutory framework) include loosening the restraints on supplemental and commuter carriers.

21. We do not necessarily imply that the typical "public interest advocate" articulates a position supportive of economic efficiency. But this can be the case. Moreover, airline market efficiency can often be in a private interest. For example, one might expect the chambers of commerce or travel bureaus of East Coast cities to advocate lower fares, as in the California intrastate markets. Successful cases in point are the advocacy roles played by the Hawaiian parties and the Puerto Rican parties in keeping fares low between their areas and the U.S. mainland. See CAB Dockets 22364 and 24353.

objectives for regulation and grants powers to the regulator which ultimately take the form of constraints on industry behavior. Reform legislation typically can take one or more of three directions. First, it might change or identify more clearly regulatory objectives; second, it might specify particular restraints on the industry, thus telling the Board more clearly what to do; or third, it might prohibit certain previously imposed restraints, thus telling the Board what *not* to do. The reforms described below contain aspects of all three.

1. *Redefine public interest to mean economic efficiency.* As described in the appendix, the legislative "Declaration of Policy," which essentially defines the term "public interest" as used in the statute, is ambiguous and contains mutually conflicting goals, some of which are inconsistent with economic efficiency. A simple legislative change which would have an important effect is replacing the Declaration of Policy with a policy statement admonishing the Board to foster efficiency in airline markets.

2. *Separate promotion activities from economic regulation.* As described above, the Board has attempted to promote air transportation and this has resulted in efficiency losses. If there are public-good aspects of the industry which require its artificial promotion, then this is better accomplished through other means. For example, as the Ash Council has recommended, transfer the promotional activities of the Board to the Department of Transportation.[22] Also, promotion, if it is to exist, should be designed to augment efficiency in the provision of the subsidized service. An example is the competitive bidding scheme proposed by the Board to assure service at low-density points.[23]

3. *Alter burden of proof.* Change the Federal Aviation Act to make entry and exit merely *consistent* with the public interest, rather than *required* by it. Make the approval of collusive agreements *required* by the public interest, instead of being "not inconsistent with the public interest." These changes-arguably would make entry and exit freer and would restrain Board sanctioned collusion.

22. President's Advisory Council on Executive Organization, *A New Regulatory Framework: Report on Selected Independent Regulatory Agencies* (1971).

23. See testimony of Board Chairman Secor D. Browne on S-3460 before the Subcommittee on Aviation of the Senate Committee on Commerce (April 10, 1972). Also see the contracting proposal outlined in George C. Eads, *The Local Service Airline Experiment* (Brookings Institution, 1972), pp. 199, 200; and the negative excise tax proposal contained in James C. Miller III, "Issues in Local Service Airline Subsidy" (paper delivered at MIT Workshop on Low/Medium Density Air Transportation, 1973; processed).

4. *Expand regulatory exemptions.* Broaden the class of exempt carriers which may provide scheduled air service. This could be accomplished in a number of ways. First, grant commuter carriers an explicit exemption and liberalize standards of aircraft size.[24] Second, allow existing charter (supplemental) carriers to engage in single-ticketed scheduled service. Third, totally deregulate the denser city-pair markets. The instances of inefficiency under complete deregulation are likely to be minimized the larger the market size; also, the greatest efficiency gains from deregulation are likely to be found in such markets.

5. *Withdraw or modify CAB power to approve intercarrier agreements.* Revise section 412 of the Federal Aviation Act to eliminate the power of the Board to circumvent the antitrust laws and approve and enforce cartel agreements. With possibly few exceptions, agreements coming under this provision for the purpose of escaping antitrust liability are inconsistent with maximizing industry performance.

Any of these proposals would significantly enhance the economic efficiency of airline markets. Although this study has not been directed toward determining the efficiency of a completely deregulated market, it would appear to us that this alternative, too, should be seriously weighed, even if the political impediments at present appear overwhelming.

Concluding Remarks

We note in conclusion two points. First, while the outcome of the DPFI is an encouraging portent for future CAB regulatory performance, we must stress that the Federal Aviation Act allows the Board considerable latitude in its policies and that regulatory philosophy at any time is greatly dependent upon the membership of the Board. Since the major decisions were rendered in that investigation, several positions at the Board have changed hands, including the chairmanship. According to pronouncements in early 1973 by the new chairman, Robert D. Timm, the Board will henceforth concentrate on maintaining a "healthy industry."[25]

24. Even more liberal than the new standard of thirty seats and 7,500 pounds net payload. CAB Order 72-7-61 (July 18, 1972).

25. "Aero Club Luncheon Address" (delivered April 24, 1973; processed), p. 2; "An Industry Champion Pilots the CAB," *Business Week,* No. 2281 (May 26, 1973), pp. 76, 77; and Albert R. Karr, "Under New Chief, CAB Bids to Lift Profits of Airlines, Annoying Consumer Advocates," *Wall Street Journal,* Aug. 7, 1973.

Several actions have been taken. As described in the previous chapter, the Board has authorized and even encouraged the carriers to reach agreements on controlling schedule capacity and has stated that such agreements would appear to be "a useful and successful regulatory device."[26] The Board has also approved fuel reduction and rescheduling agreements which have the effect of augmenting carrier profits.[27] At present a whole range of issues surrounding capacity agreements is under investigation.[28] However, there is little doubt that a presumption exists at the Board, especially on the part of its chairman, in favor of their utilization.

In other related actions, the Board summarily reversed its phase 5 DPFI decision to reduce the level of normal fares and instead merely ordered the phase-out of discount fares over an eighteen-month period.[29] On alleged energy conservation grounds, the Board authorized the carriers to discuss agreements leading to fuel conservation through reductions in aircraft speed.[30] To limit perceived destructive competition and substantial impairment of air services, the Board has permitted the U.S. international scheduled and supplemental carriers to negotiate an agreement setting minimum prices for transatlantic charter flights.[31] In November 1973, despite schedule cutbacks, which lowered costs but only marginally affected revenues, the Board approved an across-the-board fare increase of 5 percent.[32] Among specific measures envisioned are: (a) a slowdown of new route authorizations, (b) decertification of carriers in overcompetitive markets, and (c) a furthering of the policy of cross-subsidizing small city-pair markets.[33] Of course, these measures not only mark a retreat from the enlightened policy direction which we have imputed to the DPFI, but they are also anticompetitive and have significant associated efficiency costs. Whether such policies will in fact be continued or promulgated remains to be seen.

26. CAB Order 73-4-98 (April 24, 1973), p. 3.
27. CAB Order 73-10-110 (Oct. 31, 1973).
28. See CAB Order 73-7-147 (July 27, 1973), which approved the latest three-carrier transcontinental capacity agreement for an interim period of six months and set down an investigation of the capacity limitation concept.
29. See CAB Order 73-5-2 (May 1, 1973).
30. See CAB Order 73-5-123 (May 25, 1973). Said the Board, "Agreed-on flight times would lead to carrier observance of conservation procedures because no competitive advantage would be gained by beating such flight times." Ibid., p. 1.
31. See CAB Order 73-6-79 (June 19, 1973).
32. See CAB Order 73-11-93 (Nov. 20, 1973).
33. See Timm, "Aero Club Address," pp. 4, 5; and Karr, "CAB Bids to Lift Profits."

The second point we wish to note is that the analysis developed in this study should be applicable to a broad variety of other industries and regulatory phenomena. Obvious candidates include the motor trucking industry, the water carrier industry, commercial banking, state regulation of insurance, and the regulation of fees paid to securities and commodity brokers. Each has the characteristic of (approximately) zero excess industry profits at a range of feasible price-quality combinations. Similarly, other semiregulated or cartelized industries or professions may be described with this analysis. These include physicians, real estate agents, attorneys, hotel accommodations, and service industries where prices are determined by union scale, such as barber shops. In each case there appears to be price collusion, but control of output is imperfect; welfare losses would be indicated not only by excess profits, but by nonoptimal price-quality options. Finally, oligopolistic industries where prices are sticky likewise may be brought into question regarding price-quality options, and this is a dimension of efficiency analysis not yet developed in the industrial organization literature. In short, while this study concerns airline regulation specifically, we hope that it may contribute to the development of a new approach to industry efficiency appraisal.

The Industry and Its Regulators

THIS APPENDIX is descriptive, not analytical. It provides background material on the airlines for those readers who feel that an institutional orientation will aid their understanding of the main text. It also contains information on industry structure and regulation not readily available elsewhere.

Historical Sketch of the Industry and Its Regulation[1]

The first air passenger service in the United States began in 1914 (a flying boat operating between St. Petersburg and Tampa, Florida); it lasted only four months. Commercial air transport did not make significant headway until after the First World War.[2] What gave impetus to the industry was the passage of the Air Mail Act of 1925 (also called the Kelly Act), and then, a year later, the Air Commerce Act of 1926.[3] These acts were passed after a number of aircraft operators had tried to provide scheduled passenger and cargo service in the early 1920s, only to find revenues failing to cover costs. The Air Mail Act sought to promote civil aviation by ordering the carriage of airmail to be transferred from military planes flown by Army personnel to private carriers. The contractual arrangements were generous, and domestic commercial transport grew from thirteen operators and 1.3 million revenue passenger-miles in 1926 to thirty-eight operators and 85.1 million revenue passenger-miles in 1930.[4]

1. Although there are numerous interpretive essays on the history of U.S. commercial aviation (some of which are listed in this study), two of the most useful sources are government publications: U.S. Civil Aeronautics Board, *Handbook of Airline Statistics, 1971 Edition* (1972), Pt. 8, and Arnold E. Briddon and Ellmore A. Champie, *Federal Aviation Agency Historical Fact Book: A Chronology, 1926–1963* (U.S. Government Printing Office, 1966).

2. Alan H. Stratford, *Air Transport Economics in the Supersonic Era* (St. Martin's Press, 1967).

3. John H. Frederick, *Commercial Air Transportation* (3rd ed., Richard D. Irwin, 1951), pp. 81–82.

4. See CAB, *Handbook of Airline Statistics, 1971*, pp. 9, 23.

The Air Commerce Act also marked the beginning of federal regulation of aviation. The act provided that (a) all aircraft had to be registered, (b) pilots had to be certificated, (c) the secretary of commerce was to establish air traffic rules, (d) lighted civil airways and beacons for navigation were to be established, and (e) there were to be civil penalties for nonconformity with the act's provisions. The passage of the act meant that administration of powers was shared by three agencies: the Department of Commerce, which administered air safety; the Post Office Department, which let mail contracts; and the Interstate Commerce Commission, which controlled airmail rates.[5]

The depression of the 1930s saw rapid, if somewhat sporadic, growth in air service and remarkable technical advances in aircraft.[6] There was growth each year despite the general economic downturn and even in the face of a temporary suspension of certain mail contracts in 1934.[7] Like many other industries during this period, the established airline operators sought federal aid and, in particular, protection from "excessive competition." Partly as a result of industry pressure, the Air Mail Act of 1934 was passed later in the year, returning airmail contracts to the carriers and giving some minor federal control over entry.

In 1938, Congress established what has evolved into today's Civil Aeronautics Board. Entitled the Civil Aeronautics Act of 1938, the law set up a Civil Aeronautics Authority, an administrator in the authority, and an Air Safety Board. In 1940, the Civil Aeronautics Authority was supplanted by the Civil Aeronautics Board (CAB), the Air Safety Board was abolished and its functions transferred to the CAB, and both the CAB and the administrator and his staff (designated the Civil Aeronautics Administration by the secretary of commerce) were transferred to the Department of Commerce.[8] Under the provisions of the 1938 act, the federal government was charged with, among other things, (a) determining

5. Frederick, *Commercial Air Transportation,* pp. 81–82.
6. For a description of technological change in the U.S. commercial aircraft industry, see Almarin Phillips, *Technology and Market Structure: A Study of the Aircraft Industry* (Lexington Books, 1971). It was during the 1930s that the Douglas DC-3 was introduced into commercial service.
7. The reason for the suspension was alleged collusion between mail carriers and postal officials of the displaced Republican administration, and because of other abuses under the Mail Pay Act of 1930. A court case settled in 1941 reported there was no fraud in the airmail contracts canceled in 1934. See Frederick, *Commercial Air Transportation,* pp. 82, 83.
8. Samuel B. Richmond, *Regulation and Competition in Air Transportation* (Columbia University Press, 1961), p. 15.

which carriers would be allowed to serve which routes except for the routes already served by existing carriers (and thus, in a broad sense, entry into the industry), (b) the regulation of rates charged by the carriers, and (c) setting and maintaining standards for air safety.

Essentially, there were three reasons for congressional action. First, the 1934 act had distributed responsibility among three agencies, and problems of coordination proved overwhelming. According to Caves, "in the years 1934 through 1938, no agency was a staunch defender of the existing arrangements."[9] In fact, the Federal Aviation Commission recommended in 1935 a "wholesale revision that would centralize authority in a single new commission."[10] Second, the 1934 act's provision for airmail subsidy through contract bidding proved "unworkable."[11] It appeared that carriers would "buy in" routes at very low bids in hopes of making up losses over the long run through monopoly exploitation of nonmail service. Third, the industry was allegedly characterized by chaos, arising in part out of the frailties of the competitive bidding mechanism. Investment was risky, and established operators again argued that the trouble was due to "irresponsible" elements in the industry which perpetuated "overcompetition."[12] Under one provision of the 1938 act, the sixteen established operators were issued "certificates of public convenience and necessity" and were given the right and some obligation to continue serving those routes they had been serving; this later became known as the "grandfather clause."

Table A-1 summarizes the industry's growth from the establishment of comprehensive federal regulation in 1938 through 1970. At the beginning of the Second World War a number of civilian aircraft were given over to the military, and consequently traffic (in revenue ton-miles) grew at a slower rate than would have been the case without this constraint.[13] After an initial spurt following the end of the war, reflecting an increased supply of aircraft, traffic growth slowed down. In 1949, it rebounded for a rela-

9. Richard E. Caves, *Air Transport and Its Regulators: An Industry Study* (Harvard University Press, 1962), p. 124.

10. Ibid., p. 125.

11. Ibid., p. 124.

12. Despite allegations of pending collapse of the system, domestic air traffic grew from 189.2 million revenue passenger-miles in 1934 to 410.3 million in 1937. CAB, *Handbook of Airline Statistics, 1971*, p. 23.

13. Passenger load factors (the proportion of seats filled) in domestic service rose from 57.9 percent in 1940 to 89.4 percent in 1944. Ibid., p. 26.

Table A-1. Airline Traffic, Investment, and Revenue in Total U.S. Domestic Operations, 1938–70

Millions

Year	Total revenue ton-miles	Total investment (dollars)	Total operating revenue (dollars)
1938	55.7	30.7	42.8
1939	76.8	36.3	55.9
1940	114.5	55.4	76.9
1941	151.3	63.2	97.3
1942	170.0	77.9	108.1
1943	209.9	98.0	122.8
1944	278.9	129.4	160.7
1945	411.0	171.2	214.2
1946	654.4	262.5	316.7
1947	698.4	309.6	364.3
1948	733.0	335.2	442.0
1949	851.0	340.8	496.3
1950	1,070.9	356.3	578.7
1951	1,346.9	375.7	729.2
1952	1,549.4	447.5	844.0
1953	1,783.6	525.3	966.7
1954	1,989.5	561.5	1,068.2
1955	2,382.3	631.8	1,238.4
1956	2,730.1	765.2	1,399.8
1957	3,138.2	977.0	1,596.4
1958	3,120.3	1,141.6	1,693.2
1959	3,574.9	1,421.9	2,008.4
1960	3,732.9	1,703.8	2,178.3
1961	3,899.1	1,988.9	2,304.9
1962	4,440.9	2,157.3	2,588.6
1963	4,831.2	2,124.8	2,790.1
1964	5,600.6	2,252.3	3,168.8
1965	6,774.3	2,633.4	3,690.8
1966	8,053.9	3,411.3	4,171.5
1967	9,982.4	4,580.8	4,980.9
1968	11,461.6	5,705.0	5,691.4
1969	12,556.3	6,275.6	6,514.2
1970	13,877.9[a]	6,810.6[a]	7,180.1[a]

Sources: U.S. Civil Aeronautics Board, *Handbook of Airline Statistics, 1971 Edition* (1972), pp. 12, 69, 75, 395; and worksheets given the authors by the Board's Bureau of Accounts and Statistics.
a. Includes intra-Alaska and intra-Hawaii operations.

tively vigorous annual rate of growth, ranging between 12 and 26 percent, until the recession year of 1958, when traffic fell by 0.6 percent.

The longer-range and more comfortable Douglas DC-6 and DC-7 and the Lockheed Constellation and Super Constellation were introduced over the period 1947–53, followed by the British-built Vickers Viscount in 1955. The introduction of jets in 1958 unfortunately coincided with an unanticipated traffic decline, and many carriers found themselves in financial straits. However, traffic revived in the early 1960s, rising to an annual rate of about 20 percent over the period 1965–68. This growth resulted in part from lower costs, the widespread introduction of discount fares, and improved service made possible by turbine-powered aircraft.[14] The growth in air travel once again stagnated in 1970, reflecting the general economic recession, but had returned almost to historical levels by the time of the 1973 "energy crisis."[15]

During the Second World War the Board spent most of its energies making sure that the airlines cooperated with the military in the war effort, although it did bring about two substantial fare reductions in 1943 and 1945.[16] Immediately after the war, the Board initiated an experiment to provide feeder air service and gave temporary operating authority to a new class of carriers—the local service airlines, whose certificates were made permanent by law in 1955.[17] In 1949, the Board certificated four all-cargo airlines and in 1952 established a category of carriers exempt from economic regulation—those willing to operate aircraft having a maximum gross takeoff weight of 12,500 pounds or less (air taxis). Coach service, with lower fares, was introduced in 1948 and was encouraged as official policy in 1951.

The Board approved two major fare increases in 1947 and one in 1948. The widespread introduction of coach service during the early 1950s

14. Ibid., p. 13.

15. For the domestic operations of the trunk airlines plus Pan American, revenue passenger-miles grew 0.0 percent in 1970, 1.8 percent in 1971, 10.6 percent in 1972, and 6.7 percent in 1973. U.S. Civil Aeronautics Board, *Quarterly Airline Industry Economic Report* (December 1970), p. 7; ibid. (December 1971), p. 7; ibid. (December 1972), p. 7; and ibid. (December 1973), p. 7.

16. The Board found itself in a typical regulator's dilemma. With a shortage of aircraft and rising demand, price rationing would have meant fare *increases*. On the other hand, with load factors rising, per-passenger (accounting) costs were falling and thus profits were increasing. In the end the Board chose to limit profits rather than price-ration service.

17. For an analysis of the local service airlines, see George C. Eads, *The Local Service Airline Experiment* (Brookings Institution, 1972).

lowered the average fare significantly, and fares remained fairly stable until 1958, when the Board approved fare increases, in part to offset traffic declines. To establish a more formal policy toward the regulation of air fares, the Board held the General Passenger Fare Investigation over the period 1956–60.[18]

As jet aircraft became more widespread during the 1960s and as their operating economies became evident, the Board did two things. First, it encouraged the introduction of widespread availability of discount fares, thus lowering average price per ticket. Second, the Board expanded greatly air carrier route authorizations and in particular increased the number of competitors on routes between large cities. However, by the end of the decade a combination of cost inflation, a slowing down of real productivity increases, and falling traffic depressed industry profits, prompting Board approval of significant fare increases in 1969 and 1971. It was during the period between the two increases that the Board initiated and completed much of its second long-range review of fare policy—the Domestic Passenger Fare Investigation.[19]

The regulatory institution was changed somewhat in 1958 when Congress, prompted by two tragic midair collisions the year before, passed the Federal Aviation Act of 1958, setting up the Federal Aviation Agency (FAA). This had the effect of separating safety regulation, which was assigned to the FAA, from economic regulation, which remained with the CAB.[20] The act also transferred federal airport-airway support functions from the Department of Commerce to the new agency. In 1966 Congress established the Department of Transportation (DOT), renaming the FAA the Federal Aviation Administration and making it a part of DOT. The CAB remained an independent regulatory agency.

Industry Organization and Service

The airlines clearly have come to dominate the common-carrier, or commercial, market for intercity passenger trips.[21] However, they still fall

18. For a brief discussion of this investigation, see Chapter 8.
19. See Chapter 8.
20. However, responsibility for investigating regulated-carrier aircraft accidents remained with the Board until transferred to the National Transportation Safety Board in the 1966 Department of Transportation Act.
21. CAB, *Handbook of Airline Statistics, 1971*, p. 565.

Table A-2. Number of Air Carriers, Revenue Ton-Miles, Investment, and Revenue, U.S. Domestic Operations, by Carrier Group, 1970

Carrier group	Number of carriers	Revenue ton-miles Millions	Revenue ton-miles Percent of total	Investment Total (millions of dollars)	Investment Percent of total	Revenue Total (millions of dollars)	Revenue Percent of total
Trunk	11a	12,288.7b	88.1	5,708.3	87.4	6,172.4	86.5
Local service c	9d	851.5	6.1	616.5	9.4	736.8	10.3
Supplemental	13e	390.9	2.8	87.1f	1.3	95.2	1.3
All-cargo	2	301.5	2.2	62.3	1.0	49.4	0.7
Commuter	179	47.1g	0.3	h	...	h	...
Intra-Hawaii	2	39.9	0.3	24.3	0.4	44.4	0.6
Intra-Alaska	4	26.1	0.2	30.0	0.5	28.8	0.4
Helicopter	3i	1.2	*	0.4	*	8.3	0.1
Total	223	13,946.9	100.0	6,528.9j	100.0	7,135.3j	100.0

Sources: CAB, *Handbook of Airline Statistics, 1971*; CAB, *Air Carrier Financial Statistics* (December 1970), pp. 28, 29; CAB, *Commuter Air Carrier Traffic Statistics, Year Ended December 31, 1970*, p. 3, and Tables 3, 5. Figures may not add to totals because of rounding.

* Less than 0.1 percent.

a. Northeast merged with Delta August 1, 1972, which reduced the number of trunks to ten.

b. Excludes Pan American World Airways, which is certificated for international operations only, but carries some domestic traffic in connection with its international operations.

c. Revenue data include operations of Air West, whose certificate was transferred to Hughes Air Corporation d/b/a Air West, April 3, 1970.

d. Mohawk merged with Allegheny April 12, 1972, reducing the number of local service carriers to eight.

e. American Flyers merged with Universal May 27, 1971, reducing the number of supplementals to twelve.

f. Approximated by the product of (1) overall revenue and (2) the ratio of average investment to revenue.

g. Estimated from data in commuter source above, assuming 200 pounds per passenger and average stage length for freight and mail equal to that of passengers.

h. Not available. Commuter airlines do not report financial data to the CAB.

i. Reflects suspension of operations of Los Angeles Airways due to bankruptcy, October 8, 1970.

j. Excluding commuters.

far short of displacing the automobile as the most prominent mode of intercity travel.[22] In 1957, the airlines surpassed a declining railroad service, which, in turn, fell below bus service a year later.

By convention, commercial air carriers are classed into the groups indicated in Table A-2.[23]

As shown in the table, in 1970 there were eleven trunk carriers (reduced to ten in 1972 by merger). All had been operating in 1938, when the Board was established, and received grandfather rights at that time. Collectively

22. In 1967, the automobile accounted for 86.1 percent of intercity person-trips versus the airlines' share of 8.0 percent. U.S. Bureau of the Census, *Census of Transportation, 1967, National Travel Survey*, TC67-N1 (1969), p. 21.

23. Not included are the hundreds of air taxi operators who provide point-to-point service on demand, the plethora of private, general aviation aircraft, ranging from the omnipresent "Piper cub" to well-outfitted corporate jets, and the state-regulated intrastate carriers, the most notable being in the California corridor market, where Pacific Southwest Airlines (PSA) dominates, and the recent development in Texas, where a brand-new intrastate carrier, Southwest Airlines, is making significant headway into the markets of Braniff (a trunk carrier) and Texas International Airlines (one of the local service carriers).

Table A-3. Revenue Ton-Miles, Investment, and Revenue for Domestic Operations, U.S. Trunk Carriers, 1970

Carrier and group	Revenue ton-miles		Investment		Revenue	
	Millions	Percent of total	Total (millions of dollars)	Percent of total	Total (millions of dollars)	Percent of total
American	2,202.0	17.9	1,023.1	17.9	1,071.7	17.4
Eastern	1,417.9	11.5	752.0	13.2	808.3	13.1
Trans World	1,592.1	13.0	751.5	13.2	771.6	12.5
United	3,285.0	26.7	1,243.0	21.8	1,501.7	24.3
Big four	8,497.0	69.1	3,769.6	66.0	4,153.3	67.3
Braniff	426.7	3.5	207.0	3.6	233.7	3.8
Continental	698.9	5.6	335.1	5.9	289.4	4.7
Delta[a]	1,377.0	11.2	480.6	8.4	763.2	12.4
National[b]	301.8	2.5	226.1	4.0	192.0	3.1
Northwest[b]	453.9	3.7	443.3	7.8	267.1	4.3
Western	542.5	4.4	246.7	4.3	273.7	4.4
Other trunks	3,791.7	30.9	1,938.8	34.0	2,019.1	32.7
Total	12,288.7	100.0	5,708.3	100.0	6,172.4	100.0

Sources: U.S. Civil Aeronautics Board, *Air Carrier Traffic Statistics* (December 1971), pp. 11–16; and *Air Carrier Financial Statistics* (December 1970), pp. 6–9, 29. Figures may not add to totals because of rounding.

a. Includes data for Northeast, which merged with Delta on August 1, 1972.

b. National and Northwest were adversely affected by strikes during this period.

they have accounted for nearly 88 percent of domestic revenue ton-miles in recent years. This group also accounts for a similarly high fraction of industry investment and yearly revenues. (A breakdown of traffic, investment, and revenue by individual trunk carrier is contained in Table A-3.)

By the end of 1972 there were eight local service, or, more appropriately, regional, carriers which, though individually geographically concentrated, collectively blanket the country.[24] Originally these carriers were established by the Board to provide feeder service to the trunks but since have evolved into what amounts to miniature trunk airlines.[25] Together they account for approximately 10 percent of the industry revenue (Table A-2).

As of December 1970, there were thirteen supplemental carriers providing nonscheduled, charter service domestically (and in all but two cases— Johnson and McCulloch—internationally as well).[26] This group of carriers

24. They are: Allegheny Airlines, Frontier Airlines, Hughes Air Corporation (Air West), North Central Airlines, Ozark Air Lines, Piedmont Aviation, Southern Airways, and Texas International Airways. (Mohawk merged with Allegheny April 12, 1972.)

25. See Eads, *The Local Service Airline Experiment.*

26. These carriers are: American Flyers Airline Corporation, Capitol International Airways, Interstate Airmotive, Johnson Flying Service, McCulloch International Airlines, Modern Air Transport, Overseas National Airways, Purdue Airlines, Saturn Airways, Southern Air Transport, Trans International Airlines, Universal Airlines, and World Airways. American Flyers subsequently merged with Universal, effective May 27, 1971.

was established by the Board on an experimental basis in 1962, and in 1966, ten supplementals were given permanent certificates by the Board, with the approval of the President. As shown in the table, the supplementals account for only a small fraction of the industry.

There are two all-cargo carriers in domestic service, Airlift International and the Flying Tiger Line, of which the latter is larger (in domestic service).[27] First certificated in 1949, this group provides regularly scheduled cargo service between major cities in the United States as well as cargo and some supplemental passenger service abroad. As a fraction of the industry, they are about the same size as the supplementals (Table A-2).

Beginning in 1952, any airline enterprise has been able to escape CAB economic regulation (but not FAA safety regulation) by operating with aircraft having a maximum gross takeoff weight of 12,500 pounds or less. In July 1972, this size restraint was liberalized to a maximum of thirty seats and a net takeoff weight of 7,500 pounds.[28] The majority of such operators are air taxis, which provide service on demand. However, in 1970 there were 179 commuter airlines which offered regularly scheduled service, in many cases in direct competition with trunk or local service carriers. While obviously holding great potential for expanded air service, their traffic in 1970 was less than 1 percent of total commercial revenue ton-miles (Table A-2).

There are three other official CAB carrier groups. First, the intra-Hawaii carriers—Aloha Airlines and Hawaiian Airlines—provide head-to-head competition among the islands, with Hawaiian being the older and larger. Second, there are four intra-Alaska carriers—Kodiak Airways, Reeve Aleutian Airways, Western Alaska Airlines, and Wien Consolidated Airlines. Third, CAB-certificated helicopter service is provided by Chicago Helicopter Airways, New York Airways, and San Francisco–Oakland Helicopter Airlines.[29] Altogether, these three groups account for approximately 1 percent of the domestic industry (Table A-2).

This study deals primarily with the trunk carriers, which currently account for approximately nine-tenths of the domestic market. Table A-3 breaks out traffic, investment, and revenue data for each of these ten car-

27. The cargo operations of two of the trunk carriers—American and United—exceed those of Flying Tiger. CAB, *Air Carrier Traffic Statistics* (December 1971), pp. 11–16, 29.

28. Maximum passenger seating under the former restraint was typically twenty or less, depending on aircraft. See CAB Order 72-7-61 (July 18, 1972), p. 2.

29. A fourth carrier, Los Angeles Airways, suspended operations as of October 8, 1970, due to bankruptcy.

riers.[30] By convention, these carriers are divided into the "big four" and the "other trunks." Table A-3 indicates why this is a logical division. Except for Delta, none of the other trunks approaches the size of the smallest of the big four, Eastern, by any measure.[31] The smaller other trunks have yearly revenues only about one-fifth those of United, the largest carrier. By most size measures, the big four account for approximately two-thirds of the national market.

Some of the trunk carriers, such as American, TWA, and United, are far-flung geographically, whereas Western and others are primarily regional. In any case, trunk carriers typically compete with at least one other trunk carrier in significant city-pair markets. (Table 7-3 describes this characteristic of industry competition in some detail.) United, Braniff, Delta, and (until 1971) Northwest all have approximately one-third of their traffic in monopoly markets, whereas TWA, National, and Northeast have a much smaller percentage and thus are said to face more competition.

As a group, the other trunks have a slightly larger share of monopoly traffic than the big four. Overall, about 25 percent of domestic trunk traffic is carried in markets where there is no more than token competition. About one-half of the traffic is in markets characterized by competition between two trunk carriers. The remaining one-fourth of the traffic is generated in markets where there are three or more carriers, each receiving at least 10 percent of the traffic.[32]

The extent of head-to-head competition between carriers in the largest markets varies by carrier pair.[33] In two cases among the top 135 markets[34] there is no competition between carriers (Continental-Northeast and Northeast-Western) and in several others, very little (for example, American-Western, Braniff-National, Braniff-Northeast, Braniff-Western, Con-

30. Pan American World Airways (the country's largest carrier) has international authority only (although it does carry a small amount of domestic traffic strictly ancillary to its international operations), and thus is not included as a trunk in this study.

31. Until 1959, Eastern was in third place, but dropped behind Trans World Airlines to fourth in 1959 following strikes by mechanics and flight engineers in the latter part of 1958. By 1970, Eastern's revenues were higher than TWA's. United took over first place (from American) when it merged with Capital Airlines in 1961.

32. CAB Docket 22916, Exhibit BOR-R-501.

33. See U.S. Department of Transportation, "Executive Branch Criteria for Domestic Airline Merger Proposals" (Aug. 31, 1971; processed), p. 4.

34. The source cited in the previous footnote displays in tabular form for 1970 the extent of carrier-pair competition in the 135 markets representing the union of the set of 100 top city-pair markets in terms of revenue passenger-miles and the set of 100 top markets in terms of enplaned passengers. Ibid.

tinental-National, Delta-Western, Eastern-Western, and National-Western). On the other hand, competition among the big four (American, Eastern, TWA, and United) is particularly intense. Nearly one-half of the top 135 city-pair markets are served by both TWA and United. Among the other trunks, Delta, National, Northeast, and Northwest have relatively high degrees of competition from trunk carriers, whereas Western is relatively immune from competition.

Nonstop competitive air service is available among nearly all of the twenty "large hub" cities of the United States (FAA designation). As might be expected, however, such service is clearly superior to service between the large hubs and the thirty-nine "medium hubs."[35]

The major aspects of service quality are discussed in Chapter 3; however, we might mention a few additional ones here. Although this statistic is not computed directly, it appears that more than half of all service is nonstop. By the end of 1970, the domestic trunks carried 99.8 percent of their revenue passenger-miles with all-jet aircraft and local service airlines carried 70 percent. Passenger fatalities ran 1.3 per billion passenger miles flown in 1969, a rate that has varied between 1 and 4 per billion passenger-miles flown since 1961. On nearly all trunk carrier flights there is a choice of two types of service—first class and coach, with a price differential. In 1970 average airborne speed was 436 miles per hour for the domestic trunks, compared with slightly more than 200 as late as 1953. Load factors in 1970 were down to 49.3 percent, although they subsequently have risen, especially during the 1974 "energy crisis." For this service the passenger pays on the average about six cents per mile.[36]

Regulatory Agencies and Powers

Civil Aeronautics Board

The airlines' most significant and pervasive regulatory influence is the Civil Aeronautics Board. Its major functions and powers are described below.

Promotion. In the words of a public information document, "the Civil

35. These conclusions are drawn from a recent compilation of service authorizations made available to the authors by James F. Taylor of the Boeing Commercial Airline Company. To our knowledge, the CAB compiles no similar series, though official route maps are available. Essentially, the twenty "large hubs" constitute the largest city markets (Boston, New York, Philadelphia, and so on), whereas the thirty-nine "medium hubs" constitute the next largest markets (Buffalo, Richmond, Indianapolis, and so on).

36. See CAB, *Handbook of Airline Statistics, 1971*, pp. 26, 62, 81, 426, 432, 554.

Aeronautics Board promotes and regulates the airline industry."[37] In that publication, Board Chairman Charles S. Murphy said, "I wish to emphasize the fact that we are charged with responsibility to promote as well as regulate air transportation. We regard the promotional aspects of our work as very important."[38] Although the role of promotion was an innovation for a regulatory agency when the Civil Aeronautics Act was passed in 1938,[39] it may be recalled that one of the basic reasons for establishing regulation was to rationalize the government's support of civil aviation, principally its program of airmail subsidy.

The Board's present promotional activities take two forms: (a) direct subsidy, and (b) what may be termed "general." The statutory basis for subsidy is given in section 406(b) of the Federal Aviation Act. In determining pay for airmail, the Board is to consider, among other factors:

the need of each . . . air carrier for compensation for the transportation of mail sufficient to insure the performance of such service, and, together with all other revenue of the air carrier, to enable such air carrier under honest, economical, and efficient management, to maintain and continue the development of air transportation to the extent and of the character and quality required for the commerce of the United States, the Postal Service, and the national defense.

In 1951 the Board, by administrative action, separated subsidy from airmail payments.[40] The trunk carriers went off subsidy in 1959, except for minor payments to Northeast during 1964–68, and a class rate subsidy formula for local service airlines was instituted in 1961.[41] During fiscal year 1972 subsidy payments totaled $67.2 million, including $4.4 million for the Alaskan carriers.[42]

The Board promotes the airlines in other, general ways, deriving its mandate principally from the legislative "Declaration of Policy" which comprises section 102 of the Federal Aviation Act:

In the exercise and performance of its powers and duties under this Act, the Board shall consider the following, among other things, as being in the public interest, and in accordance with the public convenience and necessity:

37. CAB, *The Civil Aeronautics Board Promotes and Regulates the Airline Industry* (1968).

38. Ibid., p. iii.

39. See Horace M. Gray, "The Airlines Industry," in Walter Adams (ed.), *The Structure of American Industry: Some Case Studies* (3rd ed., Macmillan, 1961), p. 472.

40. CAB, *Handbook of Airline Statistics, 1971*, p. 484.

41. This method of payment was designed to encourage carriers to reduce their subsidy needs. See Civil Aeronautics Board, "Subsidy for United States Certificated Air Carriers" (August 1972; processed), pp. 9–10, and App. 7.

42. Ibid., App. 7.

(a) The encouragement and development of an air-transportation system properly adapted to the present and future needs of the foreign and domestic commerce of the United States, of the Postal Service, and of the national defense;

(b) The regulation of air transportation in such manner as to recognize and preserve the inherent advantages of, assure the highest degree of safety in, and foster sound economic conditions in, such transportation, and to improve the relations between, and coordinate transportation by, air carriers;

(c) The promotion of adequate, economical, and efficient service by air carriers at reasonable charges, without unjust discriminations, undue preferences or advantages, or unfair or destructive competitive practices;

(d) Competition to the extent necessary to assure the sound development of an air-transportation system properly adapted to the needs of the foreign and domestic commerce of the United States, of the Postal Service, and of the national defense;

(e) The promotion of safety in air commerce; and

(f) The promotion, encouragement, and development of civil aeronautics.

In carrying out this promotion mandate, the Board has shown particular sensitivity to downturns in industry profits and it has maintained price levels which tend to maximize industry output, discriminatory fare structures which augment quantity demanded, and price and entry regulation which promote investment in aircraft.[43]

Entry (route authorizations). Section 401(a) of the Federal Aviation Act states:

No air carrier shall engage in any air transportation unless there is in force a certificate issued by the Board authorizing such air carrier to engage in such transportation.

Section 401(d)(1) states:

The Board shall issue a certificate authorizing the whole or any part of the transportation covered by the application, if it finds that the applicant is fit, willing, and able to perform such transportation properly, and to conform to the provisions of this Act and the rules, regulations, and requirements of the Board hereunder, and that such transportation is required by the public convenience and necessity; otherwise such application shall be denied.

Finally, section 401(e)(1) gives the Board power to prescribe terms and conditions of the certificate:

Each certificate . . . shall specify the terminal points and intermediate points, if any . . . and there shall be attached to the exercise of the privileges granted by the certificate . . . such reasonable terms, conditions, and limitations as the public interest may require.

In short, this means that no carrier may operate in scheduled interstate

43. See the discussion of the Board's implied regulatory objectives in Chapter 9.

service without first obtaining CAB permission and then only on those routes for which authority is granted. Further, the Board can and often does attach restrictions, such as limiting nonstop service. The usual procedure is for the Board to hold "area investigations" during which carriers are invited to apply for extensions in their service. Carriers also can apply unilaterally. Since the Board controls entry into city-pair markets, it effectively controls entry into the industry. For example, not a single new trunk carrier has been certificated in the Board's history, although many of the local service carriers have grown into miniature trunks.[44]

Exit (abandonment). Section 401(j) of the act states:

No air carrier shall abandon any route, or part thereof, for which a certificate has been issued by the Board, unless . . . the Board shall find such abandonment to be in the public interest.

This gives the Board the power to require carriers to continue providing service even where the carrier would prefer to suspend or even abandon service altogether.

Fares. Section 404(a) of the act requires carriers

to establish, observe, and enforce just and reasonable individual and joint rates, fares, and charges. . . .[45]

Section 1002(d) states:

Whenever . . . the Board shall be of the opinion that any . . . rate, fare, or charge . . . is or will be unjust or unreasonable, or unjustly discriminatory, or unduly preferential, or unduly prejudicial, the Board shall determine and prescribe the lawful rate, fare, or charge (or the maximum or minimum, or the maximum and minimum thereof) thereafter to be . . . charged.

The terms "unreasonable" and "unjust" generally refer to whether a rate is "too high," leading to excessive return on investment, or "too low," possibly impairing other carriers and service in other markets. "Discrimination" refers to rate or fare differences between classes of consumers where there are no demonstrable like differences in costs. Finally, following the practice of the Interstate Commerce Commission, "preference" and "prejudice" are used to describe rate and fare relationships among geographical points, as, for hypothetical example, a higher fare from New York to Reno, Nevada, than from New York to San Francisco, a longer distance. Thus, the Board has considerable authority over carrier rates. But note that the power may not be exercised; that is, rates or rate changes

44. See Eads, *The Local Service Airline Experiment*, Chap. 6.
45. Joint rates are prices negotiated between carriers and charged for their collective services, as, for example, a passenger traveling from New York to Denver via Kansas City on two different carriers.

may be approved implicitly, without Board action; also the Board may choose to set only maximum or minimum rates, or both.

In determining the lawfulness of rates, the Board is required by the "Rule of Ratemaking," which comprises section 1002(e) of the act, to consider among other factors:

(1) The effect of such rates upon the movement of traffic;
(2) The need in the public interest of adequate and efficient transportation of persons and property by air carriers at the lowest cost consistent with the furnishing of such service;
(3) Such standards respecting the character and quality of service to be rendered by air carriers as may be prescribed by or pursuant to law;
(4) The inherent advantages of transportation by aircraft; and
(5) The need of each air carrier for revenue sufficient to enable such air carrier, under honest, economical, and efficient management, to provide adequate and efficient air carrier service.

Clause (1) has been interpreted as having to do with the price elasticity of demand, whereas (5) has been relied on (by the carriers at least) as justifying rate increases whenever their rate of return on investment falls below that which the Board terms reasonable.

Mergers. Section 408(a) of the act states:

It shall be unlawful unless approved by order of the Board as provided in this section—

(1) For two or more air carriers . . . to consolidate or merge their properties . . . into one person for the ownership, management, or operation of the properties.

Thus, air carriers seeking to merge must obtain prior permission from the Board. Moreover, in passing on merger proposals, the Board has the following guideline [section 408(b)]:

Unless . . . the Board finds that the . . . merger . . . will not be consistent with the public interest . . . it shall by order approve such . . . merger . . . *Provided,* That the Board shall not approve any . . . merger . . . which would result in creating a monopoly or monopolies and thereby restrain competition or jeopardize another air carrier not a party to the . . . merger.

In addition to these rather broad standards, the Board is also under some obligation to pay homage to section 7 of the Clayton Act (38 Stat. 731-32).[46]

Intercarrier agreements. In section 412(a) of the act, carriers are directed to file with the Board a copy of all agreements relating to pooling or apportioning earnings, losses, traffic, service, or equipment, or relating to the establishment of transportation rates, fares, charges, or classifi-

46. See Jessie Markham, "An Economic Study of the Competitive Effects of the Proposed American Airlines, Inc., Eastern Airlines, Inc. Merger," CAB Docket 13355, Exhibit JI-1 (1962), pp. 3–9.

cations, or for preserving and improving safety, economy, and efficiency of operation, or for controlling, regulating, preventing, or otherwise eliminating destructive, oppressive, or wasteful competition, or for regulating stops, schedules, and character of service, or for other cooperative working arrangements.

Section 412 (b) requires that
The Board shall by order disapprove any such contract or agreement . . . that it finds to be adverse to the public interest.

In fiscal year 1970 the CAB reviewed over one thousand such proposed agreements, relating generally to the operations of the Air Traffic Conference of America (ATCA) and the International Air Transport Association (IATA), problems of airport congestion, technical assistance to foreign airlines, equipment interchanges, passenger baggage and cargo practices, reservations and ticketing, interline traffic procedures, the airline mutual aid agreement (revenue sharing during strikes), the agreement between the airlines and REA Express, et cetera.[47]

Unfair methods of competition. The act gives the Board the power to regulate "destructive competition." Section 411 reads, in part:
The Board may . . . investigate and determine whether any air carrier . . . has been or is engaged in unfair or deceptive practices or unfair methods of competition. . . . If the Board shall find . . . [affirmatively] it shall order such air carrier . . . to cease and desist from such practices or methods of competition.

Quality of service. As discussed extensively in Chapters 4 and 6, the Board regulates service quality implicitly through its regulation of fares. It is important to note, however, that its direct regulation of service quality is rather limited. As mentioned before, section 401(e)(1) of the act gives the Board the power to set certain side constraints on flights, such as the number of intermediate points. However, section 401(e)(4) states that
No term, condition, or limitation of a certificate shall restrict the right of an air carrier to add to or change schedules, equipment, accommodations, and facilities for performing the authorized transportation and service as the development of the business and the demands of the public shall require.[48]

There is, of course, a common-carrier obligation and also some mention of adequacy of service. Section 404(a) reads, in part:
It shall be the duty of every air carrier to provide and furnish . . . air transportation, as authorized by its certificate, upon reasonable request therefor . . . to

47. *Civil Aeronautics Board Reports to Congress, Fiscal Year 1970*, pp. 12, 13.
48. However, under section 412 (just quoted) the Board can approve (and recently has approved) intercarrier agreements to "self-regulate" capacity, and thus quality of service. (See discussion of capacity agreements in Chapter 7.)

provide safe and adequate service, equipment, and facilities in connection with such transportation.

However, the question of service adequacy has not been determined in specific detail. For local service carriers the Board once established two round-trips per day as a minimum, but later it encouraged a "use it or lose it" policy and has allowed a number of deviations from the two-flights norm. Finally, there are numerous CAB-imposed rules designed for consumer protection and policed by the Board's Bureau of Enforcement. These include matters relating to carrier liability for passenger baggage, overbooking, passenger ticket refunds, and flight cancellation.

Procedure. The Civil Aeronautics Board promulgates rules and regulations consistent with its powers derived from the Federal Aviation Act. In carrying out its decision-making responsibilities the Board is constrained by the Administrative Procedure Act.[49] In practice, Board procedure ranges from an informal delegation of authority to staff members to handle routine intercarrier agreements, to formal, prolonged hearings in major route and rate cases. On occasion, especially where an issue is not particularly significant, the Board will issue a decision directly on the merits of the original petition (taking into consideration possible subsequent filings by interested parties). This procedure is also used in cases where time is of the essence or where a party has petitioned the Board to reconsider a recent decision.

With regard to regulations covering carrier cost reporting and other routine matters, the Board may institute a "rulemaking proceeding." The Board will publish a proposed policy and will invite written comments from interested parties. Another statement by the Board, such as a revised policy or clarification of original, may or may not follow. Then, often after oral argument by counsel to interested parties, the Board will reach a final decision.

Major issues coming before the Board, however, are usually set down for public hearing. This procedure can be rather complicated, although means exist for short-circuiting various stages. In response to the original petition, the Board will order that a hearing be held. An administrative law judge (formerly hearing examiner) is then assigned to the case. A prehearing conference is scheduled, prior to which parties usually, but not always, circulate statements of proposed issues. At the conference the scope of the

49. See Public Law 89-554 (Sept. 6, 1966), 80 Stat. 378, which supersedes the Administrative Procedure Act (60 Stat. 237), where the provision first appeared.

proceeding is defined in more detail (which issues are relevant and which are not), and parties are given an opportunity to request information, such as data on revenues, costs, and service provided, from other parties in the proceeding.

After the prehearing conference, parties exchange testimony and exhibits. Usually parties are given an opportunity for rebuttal testimony and exhibits, and sometimes even surrebuttal. After that, the public hearing is held, presided over by the administrative law judge.[50] The responsibility of this judge is to administer the hearing, certify the record as being true and accurate, and usually, but not always, render an initial decision which here commends to the Board. The Board then may on its own initiative or in response to a protest from an interested party take this decision under advisement and later render its own final decision. Otherwise, the judge's initial decision becomes the final one.

Organization. The Board itself is composed of five members, including a chairman and a vice chairman. All are appointed by the President, with approval by the Senate; no more than three members may be from the same political party. There is a managing director who is chief administrator of the Board's staff and reports to the chairman. The research staff is divided into bureaus. Of particular relevance to regulatory proceedings are the Bureau of Economics, which is a major participant in cases involving rates and fares, and the Bureau of Operating Rights, which is the major protagonist in route and merger cases.

Other Agencies

A number of other federal agencies regulate, or at least have an impact on, the commercial air carriers. The most important of these is the Department of Transportation, which influences the airlines primarily through its Federal Aviation Administration (FAA).[51] The Federal Aviation Act (section 103, as amended) states:

In the exercise and performance of his powers and duties under this Act the Secretary of Transportation shall consider the following, among other things, as being in the public interest:

(a) The regulation of air commerce in such manner as to best promote its development and safety and fulfill the requirements of national defense;

50. During the hearing, witnesses are cross-examined on testimony and exhibits.
51. Before passage of the Department of Transportation Act in 1966 the FAA was an independent agency, having been established as the Federal Aviation Agency in 1958 by the Federal Aviation Act.

(b) The promotion, encouragement, and development of civil aeronautics;

(c) The control of the use of the navigable airspace of the United States and the regulation of both civil and military operations in such airspace in the interest of the safety and efficiency of both;

(d) The consolidation of research and development with respect to air navigation facilities, as well as the installation and operation thereof;

(e) The development and operation of a common system of air traffic control and navigation for both military and civil aircraft.

Note from this legislative "Declaration of Policy" that Transportation, too, has a promotional role regarding civil aviation, and the mere existence of a publicly financed FAA attests to this fact.

The main regulatory role of the department's FAA is to set and maintain minimum standards for air safety. The administrator of the FAA, often through formal rulemaking proceedings, issues and enforces rules, regulations, and minimum standards pertaining to the manufacture, operation, and maintenance of the civil air fleet. The agency also certifies new aircraft, inspects flight navigation facilities, and certifies pilots whether for private or commercial purposes. The agency also has other functions, including registration of civil aircraft, and research and development pertaining primarily to aircraft, airport, and airway safety. Finally, two of the agency's most important functions are (a) provision of airport and airway navigation facilities and traffic control, and (b) administration of the airport-airway program arising from the Airport and Airway Development Act of 1970 and the Airport and Airway Revenue Act of 1970.[52] These two responsibilities, of course, directly affect carrier costs of operation as well as safety and convenience to passengers.

Another DOT-related agency affecting the airlines is the National Transportation Safety Board (NTSB)[53] which has, among other functions, responsibility for investigating aircraft accidents and determining their causes. If responsibility can be ascertained from the investigation and a violation of FAA safety standards is suspected, then criminal or civil charges, or both, may result.

52. Basically these acts provide for airport-airway subsidies for capital development to be financed out of user charges falling on airline passengers and, to a lesser extent, aircraft owners and operators.

53. The NTSB was established by the Department of Transportation Act of 1966. Although a part of DOT, the NTSB is semiautonomous and reports directly to Congress.

ENERGY REGULATION BY THE FEDERAL POWER COMMISSION

STEPHEN G. BREYER and PAUL W. MacAVOY

In searching for a way to deal with the energy prob lem, it is only natural to look in the direction of the Federal Power Commission. On the surface, en couragement might be drawn from its record. By the standards of the federal bureaucracy its procedure are thorough and it clears its dockets in a reasona ble time. Generally the FPC has been competentl staffed and managed, and it has avoided "capture by the industries it regulates.

Yet on the basis of econometric analysis, the authors conclude that the FPC is "effective but no efficient." Their main findings: by holding prices be low the competitive level at the wellhead in the 1960s, the commission inadvertently caused a shor age of gas and service; despite voluminous pro ceedings, pipeline rates ended up at about the level they would have reached without any regula tion; failure to move the electric power industry t higher levels of coordination prevented potentia savings of hundreds of millions of dollars a year.

For the reader interested primarily in energy po icy, a crucial issue is raised here. The regulator agency as such—an institution that Americans ten to rely on—has not been very helpful to the energ consumer. In some cases, reliance on the marke may yield greater economic benefits; in other case direct government participation may be needed. Fo the reader interested in general economic question the book is an illuminating case study that touche on three classic economic problems: utility regula tion, price control, and industrial planning.

The authors wrote this volume, ninth in the serie of Studies in the Regulation of Economic Activit as members of the Brookings associated sta Stephen G. Breyer, professor of law at Harvard Un versity, has served in the antitrust division of th Justice Department. Paul W. MacAvoy, professor economics at the Massachusetts Institute of Tec nology, is the author of several books. During 196 66, he was a senior member of the staff of th Council of Economic Advisers.

163 pp./1974/cloth